Competence Center for Central and Eastern Europe
Augasse 2-6, 1090 Wien
Tel.: +43/1/313 36/5284 · Fax: +43/1/313 36/905284
E-Mail: cee@wu-wien.ac.at · Web: www.wu-wien.ac.at/cee

Management Control in Central and Eastern European Subsidiaries

Management Control in Central and Eastern European Subsidiaries

Barbara Brenner

palgrave macmillan

© Barbara Brenner 2009

All rights reserved. No reproduction, copy or transmission of this publication may be made without written permission.

No portion of this publication may be reproduced, copied or transmitted save with written permission or in accordance with the provisions of the Copyright, Designs and Patents Act 1988, or under the terms of any licence permitting limited copying issued by the Copyright Licensing Agency, Saffron House, 6-10 Kirby Street, London EC1N 8TS.

Any person who does any unauthorized act in relation to this publication may be liable to criminal prosecution and civil claims for damages.

The author has asserted her right to be identified as the author of this work in accordance with the Copyright, Designs and Patents Act 1988.

First published 2009 by
PALGRAVE MACMILLAN

Palgrave Macmillan in the UK is an imprint of Macmillan Publishers Limited, registered in England, company number 785998, of Houndmills, Basingstoke, Hampshire RG21 6XS.

Palgrave Macmillan in the US is a division of St Martin's Press LLC, 175 Fifth Avenue, New York, NY 10010.

Palgrave Macmillan is the global academic imprint of the above companies and has companies and representatives throughout the world.

Palgrave® and Macmillan® are registered trademarks in the United States, the United Kingdom, Europe and other countries.

ISBN-13: 978–0–230–20140–8 hardback
ISBN-10: 0–230–20140–7 hardback

This book is printed on paper suitable for recycling and made from fully managed and sustained forest sources. Logging, pulping and manufacturing processes are expected to conform to the environmental regulations of the country of origin.

A catalogue record for this book is available from the British Library.

Library of Congress Cataloging-in-Publication Data

Brenner, Barbara, 1976–
   Management control in Central and Eastern European subsidiaries / Barbara Brenner.
     p. cm.
   Includes bibliographical references and index.
   ISBN-13: 978–0–230–20140–8
   ISBN-10: 0–230–20140–7
    1. International business enterprises – Management. 2. International business enterprises – Europe, Central – Management. 3. International business enterprises – Europe, Eastern – Management. I. Title.
HD62.4.B74 2009
658'.0490943—dc22
                                                      2008030131

10 9 8 7 6 5 4 3 2 1
18 17 16 15 14 13 12 11 10 09

Printed and bound in Great Britain by
CPI Antony Rowe, Chippenham and Eastbourne

Contents

List of Figures ix

List of Tables xi

List of Abbreviations xiii

1 Introduction: Problem, Relevance and Research Question 1
2 The Concept of Management Control 6
  2.1 Defining 'management control' 6
  2.2 The fundamentals of management control 10
    2.2.1 Classification of control mechanisms 14
      2.2.1.1 Formal vs. informal control 15
      2.2.1.2 Output control vs. behavior control 16
      2.2.1.3 Market, bureaucracy and clan controls 17
      2.2.1.4 Bureaucratic control vs. cultural control 18
      2.2.1.5 Result control vs. personnel/cultural control 19
      2.2.1.6 Personal and impersonal vs. planned and unplanned 20
      2.2.1.7 A synthesis of control mechanisms 21
      2.2.1.8 Control mechanisms used by this study 24
  2.3 Management control in multinational corporations 29
    2.3.1 Strategy determines organizational design and type of control 30
  2.4 Synthesis: strategy, control mechanisms and control extent 33
3 Literature Review of Current Studies on Management Control in MNCs 39
  3.1 Factors influencing management control 41
    3.1.1 Environmental context 42
      3.1.1.1 Uncertainty 46
      3.1.1.2 Heterogeneity/complexity/institutional framework 46
      3.1.1.3 Economic and technological imperatives 48
    3.1.2 Organizational context 49

			3.1.2.1	Age	49
			3.1.2.2	Subsidiary size	49
			3.1.2.3	Ownership and resource provision	50
		3.1.3	Culture		52
			3.1.3.1	Country of origin effect	66
		3.1.4	Moderators		69
			3.1.4.1	Expatriates	70
			3.1.4.2	The role of trust	72
			3.1.4.3	International experience of organizational units	74
			3.1.4.4	Organization culture	74
			3.1.4.5	Personality traits	75
		3.1.5	Interaction of strategy, power and interdependence		76
			3.1.5.1	MNC strategy	76
			3.1.5.2	Interdependence	77
			3.1.5.3	Power	78
	3.2	Discussion			78
	3.3	A comprehensive model of management control fit			81
4	Cultural Research on Central and Eastern Europe				85
	4.1	The aftermath of communism			91
5	Method				92
	5.1	Semi-structured interview			94
		5.1.1	Potential sources of bias and ways of dealing with it		97
	5.2	Qualitative content analysis			101
		5.2.1	Validity and reliability		104
			5.2.1.1	Validity and reliability check in the present study	105
	5.3	Rationale for chosen methodology			105
6	Sample				108
7	Empirical Results: Western Management Control in CEE				115
	7.1	Strategic choice: market entry strategy			115
		7.1.1	Motives for market entry		115
			7.1.1.1	Growth potential	116
			7.1.1.2	Early birds and first movers	116
		7.1.2	Market entry mode		117

7.2	Management control types in MNC headquarters		119
	7.2.1	Explicit MNC control	120
		7.2.1.1 Extent of centralization	120
		7.2.1.2 Extent of standardization	124
		7.2.1.3 Extent of formalization	129
		7.2.1.4 Extent of output & performance control	130
		7.2.1.5 Extent of expatriate control	135
		7.2.1.6 Reasons for using Host-Country Nationals (HCN)	145
	7.2.2	Implicit MNC control	149
		7.2.2.1 Control by lateral relations	150
		7.2.2.2 Control by informal communication and personal intra-group networks	154
		7.2.2.3 Control by international management training	157
		7.2.2.4 Control by organizational culture	163
	7.2.3	Communication HQ-subsidiary	167
		7.2.3.1 Intensity of communication	167
		7.2.3.2 Group language	168
		7.2.3.3 Communication functions	168
	7.2.4	Conclusion: extent and types of control classified	168
		7.2.4.1 Frequency of control types	168
		7.2.4.2 Combinations of control types	169
		7.2.4.3 Control extent: operational versus strategic control	173
7.3	Contingencies: the political and economic framework in CEE		174
	7.3.1	Political risk	176
		7.3.1.1 Political instability	176
		7.3.1.2 Bureaucracy	177
		7.3.1.3 Corruption	178
		7.3.1.4 Legal constraints	179
		7.3.1.5 Summary political risk	179
	7.3.2	Economic and firm level risk	179
		7.3.2.1 Risk of concealment of relevant information	179
		7.3.2.2 Development stage (maturity) and poor data quality	182
		7.3.2.3 Lack of understanding for Western management concepts and control	184
		7.3.2.4 Qualified personnel	185

		7.3.2.5	Summary of economic and firm level risk	185
	7.4	Culture		188
		7.4.1	Some CEE-wide parallels in cultural perceptions based on communism	189
		7.4.2	Moderators	209
			7.4.2.1 Moderators on the organizational level	209
			7.4.2.2 Moderators on the individual level	228
		7.4.3	Propositions and managerial implications	232
8	Major Findings			236
	8.1	Conclusion: cultural differences, contingencies, moderators and management control in MNCs		236
	8.2	Directions for future research		239
	8.3	Discussion		240
	8.4	Managerial implications		242
		8.4.1	Determinants of effective management control and business success in CEE	242
		8.4.2	Managerial implications of perceived cultural differences	246
		8.4.3	Strategic success factors for implementing management control	246
			8.4.3.1 Implementation challenges	246
			8.4.3.2 Implementation mediators	253
9	Summary			262
	9.1	Key findings on a glimpse		262
	9.2	Summary		265
	9.3	Culture, contingencies and MNC management control in CEE		267
	9.4	Culture		268
	9.5	Contingencies		268
	9.6	Moderators		269
	9.7	Conclusion		269
	9.8	The management challenge		270

Appendix 271

Bibliography 276

Index 303

Figures

1.1	Research design	4
2.1	Onion of organizational control and environment	11
2.2	Model of core control system	12
2.3	How organizational design affects behavior	13
2.4	Environment, strategy, organizational design, systems and processes in MNCs	30
2.5	Internal and external strategic, organizational design, control, and cultural fit	31
2.6	Organizational context	32
2.7	The integration-responsiveness framework	33
2.8	Strategy determines control mechanisms and extent	34
2.9	Interaction levels and extent of control between HQ and subsidiaries	35
3.1	Elements of contingency approach	42
3.2	Description of the environment	45
3.3	Model of resource provision, key appointments and control	52
3.4	Comprehensive framework of dynamic fit	82
4.1	Differences in 'as if' scores: Germanic versus Eastern European cluster	89
4.2	Differences in 'should be' scores: Germanic versus Eastern European cluster	90
4.3	Differences in Eastern European and Germanic leadership-profile scores	90
5.1	Four contextual levels of the research Interview in international business	98
5.2	Step model of inductive and deductive category development	102
7.1	HQ decision making and subsidiary autonomy	121
7.2	Network view on centralized control	122
7.3	Levels of standardization and formalization	124
7.4	Network view on standardization	125
7.5	A network view on formalization	129
7.6	Type of planning	131
7.7	Network view on detailed control and evaluation	132

7.8	Network view on the extent of evaluation control, planning and evaluation-reward system	134
7.9	Network view on lateral relations	151
7.10	Network view on network building	155
7.11	Network view on integrative function	157
7.12	Network view on management training	163
7.13	Pillars of intra-organizational transfer of organizational culture	164
7.14	Distribution of Harzing's control typology	170
7.15	Configurations of control mechanisms	170
7.16	Combinations of control mechanisms	172
7.17	Extent/intensity of HQ control in CEE subsidiaries	174
7.18	CEE challenges	175
7.19	Differences in 'As if' scores: Germanic versus Eastern European cluster	188
7.20	Perceived cultural differences and moderators	189
7.21	Common characteristics of CEE culture	190
7.22	North-south divide	199
7.23	Moderators on the perceived risk attributed to cultural differences on the organizational level	209
7.24	Network view on trust building	211
7.25	Network view on knowledge transfer	213
7.26	Austrian management style	221
8.1	MNC management control in CEE	237
8.2	Challenges for implementation and mediators at different levels of analysis	247
9.1	Distribution of control types	269

Tables

2.1	Definitions of management control in chronological order	7
2.2	A comparison of bureaucratic and cultural control mechanisms	18
2.3	Type of control mechanisms based on the object of control	20
2.4	Typology of control: planned/unplanned versus personal/impersonal	20
2.5	Classification of control mechanisms	21
2.6	Control mechanisms distinguished by various authors	25
2.7	Dimensions of international control in MNCs	36
3.1	Journals screened from 1996 to 2004 and number of identified relevant articles	40
3.2	Seminal contingency contributions	43
3.3	Overview of analyzed contingency-based empirical studies	44
3.4	Empirical studies on national culture and management control based on Hofstede (1980, 1991)	54
3.5	Parent nationality and management control type	69
3.6	Literature dealing with moderators	70
6.1	Interviewee sample	110
7.1	Reasons for using expatriates	136
7.2	The impact of expatriate control on headquarter-subsidiary relationships	141
7.3	Drivers for using host-country nationals in top positions	145
7.4	The impact of management training & socialization on headquarter-subsidiary relations	162
7.5	Pillars of organizational culture transfer	165
7.6	Communication functions	169
7.7	Impacts of political risk on subsidiary control	180
7.8	The impact of economic risk on management control	186
7.9	Perceived cultural differences and the managerial implications	233

8.1	Determinants of effective management control and business success in CEE	243
8.2	Implementation: challenges & facilitators of implementing HQ control	247
8.3	Implementation mediators	253
9.1	Key findings	262

Abbreviations

A	Austrian
ASEAN	Association of South-East Asian Nations
BFC	Bureaucratic Formalized Control
C	Collectivism
CD	Confucian Dynamism
CEO	Chief Executive Officer
CEE	Central and Eastern Europe: The term Central and Eastern Europe is taken here to also include Central Europe, Russia and the Newly Independent States (NIS) derived from the former Soviet Union
CFO	Chief Financial Officer
CH	Swiss
COMECON	Council for Mutual Economic Assistance
CSN	Control by Socialization and Networks
EBIT	Earnings Before Interest and Taxes
EBITDA	Earnings Before Interest, Taxes, Depreciation and Amortization
FCF	Free Cash Flow
F	Femininity
f	Female
FDI	Foreign direct investment
G	German
HCN	Host-Country National
HRM	Human Resource Management
HQ	Headquarters
IB	International Business
IJV	International Joint Venture
IC	Institutional Collectivism
ID	Individualism
JIBS	Journal of International Business Studies
JV	Joint Venture
LTI	Long-term incentives
M	Masculinity
m	Male
MA	Management Accounting
MAS	Management Accounting System

MCS	Management Control System
MIS	Management Information System
MNC	Multinational Corporation
NIS	Newly Independent States from the former Soviet Union
OC	Output Control
P #	Primary document number xx
PCC	Personal Centralized Control
PE	Performance Evaluation
PCN	Parent-Country National
PLD	Preferred Level of Disclosure
PECVD	Perceived Balance of Costs Relative to Benefits of Compliance
PD	Power Distance
RAPM	Reliance on Accounting Performance Measures for performance evaluation
PR	Performance-Based Rewards
reg	Regular / regularly
ROCE	Return On Capital Employed
ROS	Return On Sales
SAP	Systems, Applications and Products in the area of data processing
SOE	State-Owned Enterprise
SUB	Subsidiary
SPE	Subjective Performance Evaluation
UA	Uncertainty Avoidance
UAI	Uncertainty Avoidance Index

1
Introduction: Problem, Relevance and Research Question

Controlling and coordinating a network of geographically and culturally dispersed subsidiaries is probably one of the longest standing challenges in international management. For one, cost pressures, a highly competitive environment, and the dangers of inefficiencies due to double invention require the firm to integrate their far-flung operations. On the other side, persisting institutional and cultural differences as well as increasing local competition forces firms to be locally responsive at the same time. Thus, the firm's global network needs to be coordinated effectively in order to explore new local resources or to exploit resources within the international network of subsidiaries (Bartlett & Ghoshal, 1989). The great diversity of Multinational Corporation (MNC) operations increases the complexity of their system interdependence which, in turn, demands more coordination (Lawrence & Lorsch, 1967) and affects information processing and control systems (Egelhoff, 1984; Vachani, 1999). Consequently, the question of how to coordinate an MNC's dispersed value-creation activities has become prominent and widely discussed in the literature (Bartlett et al., 1989; Pugh, Hickson, Hinings, & Turner, 1968).

However, despite this ongoing and widely held discussion on coordination and control in MNCs, surprisingly few generalizable insights have endured time. For example, while many authors have argued that with increasing complexity, power changes within the network, as well as insurmountable information asymmetries, will all lead to a shift from more direct to more indirect forms of control (Doz and Prahalad, 1981; Martinez and Jarillo, 1989), empirical results are mixed (e.g., Ambos and Reitsperger, 2004; Egelhoff, 1991; Gencturk & Aulakh, 1995; O'Donnel, 2000).

Given the rapid increase in levels of Foreign Direct Investment (FDI) in Central and Eastern Europe (CEE) over the last decade (OECD, 2005), we strive to explore how Western developed management and control theories and techniques apply in CEE. While growth rates in Western Europe have fallen short for the last couple of years, the CEE region pulled in many investors with growth rates in the double-digit range (Gigouline & Iouri, 2001; Schwab & Porter, 2004). Two forces in particular drive the inflow of investments into the CEE region. First, there is a need to 'catch-up', since notable capital investment in the CEE region was not possible before the 1990s, resulting in a strong need for capital due to much needed technological and infrastructural development (Napier & Thomas, 2004; Spitz, 1995). Second, the transition process itself triggers Eastern European markets to conform to Western standards rendering the engagement of private foreign capital possible (Protsenko & Vinzenz, 1999). The key characteristic of the transition process is a fundamental change in the norms, values, and assumptions underlying economic activity (Roth & Kostova, 2003). Communism was abandoned speedily but is only slowly being replaced with new norms, values, and assumptions that are more consistent with democracy and a market-based economy (Napier et al., 2004; Newman, 2000). New capabilities such as efficiency orientation, strategic thinking, entrepreneurial initiative and proneness to take risk are required, but those develop only slowly (Newman, 2000).

Austria can be seen as a gateway to the East, since not only have Austrian firms invested heavily in CEE, but also MNCs use Austria as a hub for their regional CEE headquarters (Breinbauer & Wakounig, 2003). Increasing corporation size combined with a growing dynamic and complexity of markets in transition economies call for control mechanisms which maintain flexibility and transparency at the same time (Gigouline et al., 2001). Hence, management control plays a crucial role in effectively managing FDIs since it forms the basis for decision making in MNCs (Reichmann, 1995; Vogel, 1998). The relationship between Headquarters (HQ) and subsidiaries in MNCs deserves much needed empirical research. We respond to the call for more research on the complex issue of HQ-subsidiary relations by analyzing HQ control in CEE subsidiaries and joint ventures.

Understanding the factors that influence the adoption of HQ management control practices in CEE enhances the success with which such practices are disseminated throughout the MNC and in turn affects a firm's economic performance (O'Connor, Chow, & Wu, 2004). Diffusion difficulties arise from different business environments affecting operational outcomes, different background knowledge, and different culturally determined value systems (Noerreklit & Schoenfeld, 2000). 'The greater the difference between the institutional profiles of the home country [...] and the recipient country, the greater the likelihood that there will be a misfit between the transferred practice and the recipient environment, which, in turn, may result in difficulties or even failure of the transfer' (Kostova, 1999). However, little empirical research has been undertaken into the cross-border applicability of management and control techniques (Firth, 1996). As MNCs expand into CEE, the variety and complexity of international control tasks makes it increasingly difficult to rely on conventional standardized and bureaucratic means of control such as rules and regulations, auditing and performance evaluations. Such mechanisms, however, might be too rigid for effectively coping with a number of separate, interdependent international operations (Doz & Prahalad, 1986, 1988; Paik & Sohn, 2004). Hence, the overall performance of the organization might suffer if MNCs ignore specific host-country factors such as CEE culture or institutional specifics. The need to maintain an effective and consistent yet flexible Management Control System (MCS) to coordinate widely dispersed operations is a great challenge to MNCs (Doz et al., 1988).

This study seeks to contribute to the debate on international management control practices of MNCs by:

- providing a comprehensive framework of factors determining the cross-border diffusion of management control based on a literature review of 95 articles in international business journals;
- shedding light on the international applicability of MCS by empirically studying how Western MNCs control their subsidiaries in CEE; and
- proposing a model of fit between control mechanisms, context factors, national culture and moderators.

Therefore, our central research questions are:

1. Which MCS do MNCs use to control the activities of their foreign subsidiaries in CEE? How are those systems implemented, designed and managed?

2. How does culture influence the design and management of HQ control systems in foreign subsidiaries?
    a. What are the major cultural differences in CEE as perceived by MNC HQ personnel?
    b. What are the successful strategies adopted by MNC HQ to cope with cultural differences?
3. How do context factors, such as the environment and organizational characteristics, influence the design and functioning of coordination and MCS in the CEE subsidiaries?

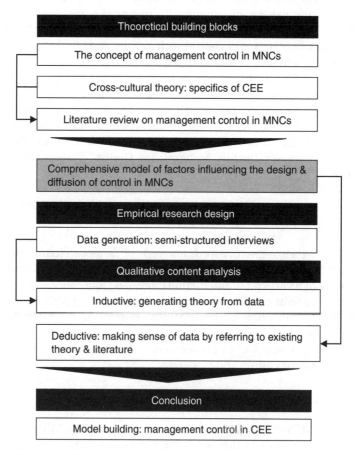

Figure 1.1 Research design.
Source: Author.

Given the novelty of analyzing HQ control in the context of CEE, this study uses a qualitative method to analyze the current state of management control in CEE and the cross-border transfer of control mechanisms between HQ and subsidiaries. The salience of context and cultural factors impacting the transfer of management practices is tested by a qualitative research design, using the method of the semi-structured interview. This allows us to follow up why and how questions while comparability of data is assured by the use of an interview guide. Interview data is analyzed with the qualitative content analysis (Mayring, 2002b). So far, empirical studies on international management control have predominantly used quantitative methods to obtain data, which might have yielded a lower level of understanding of the underlying phenomena than required. The majority of studies on the international transfer of management practices in general are based upon rather large-scale surveys, based on questionnaires (Gamble, 2003).

This study is structured as follows: (i) It starts with an introduction to the theoretical foundations of the concept of management control in MNCs and briefly presents the findings of an extensive literature review on this topic. Based on the findings in the literature, a comprehensive framework of factors impacting the adoption and diffusion of MCS is established. (ii) The rationale for choosing a qualitative research approach is given and the method discussed in some detail. (iii) Empirical findings on 40 international and/or regional HQ of MNCs are presented based on 46 semi-structured interviews with HQ executives and controllers. (iv) A fit model of contingencies, cultural differences and strategic choice is drawn based on the empirical findings. And finally (v), a short summary and the expected use of the study for scholars and practitioners are presented. Figure 1.1 depicts an overview of our research design.

2
The Concept of Management Control

2.1 Defining 'management control'

Despite the lack of a commonly accepted framework or typology of organizational controls, most authors interpret control in terms of the influence exerted on the subordinates to seek their compliance with organizational goals (Simons, 1995). 'Management control is the back end of the management process' (Merchant, Van der Stede, & Zheng, 2003). The number of definitions of management control per se is legion, however, they 'all relate to the process of organizing resources and directing activities for the purpose of achieving organizational objectives' (see Table 2.1) (Horvath, 1986; Merchant et al., 2003; Peemoeller & Keller, 1998). Merchant and Simons (1986) observed an absence of a unifying view on control in diverse areas of management and practice. Consistent with cybernetics theory (Weiner, 1954), from which the term 'control' was initially adopted, modern organization theorists tend to agree that control is a purposely designed and implemented process by which the organization achieves its goals (Yan & Yadong, 2001). 'The terms management accounting (MA), management accounting systems (MAS), management control systems (MCS), and organizational controls are sometimes used interchangeably. In general, MA refers to a collection of practices such as budgeting or product costing, while MAS refers to the systematic use of MA to achieve some goal' (Chenhall, 2003). The MCS is generally interpreted broader encompassing MAS and also other controls such as personal or clan controls.

The above definitions bear two essential messages:

- **Coordination:** Control is used as a means of directing behavior. 'Coordination means integrating or linking together different parts

Table 2.1 Definitions of management control in chronological order

Author	Exemplary definitions of management control
(Fayol, 1949)	'Control is a process by which the organization verifies the conformity of its actions to plans and directions.'
(Anthony, 1965)	'Management control [...] is the process by which managers ensure that resources are obtained and used effectively and efficiently in the accomplishment of the organization's objectives'.
(Tannenbaum, 1968)	'It is the function of control to bring about conformance to organizational requirements and achievements of the ultimate purposes of the organization'. '[c]ontrol is any process in which a person, group, or organization intentionally affects or determines what another person, group, or organization will do. [...] The purpose of control is to minimize idiosyncratic behavior and to hold individuals or groups to enunciated policy, thus making performance predictable.' (p. 238)
(Child, 1973)	'Control is essentially concerned with regulating activities within an organization so that they are in accord with the expectations established in policies, plans and targets.'
(Arrow, 1974)	'Management control refers to the process by which an organization influences its sub-units and members to behave in ways that lead to the attainment of organizational objectives'. (Arrow, 1974, Flamholtz, 1996)
(Youssef, 1975)	'The term control refers to the mechanisms used to assure the execution of organizational goals and plans.'
(Child, 1984)	'Management control is a process whereby management and other groups are able to initiate and regulate the conduct of activities so that their results accord with the goals and expectations held by those groups.'
(Geringer & Hebert, 1989)	'Control refers to the process by which one entity influences, to varying degrees, the behavior and output of another entity through the use of power, authority and a wide range of bureaucratic, cultural and informal mechanisms.' (pp. 236–237)
(Chow, Shields, & Wu, 1999b)	'Management control systems help organizations to increase the probability that employees make decisions and take actions which are in the organization's best interest'
(Anthony & Govindarajan, 2000)	'Management control is the process by which managers influence other members of the organization to implement the organization's strategies.'

Source: Author.

of an organization to accomplish a collective set of tasks' (Van de Ven, Delbecq, & Koenig, 1976). Thus, the decisive element of coordination is integrating and harmonizing different organizational parts towards a common goal (Harzing, 1999). The power element in coordination is therefore much more implicit as compared to the term control.
- **Power:** Control is an element of power in a relationship. 'Different mechanisms of control and their use in various combinations reflect the realities of political processes within the company and the struggles for control and autonomy between different interest groups that underlie them' (Ferner, 2000).

In short, 'control is a means to achieve an end called coordination, which in turn leads towards the achievement of the common organizational goals' (Harzing, 1999, p. 89). Before exploring the various types and theories of control in greater detail, the question of why coordination is needed is discussed.

Multiple theoretical assumptions on control lead to multiple answers:

Transaction cost theory
Basically, two types of control and coordination can be distinguished: market and organization. The need for coordination and control emerged from the division of labor (Smith, 1776). In a market system with perfect competition, accumulated supply and demand results in the market price, which contains all the information needed for individuals to decide whether or not to perform a transaction. Hence, the price is the control mechanism in the market system which ensures an efficient allocation process. However, there are some other factors coming into this equation, otherwise there would not be any organization present in society today. Coase (1937) concluded that there are costs involved using the price mechanism. Sometimes conducting transactions in the market system is more costly than performing transactions within an organization. Thus, the costs of internal coordination are lower than the costs involved in market transactions.

Williamson's transaction cost theory (1975; 1981) sheds more light onto this phenomenon: Williamson postulates that human beings are bound to make rational decisions but they are limited by their capacity to formulate and solve problems. Human beings are physically limited in their power to 'receive, store, retrieve and process information without error' (Williamson, 1975). The limits of rationality only come into play, if 'the limits of rationality are reached – which is to say, under conditions of uncertainty and/or complexity' (Williamson, 1975).

Consequently, an internal organization has several advantages under those conditions since it can deal with uncertainty/complexity in an adaptive, sequential way without fearing opportunism. Behaving opportunistically means using a situation to one's own advantage. Williamson (1975) argues that nobody knows beforehand if a human being is going to behave opportunistically or not. Opportunistic behavior, however, is only a problem if the number of potential trading partners is small. Internal organizations have an advantage, because parties within an organization are less likely to behave opportunistically. Moreover, an organization can be audited more easily and thereby reduce opportunistic potential. In short, transactions will take place where the cost is lowest. The costs depend on three critical dimensions of transactions – asset specificity, complexity/uncertainty, and frequency. Transactions characterized by high asset specificity, a high complexity/uncertainty and a high frequency will probably lead to the formation of an organization or as Williamson (1975) calls it 'hierarchy'.

Agency theory
Barnard (1968) states the fundamental problem of cooperation is the fact that individuals have only partially overlapping goals. Left to their own devices they pursue incongruent objectives and their efforts are uncoordinated. Thus, any organization with an economic goal must have a means of controlling diverse individuals efficiently (Ouchi, 1980). This phenomenon is addressed by classical agency theory (Berle & Means, 1932; Jensen & Meckling, 1976), which deals with the separation of ownership from control. Agency theory is frequently used to view dyadic relations (Eisenhardt, 1989a; Ghoshal & Nohria, 1989; Roth & O'Donnel, 1996), since it examines relations in which one party (the principal) delegates work to another party (the agent) under the assumption of self-interest, risk aversion, and opportunism (Eisenhardt, 1989a). Diverging interests and information asymmetry between principal and agent can trigger agency problems (Jensen & Meckling, 1976): The headquarters, the principal, depends on the unique knowledge of the subsidiary for effective decision making in the MNC and on some subsidiary specific advantages (Rugman & Verbeke, 2001). At the same time, the headquarters needs to reserve some decision making authority since its own interests and the local interests of the subsidiaries may collide (Nohria & Ghoshal, 1994). This classical agency problem provoked a debate in the literature on subsidiary autonomy and how to best govern and control an MNC's far-flung entities (see e.g., Egelhoff, 1988).

2.2 The fundamentals of management control

> If you can't measure it, you can't manage it.
> (Kaplan, Norton, 1997)

Controls have been categorized in many ways (Langfield-Smith, 1997). Before providing an overview of different classifications of control by various authors we briefly introduce the essential control functions.

Objectives and functions of management control

> In order to motivate people to behave in ways consistent with organizational goals, control systems must perform three related tasks.
> (Flamholtz, 1996)

- **Focus on goals:** People must be motivated in order to make decisions which are consistent with the organizational goals.
- **Coordination:** People's efforts must be coordinated and management control allows for decentralized structures. This need was recognized already in the early 20th century, as Alfred Sloan, in his function as managing General Motors during the 1930s stated:

> How could we exercise permanent control over the whole corporation in a way consistent with the decentralized scheme of the organization? [...] The means, as it turned out, was a method of financial control which converted the broad principle of return of investment into one of the important working instruments for measuring the operations of the divisions. (Sloan, 1965)

The underlying principle is to give autonomy to managers in their day-to-day operations, while at the time measuring the success of their decisions by a return of investment ratio.

- **Information:** Last but not least a control system is to provide information about people's performance and the results of operations.

Layers of management control
Management control is embedded within the organizational structure, organizational culture and an organization's environment. Management control is highly intertwined with other organizational tools and

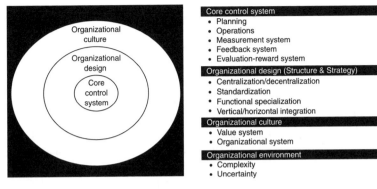

Figure 2.1 Onion of organizational control and environment.
Source: Adapted from Flamholtz (1996: 16).

systems and can be seen as a major hub of the management system. The organizational system and structure specifies roles, reporting relationships, and the division of responsibilities that shape decision making within an organization (Anthony and Govindarajan, 2000). Figure 2.1 shows how the core control system is supported by organizational structure, which is in turn embedded in the organizational culture.

In the following, the single elements of the above figure are described in some detail:

Core control system
The 'core control system' comprises four subsystems: Planning, operations, measurement, and evaluation reward (see Figure 2.2 below), which enables an organization to decide on what action should be taken and how to influence people to change behavior (Anthony and Govindarajan, 2000). **Planning** basically refers to the process of deciding on the organizational objectives and the means to attain those goals. Hall (1975) defines organizational goals as 'desired ends or states of affairs for whose achievement system policies are committed and resources are allocated'. The term 'objectives' refers to broad statements, an organization wishes to achieve, whereas 'goals' are expressed in definite operational terms. **Operations** refer to responsibilities, functions and activities specified in organizational roles to ensure a smooth run of day-to-day organizational activities (Flamholtz, 1996). The **measurement system** includes the Management Accounting System (MAS), which measures financial and managerial performance and non-financial measures such as product

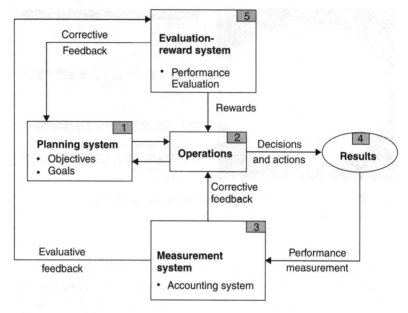

Figure 2.2 Model of core control system.
Source: Flamholtz (1996: 18).

quality, capacity utilization and so on. The function of measurement is twofold: First, the numbers and ratios generated are used to monitor the degree of goal achievement and provide the basis for corrective feedback. Second, the medium of measurement itself is a stimulus since people tend to change behavior if something is the object of measurement (Flamholtz, 1983, 1996). The **feedback loops** transport information about operations and their results. Corrective feedback provides information about performance and is designed to help adjust and improve the performance of operations. Evaluative feedback, however, is information about how well operations are doing and forms the basis for performance evaluation and rewards (Flamholtz, 1996). Lastly, the **evaluation-reward-system** assesses performance and administers extrinsic rewards (Flamholtz, 1996). Basically the core control process can be visualized as follows:

Organizational design as a control component
Organization design is determined by an organization's strategy and structure. According to Etzioni (1961); '[o]rganization structure is developed as a response to the problem of control' (see Figure 2.3).

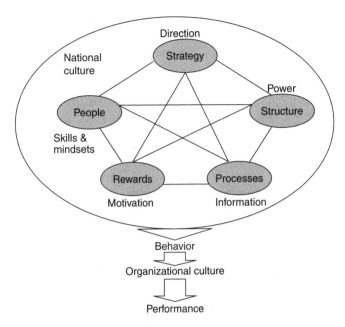

Figure 2.3 How organizational design affects behavior.
Source: Adapted from Galbraith (1995).

Indeed, structure not only specifies behavior expected from people in performance of their roles but also specifies the authority and reporting relationship of the entire set of roles existing in organizations (Flamholtz, 1996). Roles refer to the jobs people occupy in an organization and the sets of behaviors expected to be performed (Flamholtz, 1996). Structural dimensions of control are the **degree of centralization or decentralization, functional specialization**, and the **degree of vertical or horizontal integration** (Flamholtz, 1996). Galbraith (1995) visualizes the influence of structure on behavior in his well-known star model as depicted in Figure 2.3. He argues that structure becomes less important in fast-changing and complex environments, while processes, rewards and people become more important (Galbraith, 1995). We suggest adding a new dimension to the star framework by introducing national culture as an element influencing all five dimensions. Kluckhohn (1951) describes culture as 'patterned ways of thinking, feeling and reacting, acquired and transmitted mainly by symbols, constituting the distinctive achievement of human groups, including their embodiments in artifacts; the essential core of culture consists of traditional (i.e., historically derived and selected) ideas and especially their attached values'. Therefore, we conclude that national culture impacts strategy, structure, processes, reward policies and of course people's mind sets.

Major factors influencing structure are an organization's size and strategic intent, that is the degree of autonomy given within an organization (Flamholtz, 1996). As compared to the 'core control system' as outlined above, organizational design is rather static. Moreover, it can be seen as a strategic response to contingency factors, such as requirements of markets, technology and the environment per se (Miller, Droge, & Toulouse, 1988).

Organizational culture as a control component
Following our onion model depicted in Figure 2.1, the layer following organizational design is organizational culture. Organizational culture has been defined as a 'pattern of beliefs and expectations shared by the organization's members' (Schwartz & Davies, 1981) and as a subculture in the sense that it is a normative system of a group smaller than a society (Yinger, 1960). It generates a system of symbols, language, ideology, rituals, images, and myths that shapes the behavior of individuals and groups in the organization (Baliga & Jaeger, 1984). Ouchi (1979) refers to organizational culture as the broader values and normative patterns which guide worker behavior, practices and policies. Thus, organizational culture permeates many critical aspects of management control. The way people are chosen, developed, nurtured, interrelated, and rewarded in organizations is critical for organizations (Mintzberg & Quinn, 1991). For this paper, Flamholtz (1996) definition of organizational culture will be used: 'organizational culture is defined as a set of values, beliefs, and social norms which tend to be shared by its members and, in turn, tend to influence their thoughts and actions'. Organizational culture per se constitutes a control system by specifying the kinds of values, beliefs and norms which the organization supports (Flamholtz, 1996).

Lastly it is important to keep in mind that a firm's culture cannot exist independently from other dimensions as depicted in Figure 2.1. The core control system, structure and culture do influence each other (Flamholtz, 1996).

2.2.1 Classification of control mechanisms

Discussing the sheer magnitude of different typologies of management control found in literature one by one is beyond the scope of this study. Rather, different concepts of breaking down control will be discussed and compared in a table using Harzings (1999) classification of control mechanisms. However, the most seminal contributions of classifying control will be briefly introduced and discussed with a special emphasis on control in MNCs.

2.2.1.1 Formal vs. informal control

Almost any examination of control and organizations begins with Weber (1946). Weber's classical bureaucratic model of organizational control builds on explicit formal rules and regulations, thus, power and authority have a rational basis. In contrast, an organization with informal, cultural controls builds on an implicit organization-wide culture to control organization members. Power and authority are based on the customs and traditions inherent in the organizational culture (Weber, 1946). A number of scholars for example Child (1972; 1973), Ouchi (1979), Jaeger (1983) Baliga (1984), Anthony (1989), Martinez (1991) and Gupta (1991) basically build on that classification.

Formal controls consist of rules, standard operating procedures and budgeting systems. Hence, formal controls are the most visible, objective components of the control system and therefore relatively easy to research (Gupta et al., 1991; Langfield-Smith, 1997). They include output controls, which ensure the achievement of certain outcomes and involve monitoring, measuring, and taking corrective actions. Ex-ante controls, which focus on feed-forward controls, include administrative controls, personnel controls and behavior controls (ongoing monitoring of activities and decisions). Martinez and Jarillo (1991) name five control mechanisms as formal:

- *Centralization* is the extent to which decision making is located at the high levels of the chain of commands (Child, 1972; Galbraith, 1973; Lawrence & Lorsch, 1967; Martinez et al., 1991; Pugh, Hickson, Hinings, & Turner, 1969). In an international context centralization can be defined as 'the division of decision-making authority between headquarters and the various operational units' (Garnier, 1982).
- *Formalization* 'is the extent to which policies, rules, job descriptions, etc. are written down in manuals and other documents, generally leading to the establishment of standard routines' (Martinez et al., 1991).
- *Planning* comprises systems and processes such as strategic planning, budgeting, and goal setting to channel activities and actions of single units.

- *Output control/performance control* is based on the evaluation of files, records and reports by organizational units submitted to corporate management (Martinez et al., 1991; Mintzberg, 1979).
- *Behavioral control* is based on direct personal surveillance of subordinates behavior (Mintzberg, 1983; Ouchi, 1979).

Informal controls are not consciously designed. They are merely unwritten policies of an organization which derive from organizational culture. Ouchi (1979) describes 'clan controls' as a result of shared values and norms or the culture of an organization. Informal controls are nonetheless important components of MCS as the effectiveness of formal controls may depend on the nature of informal controls (Flamholtz, 1983).

Martinez and Jarillo (1991) group the following three types of managerial tools as informal:

- *Lateral relations* cut across the vertical structure and include permanent or temporary teams, task forces, integrative departments, task-related direct contacts between managers from different units, and so forth (Galbraith, 1973; Galbraith & Kazanjian, 1986; Lawrence et al., 1967).
- *Informal communication* is a network of informal and personal contacts among managers across different units of a company, supplementing formal communication channels (Kotter, 1982).
- *Organizational culture* communicates the 'way of doing things' in an organization (Pfeffer, 1982). Thus, values and objectives are communicated by socialization (Martinez et al., 1991).

Although all organizations have some sort of informal structure, subtle coordination mechanisms are only consciously developed if formal (and cheaper) coordination mechanisms do not suffice (Martinez et al., 1991). Other authors, however, including Bartlett and Ghoshal (1989) find that formal systems are the 'anatomy' of the organization and informal mechanisms are its 'physiology' and 'psychology' (Calori, Labatkin, & Very, 1994).

2.2.1.2 Output control vs. behavior control

Ouchi (1979) stresses that only two phenomena can be monitored and evaluated: behavior and output. If output measures are available and valid, then output is monitored and controlled (Baliga et al., 1984). Mintzberg (1979) calls this 'performance control'. Obviously the focus here is on 'ends' leaving some flexibility for organizational members to achieve those ends. However, if output measures are not readily available or their validity is questionable than behavior is monitored (Govindarajan & Fisher, 1990). Mintzberg (1979) labels this 'action planning'. It imposes specific decisions and actions at specific points of time (Baliga et al., 1984). If it is not possible to control for behavior or output, organizations have no choice but to indoctrinate their members with the organization's values and mission and hope that the members act accordingly. However, Harzing (1999) argues that characterizing some control mechanisms as behavior control might not be plausible, since all control mechanisms ultimately aim at changing behavior. Since output is nothing else but a behavioral result, the distinction between behavior and output control might not be very useful.

Snell (1992) adds another dimension to behavior and output control: Input control. Basically, Snell (1992) distinguishes three forms of control based on a human resource perspective: Input, behavior and output control. Input control includes the recruitment and selection of new employees and the training of individuals after they have joined the organization. Thus, input control ensures that only the 'best' applicants are selected. Furthermore, Snell defines input control as the formal bureaucratic human resource management systems, such as the selection and training, rather than the less observable influences such as socialization or clan control. Input controls regulate the antecedent conditions of performance including the knowledge, skills, abilities, values and motives of employees. From a control perspective, thus, the recruitment process itself is an important control regulative.

2.2.1.3 Market, bureaucracy and clan controls

Ouchi (1979; 1980) distinguishes three fundamental mechanisms through which organizations can cope with the problem of evaluation and control: markets, bureaucracy and clans. **Markets** deal with the control problem through their ability to precisely measure and reward individual contributions (Ouchi, 1979). The work of a purchasing agent, for example, is largely subject to the market mechanism, as the price conveys all the information needed for decision making. **Bureaucracies** rely on a mixture of close evaluation with a socialized acceptance of common objectives (Ouchi, 1979). Ouchi describes warehousing as being subject to a variety of explicit routines of monitoring and directing, basically reflecting the bureaucratic model described by Weber (1947). The rules differ from the price in that they are rather a partial bundle of information or an arbitrary standard to which a comparison has yet to be made (Ouchi, 1979). In a bureaucratic relationship, each party contributes labor to a corporate body which mediates the relationship by placing a value on each contribution and then compensating it fairly. **Clans** rely on a rather complete socialization process which effectively eliminates goal incongruence between individuals. Ouchi (1979) uses the example of a foreman in a warehouse who is promoted on the basis of his high internal commitment to a firm's objectives. The appropriateness of the different forms of controls in organizations depends on social and informational requirements.

2.2.1.4 Bureaucratic control vs. cultural control

Along those lines, Jaeger (1983) and Baliga and Jaeger (1984) distinguish between bureaucratic control and cultural control. Based on the distinction between output and behavior control (e.g., Ouchi, 1979), and formalized and cultural control, Baliga and Jaeger (1984) distinguish four types of control as shown in Table 2.2.

Behavior control consists of monitoring behavior of organization members and providing feedback to correct any discrepancies from desired behavior (Thompson, 1967). According to Ouchi (1980) and Etzioni (1980), attention must also be paid to the selection, training and socialization of organizational members.

Bureaucratic control consists of using a limited and explicit set of codified rules and regulations which delineate desired behavior (Child, 1973; Jaeger, 1983). Individuals who become functional members must accept the legitimacy of the organization's authority and obey its rules and regulations. The bureaucratic model is widely used in modern organizations and only few alternatives are offered by the literature. However, Jaeger (1983) sees control by organizational culture as an alternative to bureaucratic control and refers to large Japanese organizations which rely on informal and implicit control mechanisms

Table 2.2 A comparison of bureaucratic and cultural control mechanisms

Object of control	Type of control	
	Pure bureaucratic/ formalized control	Pure cultural control
Output	Formal performance reports	Shared norms of performance
Behavior	Company manuals	Shared philosophy of management

Source: Baliga and Jaeger (1984).

(Clark, 1979; Johnson & Ouchi, 1974). Jaeger (1983) identifies the Z-type organization which is in many ways similar to the Japanese organization: Even though formal control mechanisms are in place, control is mainly based on organizational culture (Jaeger, 1983).

2.2.1.5 Result control vs. personnel/cultural control

Building on the work of Geringer and Herbert (1989), Groot and Merchant (2000) provide a useful framework of classifying control of international ventures, by distinguishing control mechanisms, control focus, and control tightness. A good way to classify control mechanisms is according to the object of control, whether control is exercised over *actions, results or personnel/organizational culture* (Groot et al., 2000). Partners in International Joint Ventures (IJV) can make sure that desirable actions are taken by ensuring that they have the right to make certain key decisions or they can require certain personnel policies to be adhered to. Perlmutter (1969) distinguishes three mindsets concerning international staffing:

- Ethnocentric staffing implies that management style and values from the home country are considered to be superior to those of the host country. Thus only Parent-Country Nationals (PCN) are thought to be suitable for top-management positions. Headquarters influence on subsidiaries is high.
- The polycentric point of view, however, favors local nationals for management positions on the subsidiary level. Moreover, subsidiaries enjoy a considerable degree of autonomy and there is rather little communication between HQ and subsidiary.
- The geocentric perspective embraces a world-orientation. Managers are appointed regardless of their nationality on both, HQ and subsidiary level.
- Later, Perlmutter added a fourth dimension, which he called regiocentric. It is basically similar to the geocentric view only with a regional instead of a world orientation.

Obviously, those approaches have differing advantages and drawbacks: Although ethnocentric staffing provides a greater extent of control for the parent, it also involves a greater potential for conflict arising through cultural differences and conflicting national loyalties (Dowling, Welch, & Schuler, 1999). Moreover, an 'overuse' of PCNs can encourage a sense of differentiation between parent-country and Host-Country Nationals (HCN) (Lawrence et al., 1967).

Action control can be combined or replaced by result control. The latter means monitoring results and intervening whenever necessary. Alternatively, steps can be taken to ensure that the personnel are willing to perform well or that the organizational culture provides the framework for good performance. Table 2.3 contrasts result and personnel/cultural control.

2.2.1.6 Personal and impersonal vs. planned and unplanned

Flamholtz (1996) categorizes control mechanisms/systems along the dimensions personal/impersonal and planned/unplanned. Table 2.4 provides an overview on their control typology.

Ad hoc Supervision refers to day-to-day scheduling and stands for a process that occurs ad hoc rather than planned. This method of control is quite common in small firms (Flamholtz, 1996). Leadership as a method of control differs from supervision in that there is a predefined set of processes, such as performance goal settings, work facilitation and

Table 2.3 Type of control mechanisms based on the object of control

Object of control	
Result controls	**Personnel/Cultural controls**

• Set performance targets and monitor performance reports. Ask for explanations and:
  ○ Give advice where appropriate
  ○ Intervene when necessary
  ○ Promise and provide rewards for good performance
	• Select partners (in acquisition, IJVs, etc.) who can be trusted (e.g., reliable history, shared management philosophy)
	• Place qualified personnel in key positions
	• Require specified training
	• Look for specific personality traits of key personnel

Source: Based on Groot (2000).

Table 2.4 Typology of control: planned/unplanned versus personal/impersonal

	Typology of control	
	Personal control	Impersonal
Planned	Leadership	Formal control system
Unplanned	Ad hoc supervision	Ad hoc techniques

Source: Flamholtz (1996).

personal support, of which leaders are expected to make use (Flamholtz, 1996). Ad hoc control techniques are job descriptions, rules, standard operating procedures, budgets, appraisal systems, and so on. They are typically added one-at-a-time as an organization grows. However, ad hoc techniques are rather a collection of control mechanisms than a concisely designed system. Finally, formal control systems refer to a set of processes and techniques which have been designed explicitly as a system to influence behavior (Flamholtz, 1996). However, the need for a specific control method depends on the stage of development and the size of a firm. The larger and more complex an organization gets, the greater the need for a more sophisticated and integrated control system (Flamholtz, 1996).

2.2.1.7 A synthesis of control mechanisms

Given the sheer amount of different classifications, this paper is based on Harzing's (1999) framework of control which allows synthesizing and comparing virtually all of the control concepts. According to Harzing (1999) control mechanisms in MNCs can be subsumed along the following four dimensions outlined in the Table 2.5 below.

Table 2.5 Classification of control mechanisms

	Classification of control mechanisms on two dimensions	
	Personal/Cultural (founded on social interaction)	Impersonal/Bureaucratic/Technocratic (founded on instrumental artifacts)
Direct/ Explicit	**Category 1:** **Personal centralized control** • High centralization of decision making • Direct, personal supervision • Expatriate control	**Category 2:** **Bureaucratic formalized control** • High degree of standardization • High degree of formalization
Indirect/ Implicit	**Category 4:** **Control by socialization and networks** • Socialization: common corporate culture • High degree of informal communication • International management training	**Category 3:** **Output control** • Continuous evaluation of results • Detailed planning

Source: Harzing (1999; 2003).

In general, control mechanisms in the first and second category aim at controlling behavior directly and explicitly, while control mechanisms in the third and fourth category do so indirectly and implicitly (see also Groot et al., 2000).

Personal Centralized Control (PCC) includes mechanisms such as *hierarchy, centralized decision making* and personal surveillance of carrying out orders.

- *Centralization/autonomy*: Decision making is largely centralized at headquarters; subsidiaries do not have a large amount of autonomy to decide their own strategies and policies.
- *Direct supervision*: Headquarters managers strive for a close personal surveillance on the behavior of their subsidiaries.
- *Expatriate control*: Parent-country nationals are assigned to subsidiaries to ensure that headquarters policies are carried out (Harzing, 2003).

Bureaucratic Formalized Control (BFC) describes impersonal mechanisms which aim at pre-specifying behavior expected from employees. Terms used by authors that fit into this category include formalization, rules, regulations, paper systems and programs. They all refer to some sort of 'written manual', thus employees are expected to refer to the 'manual' instead of being directly told what to do. Hence, *standardization* is a pre-requisite for this form of bureaucratic control.

- *Standardization*: All subsidiaries are supposed to operate in more or less the same way.
- *Formalization*: The MNC has written rules and procedures for everything and employees are expected to follow these procedures accurately (Harzing, 2003).

Output Control (OC) bears the largest resemblance to the market way of coordination as the authors grouped in this category do not distinguish any control mechanisms. The focus is on *outputs realized* rather than on behavior. Outputs are usually made transparent by monitoring or reporting systems.

- *Output evaluation*: MNCs exert a high degree of output control, by the means of a continuous evaluation of the results of subsidiaries.
- *Planning*: MNCs have a very detailed planning, goal setting and budgeting system that includes clear-cut (often quantitative) objectives to be achieved at both strategic and operational levels (Harzing, 2003).

The category ***Control by Socialization and Networks*** (CSN) includes all types of control which do not fit into the first three categories. Such control mechanisms are not hierarchical, not bureaucratic, not formal, and there are no fixed targets. Rather, social control mechanisms are *informal, subtle, and sophisticated* (Harzing, 1999). Thus, social control depends on developing some identification with and commitment to the values and objectives of the corporation (Child, 1984). Van Maanen and Schein (1979) define organizational socialization as the process by which 'an individual is taught which behaviors and perspectives are customary and desirable within the work setting'. For this study we use Gupta's (1991) definition which puts corporate socialization in an MNC context by stating that 'corporate socialization [...] are processes through which subsidiary-managers' norms and values become closely aligned with those of the parent corporation'. Classic means of social control are international exchanges of personnel between different units of an organization and structured personal interaction and training (Das & Teng, 1998; Edstrom & Galbraith, 1977; Ferner, 2000; Fryxell, Dooley, & Vryza, 2003). Ultimately, the efficacy of social control mechanisms depends on the level of trust between the different units (Das et al., 1998). Although all organizations have informal networks, the conscious development of such subtle measures appears only when formal and cheaper means of control do not suffice (Martinez et al., 1991). At the same time, social control mechanisms have the potential to reduce formal monitoring costs and permit flexibility and adaptability (Dyer, 1997). In general, MNCs which rely on CSN rely on the following practices (Harzing, 2001a):

- *Socialization*: MNCs attach a lot of value to a strong 'corporate culture' and try to ensure that all subsidiaries share the main values of the firm.
- *Informal communication*: MNCs have a very high degree of informal communication among executives of the different subsidiaries and HQ and do not rely on formal communication channels.
- *International management training*: MNCs make extensive use of international (as opposed to purely national) management training programs. In these programs executives from different subsidiaries and the HQ follow courses that deal mostly with the transfer of company-specific knowledge (Harzing, 2003).

In sum, different control mechanisms should rather be seen as complements than as substitutes. Nevertheless, some combinations are more likely to occur than others. For example, PCC and BFC are more likely to go together than other combinations (Child, 1984). Table 2.6 gives an overview of control mechanisms distinguished by various authors who are categorized using Harzing's framework of PCC, formal bureaucratic control and CSN.

2.2.1.8 Control mechanisms used by this study

Based on Harzing (1999) and Martinez (1991) we developed the following categorization of control mechanisms. This categorization comprises all subcategories of Martinez (1991) classification and also allows us to group the control mechanisms into Harzing's broader categories of PCC, BFC, OC and CSN.

Explicit control mechanisms

- *Extent of centralization*: The extent to which decision making takes place at the HQ. A high centralization implies that decision making is largely centralized at the HQ and subsidiaries do not have a large amount of autonomy to decide on their own strategies and policies.
- *Extent of standardization*: The extent to which all subsidiaries are supposed to operate in more or less the same way.
- *Extent of formalization*: The extent to which an MNC has written rules and procedures for everything and employees are expected to follow these procedures accurately.
- *Extent of output & performance control*: The extent to which an MNC exerts output control by the means of a continuous evaluation of the results of subsidiaries. It comprises three elements:
  ○ Extent of planning (top-down, bottom-up)
  ○ Extent of output control
  ○ Extent of evaluation reward systems
- *Extent of expatriate control*: The extent to which expatriates are assigned to subsidiaries to ensure that headquarters' policies are carried out.

Implicit control mechanisms by socialization and networks

- *Control by lateral relations* cuts across the vertical structure and includes permanent or temporary teams, task forces, integrative departments, task-related direct contacts between managers from different units, and so forth (Galbraith, 1973; Galbraith et al., 1986; Lawrence et al., 1967).
- *Control by informal communication and personal intra-group networks* are an intra-group network based on informal communication and

Table 2.6 Control mechanisms distinguished by various authors

Author(s)	Personal centralized control	Formal bureaucratic control	Output control	Control by socialization and networks
March & Simon (1958) Blau & Scott (1963)	Coordination by feedback Control through personal supervision	programs (activity coordination) rules and regulations	programs (output coordination) performance records (results achieved)	coordination by feedback recruitment and training
Lawrence & Lorsch (1967)	Managerial hierarchy	paper system		direct managerial contact; individual/team or departmental integrative devices
Thompson (1967)	(Coordination by mutual adjustment)	standardization (routines or rules)	coordination by plan (schedules)	coordination by mutual adjustment
Child (1972; 1973)	Centralization	bureaucratic (formalization, standardization)		
Galbraith (1973)	Hierarchy	rules and programs	planned targets/ goal setting	creating lateral relationships (a.o. direct contact, task forces)
Edström & Galbraith (1977)	Centralizing control strategy (personal/direct)	bureaucratic strategy (impersonal/indirect)		control by socialization
Ouchi (1977; 1979; 1980)	Behavior control (direct personal surveillance)	behavior control (rules and procedures)	output control	clan control (indoctrination, socialization)

Continued

Table 2.6 Continued

Author(s)	Personal centralized control	Formal bureaucratic control	Output control	Control by socialization and networks
Mintzberg (1979; 1983)	Direct supervision	standardization of work processes	standardization of output	mutual adjustment; socialization; standardization of skills)
Doz/Prahalad (1981)	Direct personal: managers' management mechanism (choice of key managers, reward & punishment, management development)	indirect, formal: data management mechanism (information systems, measurement systems, resource allocation procedures, strategic planning, budgeting)		socialization: Conflict Resolution Mechanism (decision responsibility assignment, integrators, business teams, coordination committees, task forces, issue resolution process)
Baliga & Jaeger (1984)	Cultural (personal)	Bureaucratic (behavior)	Bureaucratic (output)	Cultural (socialization)
Child (1984)	Personal centralized control	Bureaucratic control (a.o. Formalization, routinization)	Output control	Cultural control (a.o. Socialization, emphasis on selection, training and development)
Kenter (1985)	Personal control mechanisms (personal instructions)	Technocratic control mechanisms (formalization)	Technocratic control mechanisms (planning)	Personal control mechanisms (socialization)
Merchant (1985; 1996)	Action (a.o. Centralization)	Action (a.o. Bureaucratic)	Result	Personnel (a.o. Selection, training, cultural control)

Author		Bureaucratic behavior	Bureaucratic (output)	Cultural (socialization)
Pucik & Katz (1986)				
Bartlett & Ghoshal (1989)	Centralization (direct intervention)	Formalization (formal systems, policies and standards)		Socialization (recruitment, development, acculturation)
Martinez & Jarillo (1989)	Structural and formal (behavior control/direct supervision, centralization)	Structural and formal (departmentalization, centralization, formalization, standardization)	Structural and formal (output, planning)	Informal and subtle (lateral relations, informal communication, socialization)
Gupta & Govindarajan (1991)	Centralization and formalization			
Hennart (1991)	Hierarchy (personal)	Hierarchy (impersonal through rules and regulations)	Price	Selection/socialization
Macharzina (1993)	Personal coordination	Structural coordination, Technocratic coordination		Personal coordination
Sohn & Paik (1994; 1996) Paik & Sohn (2004)				Expatriates as social control
Flamholtz (1996)	Ad hoc supervision (unplanned personal control), Leadership (planned personal control)	Ad hoc techniques (impersonal, unplanned control), Formal control system (impersonal, planned control)		

Continued

Table 2.6 Continued

Author(s)	Personal centralized control	Formal bureaucratic control	Output control	Control by socialization and networks
Ferner (2000)		Bureaucratic control mechanism		Social/personal control
Groot and Merchant (2000)	Personal control		Result control	
Hamilton & Kashlak (1999)	Input control (behavior control)		Output control	Input control (management training)
Harzing (1999; 2001b; 2001c)	Staffing as a means of control			
Konopaske, Werner & Neupert (2002)	Staffing control			
Kim, Park & Prescott (2003)	Centralization based integration	Formalization based integration	Information based integration	People based integration

Source: Amplified and updated based on Harzing (1999).

personal relations among managers from different units of a company, supplementing formal communication channels.
- *Control by socialization via organizational culture*: MNCs attach a lot of value to a strong 'corporate culture' and try to ensure that all subsidiaries share the main values of the firm. Thus, values and objectives are communicated by socialization (Martinez et al., 1991).
- *International management training*: MNCs make extensive use of international (as opposed to purely national) management training programs. In these programs executives from different subsidiaries and the HQ follow courses that deal mostly with the transfer of company-specific knowledge (Harzing, 2003).

2.3 Management control in multinational corporations

When firms expand overseas, both complexity and diversity increases and although exercising control in international ventures has no fundamental conceptual difference from controlling single companies, the demand for monitoring, coordinating and integrating activities and resources increases (Yan et al., 2001). Controlling and coordinating a network of geographically and culturally dispersed subsidiaries is far more challenging than controlling a purely domestic firm. The type of control employed and the organizational structure of an MNC is determined by the international strategy it pursues (Hamilton et al., 1999) and by various contingencies. In order to explore new local resources or to exploit resources within the international network of subsidiaries (Bartlett & Ghoshal, 1989) effective coordination and control is needed. The great diversity of MNC operations increases the complexity of its system interdependence which, in turn, demands more coordination (Lawrence & Lorsch, 1967) and affects information processing and control systems (Egelhoff, 1993; Vachani, 1999).

According to Cray (1984) a parent firm does not attempt to maximize predictability through control due to two considerations: The first is flexibility, since an organization must maintain freedom of action when faced with a changeable environment (Burns & Stalker, 1961; Lawrence et al., 1967). This holds all the more true if the environment of the subsidiary and the one of the parent differs substantially. The other consideration is the cost of control. Thompson (1967) argues that the cost of communication and control can be minimized if the cost of integration is lowered. Therefore, the level of control exerted over a sub-unit represents a compromise between the desire for control, the need for flexibility and the cost of maintaining control (Cray, 1984). In any case, management control has to ensure that an MNC HQ has all the information necessary to pursue its strategy effectively.

2.3.1 Strategy determines organizational design and type of control

> A strategy that cannot be evaluated in terms of whether or not it is being achieved is simply not a viable or even a useful strategy.
>
> (Roush & Ball, 1980)

Strategy has been used as a major variable in MCS research since the 1980s (Langfield-Smith, 1997). Mintzberg (1978), for example, describes strategy as a pattern of decisions about the organizations future. Strategy becomes meaningful through implementation in the organization's structure and processes (Miles & Snow, 1978). Strategic management is conceptualized as the progression from strategy formulation to strategy implementation (Langfield-Smith, 1997). A firm's strategy is influenced by the pattern of the international competition and determines the organizational design and control system. As already outlined in Figure 2.1, an organizational environment influences the type of control employed in an organization. Figure 2.4 depicts how strategy building and control mechanisms are affected by changes in the international environment.

The link between strategy and structure/control has been discussed extensively in literature and many scholars have argued that strategy

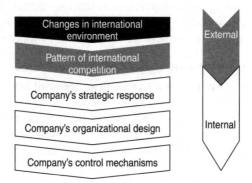

Figure 2.4 Environment, strategy, organizational design, systems and processes in MNCs.

Source: Based on Martinez and Jarillo (1989).

might be as dependent on structure as structure is on strategy (e.g., Amburgey & Dacin, 1994; Burton & Obel, 2004; Chandler, 1962). 'Structure no more follows strategy than the left foot follows the right in walking' (Mintzberg et al., 1991). Nevertheless, all elements of an organization must 'fit' to be in 'harmony' with each other (Mintzberg et al., 1991). 'An effective organization is one that has blended its structure, management practices, rewards, and people into a package that in turn fits with its strategy' (Galbraith, 1983). Recent management literature has moved away from the 'one best way' approach of management toward an 'it all depends' approach, formally known as 'contingency theory' (Mintzberg, 1979).

Organizational design, strategy, organizational culture, and control must not only be designed to provide an 'internal fit', but also ensure a smooth fit with the environment (Chapman, 1997). As Figure 2.5 shows, an MNC's effectiveness is a function of fit between its international strategy, its organizational design, its control and its environment (Roth, Schweiger, & Morrison, 1991).

Design 'is concerned with how things ought to be, with devising structures to attain goals' (Simon, 1981). An organization's mission and goals form the basis for organizational design (see Figure 2.6). The multiple contingency model states that the organizational structure depends on multiple dimensions as outlined below.

According to Mintzberg (1979), a firm's structure and strategy are determined by its environment to a large extent. 'In organizational

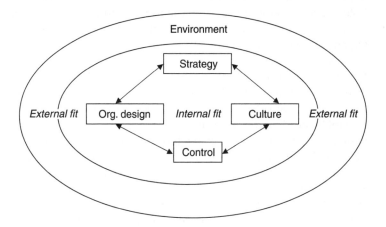

Figure 2.5 Internal and external strategic, organizational design, control, and cultural fit.
Source: Adapted from Hoffmann (1996).

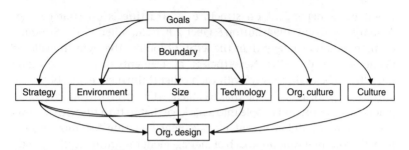

Figure 2.6 Organizational context.
Source: Adapted from Burton & Obel (2004).

theory it is beyond dispute that the organizational structure changes during the process of internationalization' (Mintzberg et al., 1991; Wächter, 2003). The internationalization of the world economy is the most important trend for internationally operating organizations (Bartlett et al., 1989). Analyzing industry, structure and strategy, Bartlett & Ghoshal (1989) use the following terms: multidomestic, international, global and transnational.

- **Multidomestic:** A multidomestic industry is characterized by cultural, social and political differences between countries. Thus, companies operating in these industries usually follow a strategy that holds national responsiveness as the most important factor. Therefore, products/services and policies are tailored to local needs. Organizational structures are characterized by decentralized assets and decision making.
- **International:** The internationalization process reflects the international product life cycle. Thus, the knowledge transfer from the parent to units abroad plays a pivotal role. Close coordination and control by headquarters is necessary.
- **Global:** A global industry is characterized by standardized consumer needs and economies of scale; hence centralization and integration are high. Both resources and decision making are centralized.
- **Transnational:** Companies operating in transnational industries are required to respond to the conflicting needs of global efficiency, national responsiveness, and world-wide learning at the same time. This makes it impossible to speak of one appropriate strategy; rather the strategy is to stay flexible by all means. This need is also reflected by a network-like organizational structure to ensure flexibility at all levels.

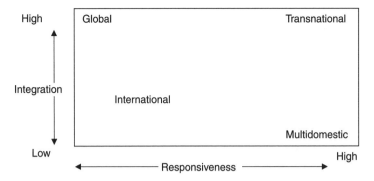

Figure 2.7 The integration-responsiveness framework.
Source: Prahalad & Doz (1987).

Those four combinations of industry, strategy and structure are presented in the integration/responsiveness framework by Prahalad and Doz (1987) shown in Figure 2.7. Integration represents the level of global integration. Responsiveness shown on the horizontal axis represents the desired influence of subsidiaries in strategic and operational decisions.

In a study based on nine MNCs in three industries Bartlett and Ghoshal (1989) found that the international organizational model is the dominant model for American MNCs, the global model for Japanese MNCs and the multi-domestic model for European MNCs. However, it is important to note that the transnational type shown in the upper right corner does not necessarily rank high on both integration and responsiveness. Rather, the transnational approach chooses whether high integration or high responsiveness suits best in a given situation. Interestingly, recent literature (Forsgren, 1990; Harzing, 1999; Taylor, 1991) sees the transnational model as the most suitable configuration for MNCs.

2.4 Synthesis: strategy, control mechanisms and control extent

This chapter strives to bring together the MNC's strategy, the resulting roles of the parent and subsidiaries, the type of management control and the extent of control. Figure 2.8 depicts the relationship between strategy, control mechanisms and control scope: HQ determines the framework for the control systems in place, hence, differences in the management style of the parent are reflected in the choice of control mechanisms and the object and scope of control. The chosen control type and the extent of

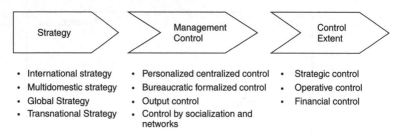

Figure 2.8 Strategy determines control mechanisms and extent.
Source: Author.

control exercised by a parent is based on its strategy and environmental conditions. As discussed at length before, control mechanisms can be classified into four categories: PCC, BFC, output control and CSN (Harzing, 1999). Depending on the extent of control exercised by the parent, three types of control extent can be distinguished: financial, strategic, and operational (Bendak, 1992; Goold & Campbell, 1987; Schwarzburg, 2001). Control extent can either be broad, if the parent attempts to control the entire range of a subsidiaries activities, or narrow, if control is focused on some aspects only, for example. only on some key performance measures (Groot et al., 2000). Hence, each control type can be used to affect tighter or looser control (Merchant et al., 1986).

In an international context, Prahalad and Doz (1981) define **strategic control** as 'the extent of influence that an HQ has over a subsidiary concerning decisions that affect subsidiary strategy'. Child (1984) defines strategic control as 'control over the means and methods on which the whole conduct of an organization depends', including the deployment of capital, the determination of strategic priorities and deciding on senior appointments. Goold and Quinn (1990) define strategic controls as formulating competitive benchmarks and using non-financial performance measures as a basis for developing short term indicators that are linked to the achievement of long-term strategic goals. Johnson (1987) states that strategic controls are concerned with matching organizational activities to its environment and resource capabilities, the allocation of major resources within the organization, and consideration of the expectations and values of the organization's stakeholders. The interface between the subsidiary and the HQ is situated on the strategic level, with the HQ governing and coordinating its subsidiaries to ensure that a common strategic goal is reached (Liessmann, 1990). Consequently, the role of the HQ is often named as a 'strategic holding'. In the past, MCS research focused on senior management in strategic control (Simons, 1995). However, many scholars share the belief that lower level employees are becoming more actively involved in activities of strategic significance. The orientation towards accounting controls and accounting information, which has dominated MCS research, might not be broad enough to analyze more modern approaches to effective control (Langfield-Smith, 1997).

Operational control is control over the essential processes within an organization, in the sense of determining how employees of an organization perform their work (Child, 1984; Groot et al., 2000). The interface between the HQ and the subsidiary is located on the operative management level, and the extent and intensity of control and related activities is high. Furthermore, there is a high intensity of communication between the HQ and its subsidiaries. *Detailed budgets* serve as a major governance and control mechanism. Motivation and regulation of operational control is often affected by *personal and social coordinating mechanisms*, since centrally planned transfer prices distort returns of single ventures (Bendak, 1992). The HQ involvement in planning and control combined with a standardized reporting system creates group-wide transparency. At the same, however, subsidiary responsibility and corporate culture and mission statements play an important role in operational control (Gigouline et al., 2001). In general, operational control is a much tighter form of control than strategic control and financial control.

Finally, **financial control** is the most minimalist form of control since financial management is the only interface between the HQ and its subsidiaries. Each subsidiary is fully responsible for both strategic and operational control systems (Bendak, 1992). The only governing and control mechanisms of the HQ are key financial ratios (Dieckhaus, 1993).

Figure 2.9 depicts the different interaction levels of financial, strategic and operational control; and links it to the control extent, standardization, centralization, communication and subsidiary autonomy.

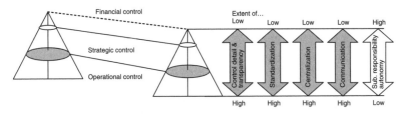

Figure 2.9 Interaction levels and extent of control between HQ and subsidiaries.
Source: Author.

Table 2.7 Dimensions of international control in MNCs

Characteristics	Dimensions of management control			
	Financial control	Strategic control	Operational control	
Type of investment	Capital investment	Capital- and cooperative investment	Cooperative investment	
Role of parent	Financier	Moderator/catalyst	Architect/navigator	
Type of parent	'Financial holding'	'Strategic holding'	'Operative holding'	
Leadership style	Demanding	Coordinating/supporting	Shaping/directing	
Level of interference	Little HQ interference	Intermediate HQ interference	High HQ interference	
Objective	Profitability	Immaterial synergies	Material synergies	
Strategy type	Portfolio management	Know-how transfer	Task centralization	
Intensity of control	Minimal control	Minimal or regular control	Regular or intensive control	
Centralized (no autonomy) Responsibility assignment *Decentralized* (high autonomy)	Strategy / Operation	Strategy / Operation	Strategy / Operation	
Degree of subsidiary autonomy	High (little integration)	Intermediate (intermediate integration)	Low (high horizontal and vertical integration)	
Interface to subsidiary	Financial management	Strategic management	Operative management	

Control mechanisms				
Possible type of control mechanism (Harzing)	• Output control (but only rough planning)	• Bureaucratic formalized control • Output control • Control by socialization And networks		• Personal centralized control • Bureaucratic formalized control
Vertical	*Financial output control* Presetting financial target ratios	*Output and behavior control* Presetting of strategic guidelines, strategic milestones and operational ratios No detailed budget control		*Budget – actual comparison* Presetting detailed budgets
Horizontal	No need (market mechanism)	Decentrally negotiated transfer prices		Preset central transfer prices
Supportive	No need	Strategic framework plan, common projects		Operative framework plan, Central projects, mission statement
Planning direction	Top-down by financial ratios	Combined		Top-down in detail by HQ
Pros & cons				
Potential problems	Information shortage at HQ, Difficult to assess business performance in business units	High mgt complexity due to decentralized structures		Rigidity, innovative potential, multiple responsibility of HQ
Advantages	Low complexity High motivation for management, high innovative potential	Structural flexibility		Synergies Internal cooperation

Source: Author partly based on (Bendak, 1992; Goold et al., 1987: 152; Groot et al., 2000).

Table 2.7 provides a summary of all discussed dimensions of control in MNCs by comparing control extent – financial, strategic and operational control – with the role and type of the parent and HQ-subsidiary interaction levels. Furthermore, control mechanisms are linked with the role of the parent and the control extent employed, and potential pros and cons of the various forms are listed.

3
Literature Review of Current Studies on Management Control in MNCs

We conducted an extensive literature review of Management Control Systems (MCS) used in MNCs in leading management journals in International Business (IB). The journals were selected based on their relevance and input in the field of management control in international ventures. Table 3.1 gives an overview of the journals screened and the number of articles found relevant for the topic. Approximately 8,000 articles from 19 leading journals in international management and control over the period from 1996 to 2004 were screened and 95 articles were analyzed in depth.

All articles were analyzed using the following criteria:

- What is researched? Which variables are analyzed? What are the dependent and the independent variables?
- What is the direction and shape of the explanatory links proposed; what is the causal model?
- What is the level of analysis?
- Which context factors impact the applicability and transfer of management control practices?
- How can management control practices be transferred successfully from one international organizational unit to another?
- How does culture influence management control (both explicit and implicit forms)?

Basically we found two approaches in the literature on cross-cultural studies on management control: (i) research based on the structural contingency argument, which considers contextual variables as major

Table 3.1 Journals screened from 1996 to 2004 and number of identified relevant articles

Journals screened	Relevant articles
Academy of Management Journal	3
Academy of Management Review	1
Accounting, Organizations and Society	27
European Management Journal	1
Journal of Business Research	1
Journal of International Business Studies	6
Journal of Management	3
Journal of International Management	1
Journal of Management Studies	9
Journal of World Business	7
Journal of International Accounting, Auditing and Taxation	1
Journal of Organization Studies	8
Management Accounting Research	1
Strategic Management Journal	1
The International Journal of Accounting	21
European Accounting Review	1
Business History Review	1
The International Journal of Human Resource Management	1
International Marketing Review	1
Total number of relevant articles	**95**

determinants of the applicability of MCS; and (ii) the culture based perspective, which sees culture as a determinant for human action and, hence, explaining international variations in management practices.

Studies based on the contingency argument predicate on environmental characteristics (Crozier, 1964; Freeman, 1973; Meyer & Rowan, 1977; Pfeffer & Salancik, 1978; Pugh et al., 1969; Thompson, 1967) such as uncertainty, heterogeneity/complexity, and/or organizational characteristics (Bendix, 1956; Pugh et al., 1969; Taylor, 1911; Weber, 1946; Wong & Birnbaum-More, 1994) (such as age, size, level of interdependence, ownership and organizational culture), as decisive factors.

Studies based on cultural theories, however, claim that differences in management practices are due to cultural discrepancies. They see the country of origin as the dominating factor determining what types of management practices are used in a foreign subsidiary. Basically, they assume that the more culturally distant the host country is from the home country the more difficult it is to transfer management practices (Beechler & Yang, 1994). The great majority of studies investigated use a value-dimensional conception of culture, and, since the late 1980s,

Hofstede's dimensions (Arnold, Bernardi, & Neidermeyer, 2001; Awasthi, Chow, & Wu, 2001; Chow, Hwang, Liao, & Wu, 1998; Chow, Kato, & Merchant, 1996; Chow et al., 1999b; Harrison, McKinnon, Panchapakesan, & Leung, 1994; Harrison & McKinnon, 1999; Williams & Seaman, 2001).

This review is structured as follows: First, empirical contributions to the diffusion of MCS based on contingency theory are introduced, thus, the influence of organizational characteristics and environmental factors on MCS are discussed. Second, articles dealing with the role of culture regarding the MCS and the cross-border transfer of MCS are analyzed. Third, factors which were found to have a moderating effect on the applicability and transfer of managerial control are analyzed. Finally, a comprehensive model combining all discussed forces on the diffusion process is proposed.

3.1 Factors influencing management control

Contingency-based research assumes that managers act with an intent to adapt their organizations to changes in contingencies in order to attain a fit and enhance performance (see Chenhall 2003 for a review). The term contingency basically implies that something is true only under specified conditions (Chenhall, 2003). In its core, contingency theory explains the effectiveness of MCS design that suits the nature of the environment, technology, size, structure, institutions, and strategy. It is assumed that patterns of perception and preferences of organizational members are dictated by the environment and are therefore not universal across borders. Many contemporary studies still draw on the seminal structural contingency frameworks developed by organizational theorists such as Burns and Stalker (1961), Woodward (1965), Lawrence and Lorsch (1967), Perrow (1970), Thompson (1967), Pugh et al. (1968), and Galbraith (1973). The most recent stream of contingency literature has been related to the role of strategy in MCS design (Chenhall, 2003). Important links between strategy, the environment, technology, organizational structure, and MCS have been established (see Langfield-Smith 1997 for a review).

Basically, organizational theory offers two approaches explaining organizational structure: One approach explains differences in organizational structure by the organization's environment (Crozier, 1964; Freeman, 1973; Meyer et al., 1977; Pfeffer et al., 1978; Pugh et al., 1969; Thompson, 1967), while the other approach explains variations in structure internally by the context in which the organization operates, such as technology, size, ownership and dependence (Bendix, 1956;

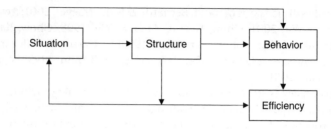

Figure 3.1 Elements of contingency approach.
Source: Kieser (1998).

Pugh et al., 1969; Taylor, 1911; Weber, 1946). Figure 3.1 depicts the basic relations of the contingency approach.

Some of the analyzed articles in our literature review from 1996 to 2004 build on seminal contingency contributions which were beyond the time scope of this literature review. Since those contributions are nevertheless highly important for the understanding of current contributions and for our ultimate goal of drawing a model of fit of international management control, the insights of seminal contingency studies will also be included in the discussion of the literature. Table 3.2 depicts an overview of 19 seminal contingency contributions in the form of books and articles which impacted later work on MCS.

Table 3.3 gives an overview on empirical contributions analyzed in the literature review which looked at the influence of various contingency factors and their impact on control mechanisms in MNCs. Thus, the dependent variables in all those studies are a variety of control mechanisms (such as output control, the use of budgets, costing and budget controls, personal control, and extent of control) which are explained by contingency variables of the organization (e.g., size and age of the subsidiary; HQ ownership structure), or by contingency variables of the environmental context (e.g., uncertainty, economic transition and industry), or by contingency variables of the country of origin such as national institutions which shape an MNC's control system. The table below gives an overview of analyzed articles explaining MCSs by environmental, organizational and institutional contexts.

In the following, the analyzed literature is discussed in more detail.

3.1.1 Environmental context

The IB environment has been categorized in many ways (Burton et al., 2004). In contingency theory, variables related to uncertainty measures

Table 3.2 Seminal contingency contributions

Seminal contingency contributions	
Authors	Variables
Burns and Stalker (1961)	External: environment
Crozier (Crozier, 1964; Freeman, 1973; Meyer et al., 1977; Pfeffer et al., 1978; Pugh et al., 1969; Thompson, 1967)	External: environment
Lawrence and Lorsch (1967); Lawrence (1981)	External: environment
Thompson (1967)	External: environment
Perrow (1970)	External: environment
Pugh et al. (1968)	External: environment
Freeman (1973)	External: environment
Galbraith (1973)	External: environment
Meyer (1977)	External: environment
Pfeffer (1978)	External: environment
Weber (1946)	Internal: organization
Bendix (1956)	Internal: organization
Blau (1970; 1963)	Internal: organization
Woodward (1965)	Internal: organization
Pugh (1969)	Internal: organization
Pondy (1969)	Internal: organization
Hickson (1974)	Internal: organization
Singh (1986)	Internal: organization

Source: Author.

have been used most in empirical investigations of the business environment. In their seminal work, Lawrence and Lorsch (1967) measured uncertainty as a perceptual measurement of clarity of information, certainty of causal relationships, and time spans of definite feedback. Lawrence (1981) combines the instability as the rate of change, ignorance of data, and cause and effects, into unpredictability. Additionally, he groups the number of variables, the homogeneity and heterogeneity, and interdependency of variables into complexity. Figure 3.2 depicts how unpredictability and complexity are then aggregated into uncertainty.

Duncan (1972), developed a two-dimensional measure of environmental uncertainty, consisting of environmental change or dynamism (unstable to stable) and environmental complexity (simple to complex). The environmental change dimension encompasses that the environment can change in both predictable and unpredictable ways, while environmental complexity refers to the number of elements in an organization that are important to organizations. Khandwella (1977) provides a useful taxonomy of environmental variables, such as

Table 3.3 Overview of analyzed contingency-based empirical studies

	Context: environment	
Authors	Explanatory variable category	Sign. Corr.
O'Connor, Chow & Wu (2004)	Environment: economic	Mixed
Fisher (1996)	Environment: uncertainty	No
Firth (1996)	Environment: economic	Yes
Collins, Holzmann & Mendoza (1997)	Environment: economic	Yes
Guilding, Lamminmaki & Drury (1998)	Environment: technological	No
Uddin & Hopper (2001)	Environment: economic	Yes
Williams & Seaman (2001)	Environment: economic	Yes
Eden, Dacin & Wan (2001)	Environment: economic	Yes
Dedoussis (1995)	Environment: economic	Yes
Kim, Park & Prescott (2003)	Environment: economic	Yes
Luo (2003)	Environment: economic	Yes

	Context: organization	
Authors	Explanatory variable category	Sign. Corr.
O'Connor, Chow & Wu (2004)	Size, age	Size yes; age no
Fryxell, Dooley & Vryza (2003)	Age, size	Age yes; size no
Wong & Birnbaum-More (1994)	Age, size	Size: yes;
Erramilli (1996)	Size (home-country market size)	Yes
Li, Karakowsky & Lam (2002)	Age	Yes
Firth (1996)	Ownership, size	Size yes; ownership no
Lee (1998)	Ownership	Yes
Wang & Wee (Wang & Wee, 1999)	Ownership	Yes
Child & Yan (1999)	Ownership	Yes
Chang & Taylor (1999)	Ownership	Yes
Whitley & Czaban (1998)	Ownership	Yes
Groot & Merchant (2000)	Ownership, strategy	Strategy yes; ownership no
Chang-Bum & Beamish (2004)	Strategy	Yes

	Context: institutions country of origin	
Authors	Explanatory variable category	Sign. Corr.
O'Connor, Chow & Wu (2004)	Institutions: all categories	Yes
Favere-Marchesi (2001)	Institutions: legal systems	Yes
Jaggi & Low (2000)	Institutions: legal systems	Yes

Continued

Table 3.3 Continued

	Context: institutions country of origin	
Authors	Explanatory variable category	Sign. Corr.
Mayer & Whittington (1994)	Institutions: all categories	Yes
Nagy & Neal (2001)	Institutions: all categories	Yes
Goddard, Andrew (1997)	Institutions: all categories	Yes
Lin & Chan (2000)	Institutions: education system	Yes
Wijewardena & De Zoysa (1999)	Institutions: education system	Yes
Lam (2003)	Institutions: HQ nationality,	Yes
Davies & Ma (2003)	Institutions: HQ nationality	Yes
Geppert, Williams & Matten (2003)	Institutions: HQ nationality	Yes
Collins, Holzmann & Mendoza (1997)	Institutions: all categories	Yes
Mendoza, Collins, F. & Holzmann (1997)	Institutions: all categories	Yes
Richards (2000)	Institutions: HQ nationality	Yes

Source: Author.

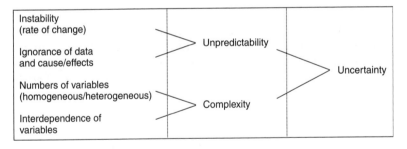

Figure 3.2 Description of the environment.
Source: Lawrence (1981).

turbulence (risky, unpredictable, fluctuating, ambiguous), hostility (stressful, dominating, restrictive), diversity (variety in products, inputs, customers), and complexity (rapidly developing technologies).

Given that MNC HQ have to rely on their national subsidiaries to interpret the local environment for them, this gives the local management a rather strong position in their relationship with HQ. Consequently, the level of uncertainty and complexity has a bearing on the type of management control exerted on subsidiaries.

3.1.1.1 Uncertainty

Environmental uncertainty in MNCs requires creativity and adaptability of the international sub-units, but at the same time integration of the single sub-units within the MNC (Merchant, 1984). 'These two objectives, however, usually conflict. It is virtually impossible to design and operate a planning and budgetary system that can serve both of them optimally (Merchant, 1984).' A highly dynamic, unpredictable and complex environment creates the need for flexibility to cope with unfolding unpredictability and rules out formalized bureaucratic control and personal centralized control (Burns et al., 1961; Chenhall, 2003; Child, 1984; Fisher, 1996; Lawrence et al., 1967; Mintzberg et al., 1991) since those forms would be too slow and inflexible in processing information (Child, 1984; Galbraith, 1973, 1995). Therefore, control by networks and socialization seems to be the most effective control mechanism (Child, 1984; Harzing, 1999). However, empirical findings on the effectiveness of output controls in highly dynamic environments are found to be contradictory: While Harzing (1999) found that output control also represents an effective way of control in highly uncertain environments, others (e.g., Brownell, 1987; Chapman, 1997) show that a strong reliance on accounting performance measures is incompatible with high levels of environmental uncertainty.

Reviewing contingency studies on MCSs in the past 20 years Chenhall (2003) comes up with the following: First, the more uncertain the external environment the more open and externally focused the MCS. Second, the more hostile and turbulent the external environment the greater is the reliance on formal controls and the emphasis on traditional budgets. Third, in case of MNCs having a tight financial control focus despite uncertain and flexible environments, interpersonal interactions are emphasized as additional control mechanisms.

3.1.1.2 Heterogeneity/complexity/institutional framework

Institutions. A substantial body of research has shown that MNCs are forced to adapt to the constraints imposed by the institutional framework of the host country in which they operate (Ferner, Quintanilla, & Varul, 2001; Lam, 2003; Mayer et al., 1994; Nagy et al., 2001). Therefore, strategic choice of MNCs is somewhat limited (Davies et al., 2003). Systems of wage determination, models of employee consultation, regulation of work time, vocational education and training, and the role of unions are likely to be highly constrained by local institutional arrangements (Child, Faulkner, & Pitkethly, 2001; Dickmann, 1999; Ferner et al., 2001; Goddard, 1997). For example, Japanese accountants are usually not accounting majors at university, much rather they are internally trained on the job, in contrast to their Western counterparts (Lin et al., 2000; Wijewardena et al., 1999). Governmental and other institutional constraints were found to be major obstacles in transferring Western MCS to Chinese enterprises (O'Connor et al., 2004).

Different legal systems are a case in point. The legal system plays a pivotal role regarding transparency requirements in accounting, for example financial disclosures by firms from common law countries are significantly higher compared to firms from code law countries (Collins et al., 1997; Jaggi et al., 2000). Favere-Marchesi (2001) provides insight of the legal environment affecting the role of statutory auditors and auditing quality in the Association of South-East Asian Nations (ASEAN) region. Unifying laws and upgrading differing regulations to match international audit standards seems essential in order to attract FDI in Asia (Favere-Marchesi, 2001).

The more complex and subject to change the environment, the more flexible organizational structures are required. Organizations operating in complex environments often differentiate the organization, creating different units to deal with different elements of the environment, and decentralize decision making (Harzing, 1999). The more subsidiaries are oriented towards understanding the national environment and supplying the local market the more problematic formal systems of control become (Ferner, 2000). Decentralized decision making is incompatible with personal centralized control and bureaucratic formalized control forms. Thus, again, control by socialization and networks fits best in a highly complex environment, while output control is possible too.

However, an alternative response to the risk presented by environmental complexity is to attempt to reduce the risk through exercising even greater control over both the environment (e.g., political lobbying), and over the venture itself (Boisot & Child, 1999; Child & Yan, 2003). Many larger firms in China have been adopting this approach (Child et al., 2003).

In general, MNCs act as a two-way vector of dynamic change within national business systems by introducing their own distinctive ways of doing things and at the same time taking lessons from the host environment (Ferner et al., 2001). Often, a hybrid approach, which adapts a home-country ethos to local realities, appears to be effective (Ferner et al., 2001). Nevertheless, a number of authors (e.g., Hunt, 2000; Mueller, 1994; Omhae, 1990; Parker, 1998) argue that technological, economic, political and cultural sources are the driving forces of globalization, leading to a 'stateless' or global firm weakening the effect of national societal institutions.

3.1.1.3 Economic and technological imperatives

The transfer of managerial practices is highly affected by economic considerations (Collins et al., 1997; Guilding et al., 1998; Uddin et al., 2001; Williams et al., 2001). Dedoussis (1995), for example, found that low-cost practices of Japanese parents were readily transferred to their overseas subsidiaries while high-cost practices were not. Therefore, it is argued that the transfer of management practices is primarily affected by economic and efficiency imperatives rather than by socio-cultural constraints (Dedoussis, 1995).

The same economic logic seems to be prevalent on the macro-level too: The greater the economic size and power of one country relative to another, the stronger the motivation to be the standard setter, the greater the volume and types of cross-border linkages between two countries, and the stronger the motivation for and the earlier the timing of cross-border diffusion (see Eden et al. (2001) for an example of the diffusion of the U.S. arms length standard into other nations). Rapid liberalization of the economy and the need for financial discipline imposed by competitive markets created an environment where Sino-foreign Joint Ventures (JVs) adopted Management Accounting practices of the foreign parent much faster than their counterparts in less exposed industries (Firth, 1996; O'Connor et al., 2004). A sudden shock to the economic system seems to act as a great stimulus to the diffusion of accounting ideas. In general, the implications for management and MCS of global competition and operations are increasingly important, as the boundaries between what is external and internal become increasingly blurred and organizations get involved in networks such as strategic alliances (Chenhall, 2003).

Kim, Park & Prescott (2003) found that in global industries, certain integration and control modes are more effective than others. In fact, people-based and information based modes of control are more effective than formalization based and centralization based modes of coordinating and controlling business functions worldwide.

Finally, the technology of the host country impacts MCS. The more standardized and automated processes are readily available the more formal are the control mechanisms in use (Chenhall, 2003).

3.1.2 Organizational context

Contingency theorists postulate that organizational behavior can never be perfectly determined by external global effects (Weick, 1979), but also organizational characteristics have a bearing on structure and control systems. The following categories for organizational contingencies impacting international organizational MCS design were identified in the literature screen:

3.1.2.1 Age

The older an organization, the larger its size, and the older the industry in which it operates, the more bureaucratic and centralized the organization tends to be (Baliga et al., 1984; Blau et al., 1963; Khandwalla, 1977; Kimberly, 1976; Pugh et al., 1969). However, Garnier (1982) and Gates & Egelhoff (1986) found that the older the subsidiary the lower the level of centralization by the HQ.

In an empirical study of U.S.-based International Joint Ventures (IJV) Fryxell et al. (2003) found that social control mechanisms are positively correlated with the age of the IJVs. It appears that after IJV formation formal controls fit with the requirements of a competitive environment and the needs of both partners. However, soon the advantages of formal control wane as shown by the negative correlation between IJV performance and formal control mechanisms in older IJVs (Fryxell et al., 2003). Also inter-organizational trust was found to grow with the length of operations.

Moreover, subsidiary age has a moderating effect on the impact of cultural distance which may disappear as firms gain more experience in operating in foreign countries and only firms in their initial stage of expansion show preferences for investing in culturally similar countries (Li et al., 2002).

3.1.2.2 Subsidiary size

As organizations grow in size, various components, such as time horizons, goals, interpersonal orientation, and the degree of formalization, are affected (Baliga et al., 1984). The larger an organization is in terms of employees, and the more diversified its operations, the greater is the importance of standardization and formalization (Chenhall, 2003) and the less important is centralization (Pugh et al., 1969; Pugh et al., 1968; Wong et al., 1994). Harzing (1999) found that subsidiary size is positively correlated to the use of more indirect control mechanisms such as bureaucratic formalized control. Furthermore, the larger an organization is, the more elaborate is its structure and degree of specialization (Mintzberg et al., 1991). A large size is associated with an emphasis on and participation of budgets and sophisticated administrative controls (Bruns & Waterhouse, 1975; Merchant, 1981, 1984). The role of MCSs in small or medium sized units has received little scholarly attention, nor has the role of MCS in case of sudden changes in size such as mergers been explored sufficiently (Reid & Smith, 2000). According to Harzing (1999) there is a positive relationship between MNC size and bureaucratic formalized control in France, the United Kingdom and Switzerland, while a negative relationship is found for Finland and Sweden.

However, analyzing size from a subsidiary level, size can have a twofold meaning for the scope of control exercised by the HQ: On the one hand, increased size means that a subsidiary can build up its own resources and reach a greater level of independence from the HQ. On the other hand, a large subsidiary can be of great importance to the HQ and therefore be monitored closely (Hedlund, 1981). Results of empirical research on the relationship between size and scope of HQ control are rather mixed too (Cray, 1984; Hedlund, 1981). For example, Chang & Taylor (1999) found subsidiary size to have a moderating effect on the amount of control exercised on the United States and Japanese subsidiaries in Korea, while Wong & Birnbaum (1994) found subsidiary size to be positively correlated with the scope of HQ control. Rates and adoption speed are also found to be influenced by the size of subsidiaries and JVs (Firth, 1996).

3.1.2.3 Ownership and resource provision

Resource-provision and control. The resource-dependence theory of interorganizational power suggests that the extent to which MNC HQ enjoy strategic and operational control over their international units depends partly on their ability to provide resources needed for their units. Thus, a parent who contributes a vital resource will gain more power over its subsidiaries. According to Barney (1991) 'firm resources include all assets, capabilities, organizational processes, firm attributes, information, knowledge, and so on. controlled by a firm that enable the firm to conceive of and implement strategies that improve its efficiency and effectiveness'. More specifically, Yan and Grey (1994) distinguish two categories of resources: (i) equity, and (ii) non-equity, resources. Equity resources are 'capital resources', such as cash, land, buildings and plants. Non-equity resources include 'technology, management expertise, local knowledge, raw material procurement channels, product distribution and marketing channels, and global service support' (Yan et al., 1994). This distinction is relevant with regards to control as each type of resource provides the basis for a different source of power and a different source of influence (Child et al., 2003). Newburry and Zeira (1997) point out that the nature and ownership level of the foreign investment, such as equity international JVs, international acquisitions and international Greenfield investments, determines the level of control exercised.

Capital resources and ownership structure & market entry mode. The choice of a desired ownership level reflects the interplay between a firm's desire to secure control and its attitudes towards investment risk. 'Investment is defined as the commitment of capital and non-capital resources to a venture's infrastructure and capabilities' (Child et al., 1999). Although exercising control over JVs and subsidiaries can also be gained through non-equity-based mechanisms, a high equity position in a local unit remains the most significant determinant of a parent's ability to control (Barden, Steensma, & Lyles, 2005; Geppert et al., 2003; Paik et al., 2004; Wang et al., 1999; Yan et al., 1994; Yan et al., 2001). Equity share, especially majority share, provides certain legal rights to determine the overall direction of a venture (Erramilli, 1996; Groot et al., 2000; Peterson, Napier, & Shim, 1996; Wang et al., 1999). Lecraw (1984) found a positive correlation between the equity share held by MNCs in 153 Asian subsidiaries and the level of overall management control exercised over those subsidiaries. In a similar vein, Chang and Taylor (1999) found empirical evidence for their hypothesis, positing that as the degree of ownership increases, the degree of output control and staffing control also increases. A right typically associated with an equity position is the right to appoint board members (Wang et al., 1999). Board members not only approve strategic decisions but also have the ability to influence appointments of key executives (Child et al., 1999).

How a foreign subsidiary is set up also has a share in the level of HQ interference and control: MNCs setting up a Greenfield site are able to bring in their managerial practices more easily as compared to taking over an already existing firm or entering into a JV (Tayeb, 1994). The legal form of ownership also determines the diffusion rates of MCSs. Chinese State-owned Enterprises (SOE) which found JVs with foreign partners tend to have higher diffusion indices of management accounting systems than their non-JV SOE counterparts (Firth, 1996).

Non-capital resources. Non-capital resources secure other bases of control. The use of proprietary technology or brand names, or the transfer

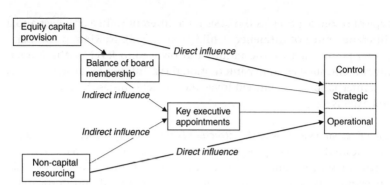

Figure 3.3 Model of resource provision, key appointments and control.
Source: Adapted from Child and Yan (1999).

of managerial expertise, for example, creates dependency on the provider. In an empirical study of 67 manufacturing IJVs formed with Chinese and foreign partners headquartered in the United States, Western Europe, Japan or in overseas Chinese territories, Child and Yan (1999) found that equity share is the only significant predictor of strategic control, and providing non-capital resources has a bearing on IJV operational control (Yan et al., 2001). Figure 3.3 depicts the relation between capital resources and non-capital resources and their impact on managerial HQ control.

Nonetheless, evidence on the performance of shared controlled IJVs as compared to dominantly controlled IJVs or fully owned subsidiaries is mixed. A number of authors (Bleeke & Ernst, 1993; Child et al., 2003; Li et al., 2002) found positive correlations for IJVs with a balanced cultural diversity in management boards or shared IJV control and performance measures, while others (Lee et al., 1998; Shaw, 1998) found no such effects.

3.1.3 Culture

Cultural research on MCS design mainly dates back to the 1980s, and may still be considered exploratory. However, evidence accumulates that people from different nations not only differ in work-related values but also in how they react to management practices (Adler, 2002;

Birnberg & Snodgrass, 1988; Chow et al., 1998; Chow et al., 1999b). The great majority of studies on MCS and culture are using the value-dimensional conception of culture and, since the late 1980s, Hofstede's dimensions. Studies are predominantly focused on comparisons between a variety of Asian and Anglo-American nations. As Table 3.4 shows, the dependent variables of these studies cover a broad spectrum, ranging from preferences for controls (Chow et al., 1994), to the design of controls (e.g., control system tightness in Chow et al., 1996), Team Rewards (TR) (Merchant, Chow, & Wu, 1995), the effects of controls (e.g., performance in Luo 2003), or job tension and satisfaction (Harrison, 1992; 1993). Most of these studies include only some aspects of management control, preferably such which were hypothesized to have a clear-cut relationship with one or more of Hofstede's dimensions (Chow, Harrison, McKinnon, & Wu, 1999a). Furthermore, authors made different interpretations of Hofstede's cultural dimensions; for example Harrison et al. (1994) postulated that long-term planning is related to Confucian Dynamism (CD) and Individualism (ID), while at the same time Ueno and Wu (1993) posited that using long-range budgets is an indicator for high Uncertainty Avoidance (UA). Regarding methods, the survey questionnaire was used predominantly. Table 3.3 depicts an overview of the single studies using Hofstede's dimensions as explanatory variables, indicating the nature of the sample, the method, the dependent variables, and the postulated relations. An explanation of Hofstede's (1980a) dimensions can be found in the appendix.

Although some support could be found for the effects of culture on MCS preference and design, the results of many tests have been either non-significant, or the form of interaction was opposite to the hypothesis. Some of the contradictory or unexpected results might be due to non-controlled contingency variables, for example distortions caused by using samples of managers who work for a great variety of firms in all sizes and in different countries. Furthermore, data was collected from divergent sources, ranging from profit-center managers (Chow et al., 1996), manufacturing managers (Harrison et al., 1994), to business students (Chow et al., 1991, 1994). Thus, comparability of results would require a meta-analysis.

Summarizing management control research based on Hofstede's dimensions, the following can be said (e.g., Arnold et al., 2001; Awasthi et al., 2001; Calori et al., 1994; Chow et al., 1996; Chow et al., 1998; Chow et al., 1999a; Chow et al., 1999b; Fryxell et al., 2003; Ganguly & Turner, 2000; Garcia-Sordo & Wong Baren, 1999; Hussein, 1996;

Table 3.4 Empirical studies on national culture and management control based on Hofstede (1980, 1991)

Study	National cultures included Sample size	Method	Dependent variable	Explanatory variable	Prediction	Result = Prediction (sign)	Non-significant result	Significant unpredicted result
Arnold et al. (2001)	Europe (181) (Denmark, Ireland, Italy, Spain, Sweden, Netherlands and the UK) and US (83)	Experiment/ case study	Materiality estimates	UA	Materiality estimates = f (UA)	Yes		
Awasthi et al. (2001)	US (75) and Taiwanese (75) with Chinese ethnicity (MBA students)	Experiment	Team based performance evaluation	ID, PD	Performance = f (ID, PD, team performance pay)	Yes		
			Individualistic performance evaluation	ID, PD	Performance = f (ID, PD, individualistic performance pay)		Yes	
					Satisfaction = f (self selected performance pay vs. Imposed performance pay)	Yes		

Calori, Lubatkin & Very (1994)	France, US and UK 161 top managers from 75 firms	Survey questionnaire	Degree of formalization, centralization, informal control	PD, UA	H1a: French higher formal control than US;	Yes	
					H1b: U.S. higher formal control over individual managers and financial resources than French;		Yes
					H1c: U.S. higher formal control through procedures than French;		Yes
					H1d: U.S. higher informal control through teamwork than French;	Yes	
					H2a U.S. higher formal control by centralization than British;		Yes
					H2b: Americans higher formal control through procedures than British.	Yes	

Continued

Table 3.4 Continued

Study	National cultures included Sample size	Method	Dependent variable	Explanatory variable	Prediction	Result = Prediction (sign)	Non-significant result	Significant unpredicted result
Chow et al. (1991)	Singapore (96) and the US (96)	Experiment	Team pay	ID	Performance = f (ID, team pay, task)		Yes	
Chow et al. (1996)	Japan (28) and US (54)	Survey questionnaire	Control system tightness	ID	Control system tightness = f(ID)		Yes	
			Procedural controls	UA	Procedural controls = f (UA)	Yes		
			Centralized directives	PD	Centralized directive = f (PD)	Yes		
Chow et al. (1994)	Japan (39) and US (54)	Experiment	Controllability Filter (CF)	UA	CF = f (Uncertainty, UA)		Yes	
			Centralized Planning (CP)	PD	CP = f (Centralization, PD)		Yes	
			Team rewards (TR)	ID	TR = f (Interdependence, ID)			n.sign.

Study	Sample	Method	Variable(s)	Cultural dimensions	Findings	Culture matters?
Chow et al. (1998)	US (72) and Chinese (72) in Taiwan	Experiment	Misrepresentation (MR) of private information Face-to-face interactions Performance-pay scheme	CD, 'Face', ID/C	MR = f (CD, ID, pay scheme) MR = f (CD, ID, face-to-face and pay)	Yes
Chow et al. (1999b)	US, Japan, Taiwan (159 Taiwanese managers working in 6 each of Japanese-, Taiwanese-, and U.S.-owned firms in Taiwan)	Survey, two-stage process: 1. personal interviews in situ/2. survey questionnaire	Decentralization Structuring of activities Participative budgeting Standard tightness Participative performance evaluation Controllability filters Performance contingent financial rewards	ID, PD ID, PD, UA ID, PD M, UA ID, PD ID, UA ID, M, UA	Decentralization = f (ID, PD) Structuring = f (ID, PD, UA) Participative budgeting = f (ID, PD) Standard tightness = f (M, UA) Participative p. eval. = f (ID, PD) Controllability filters = f (ID, UA) Performance pay = f (ID, M, UA)	Mixed findings; See paper
Chow et al. (1999a)	Australia and Taiwan (52 middle managers from 13 Taiwanese firms and 50 middle managers from 14 Australian firms)	Personal interviews & survey questionnaire	Informal information sharing	ID	Information sharing = f (ID)	Yes

Continued

Table 3.4 Continued

Study	National cultures included Sample size	Method	Dependent variable	Explanatory variable	Prediction	Result = Prediction (sign)	Non-significant result	Significant unpredicted result
Erramilli (1996)	217 subsidiaries of U.S. MNCs in Europe and 120 subsidiaries of European MNCs in Europe	Survey questionnaire	Control by majority ownership	PD, UA	Majority ownership control = f (PD) Majority ownership control = f (UA)	Yes Yes		
Harrison (1992)	Australia (96) and Singapore (115)	Survey questionnaire	Participative Budgeting (PB) Budget Emphasis in performance evaluation (BE)	ID/PD	Job tension, satisfaction = f (PB, BE) and not = f (PB, BE, ID/PD)	Yes		
Harrison (1993)	Australia (96) and Singapore (115)	Survey questionnaire	Reliance on Accounting Performance Measures for performance evaluation (RAPM)	ID	Job tension, satisfaction = F (RAPM, ID)	Yes		

Study	Sample	Method	Variable	Cultural dimension	Relationship	Supported
Harrison et al. (1994)	Australia (140), US (104), Hong-Kong (55) and Singapore (65)	Survey questionnaire	Decentralization	ID/PD	Decentralization = f (ID/PD)	Yes
			Responsibility centers	ID/PD	Responsibility centers = f (ID/PD)	Yes
			Long-term planning	CD, ID	Long-term planning = f (CD, ID)	Yes
			Formalization of planning and control	PD	Formalization = f (PD)	Yes
Hussein (1996)	US and the Netherlands	Data analysis	Measurement practices = f (ID)	ID	Measurement practices = f (ID)	Yes
			Disclosure (social, environment)	M/F	Disclosure = f (M/F)	Yes
Garcia-Sordo, Juan B.; Wong Baren, Adrian (1999)	MBA students, 85 US and 36 Mexican students, average of 6 years full-time working experience	Laboratory experiment		PD, UA, ID		
Merchant et al. (1995)	Taiwan (23) and US (54)	Open-ended in-depth interviews	Performance-Based Rewards (PR)	ID, M, UA	PR = f (ID, M, UA)	Yes
			Team Rewards (TR)	ID, UA	TR = f (ID, UA)	Yes
			Long-Term Incentives (LTI)	CD, ID	LTI = f (CD, ID)	Yes
			Subjective Performance Evaluation (SPE)	PD, UA	SPE = f (PD, UA)	Yes

Continued

Table 3.4 Continued

Study	National cultures included Sample size	Method	Dependent variable	Explanatory variable	Prediction	Result = Prediction (sign)	Non-significant result	Significant unpredicted result
O'Connor (Beatty, 1995)	Singapore (125) (local- and foreign owned firms)	Survey questionnaire, and pre and post hoc interview	Participative Budgeting (PB) Participative Performance Evaluation (PE)	PD PD	Role ambiguity = f (PB, PD) Role ambiguity = f (PE, PD)		Yes Yes	
Salter and Sharp (2001)	US (201) Canada (98)	Survey questionnaire	Adverse selection	ID	Adverse selection = f (I)	Yes		
Schultz and Lopez (2001)	US, Germany and France	Experiment	H1 = US recommend less cautions estimates than F and G; H2 = warranty estimates (given a low to high monetary order) will be greatest for the French accountants, with German and American accountants following in that order	UA	Warranty estimates = f (UA)	Yes		

Author	Sample	Method	Variables studied	Cultural dimensions	Findings	Supported?
Tsui (1996)	Big six CPA firms in Hong-Kong	Experiment	P-Score = auditors ethical reasoning		P-Scores (=auditors ethical reasoning level) = f (ID, PD, and long vs. short time orientation)	Yes
Tsui (2001)	China (51) Western expatriates in Hong-Kong (38)	Survey questionnaire	Participative budgeting (PB) Management Accounting System (MAS)	PD, ID, CD	PB = f (PD, ID) positive correlation with Western expats, negative correlation with Chinese	Yes
Ueno and Sekaran (1992)	Japan (149) US (70)	Survey questionnaire	Communication and Coordination	ID	Communication = f (ID)	Yes
			Planning time horizon	UA	Planning time = f (UA)	Yes
			Structuring of budget process	ID, UA	Structuring = f (ID, UA)	Yes
			Budget slack	ID, UA	Budget slack = f (ID, UA)	Yes
			Budget controllability	ID	Budget controllability = f (ID)	Yes
			Budget performance evaluation time horizons	ID	Budget performance time = f (ID)	Yes

Continued

Table 3.4 Continued

Study	National cultures included Sample size	Method	Dependent variable	Explanatory variable	Prediction	Result = Prediction (sign)	Non-significant result	Significant unpredicted result
Ueno and Wu	Japan (247) and US (205)	Survey questionnaire	Participative budgeting	ID	Participative budgeting = f (ID)	Yes		
			Long-range budgets	UA	Long-range budgets = f (UA)		Yes	
			Structure of budget process	UA	Structure = f (UA)		Yes	
			Budget slack	ID	Budget slack = f (ID)	Yes		
				ID	Controllable budgets = f(ID)	Yes		
			Long-term performance-evaluation horizon	ID	Performance evaluation = f (ID)	Yes		
Van der Stede (2003)	Canada and Singapore	Survey questionnaire	Tight and loose budget system	ID	'looser' budget system = f (ID)	Yes		
				PD, UA, ID, M/F	MIS design = f (PD, UA, ID, M/F)			Yes

Study	Country	Method	DV	IV	Relationship	Supported
Williams and Towers (1998)	Singapore and Australia	Survey questionnaire	'Secrecy' Preferred Level of Disclosure (PLD) Perceived Balance of Costs Relative to Benefits of Compliance (PECVD)	UA, C, F, PD, CD,	PLD = f (UA, C, F, PD, CD)* PECVD = f (UA, C, F, PD, CD)	Yes* Yes*
Williams and Seaman (2001)	Canada (24) Singapore (total 93, manufacturing 25	Survey questionnaire	MCS are amendable to change	PD	Change = f (structure/PD)	Yes
Wong (1994)	US, UK, Netherlands, Canada (Hong-Kong, Singapore, India, Philippines, Germany, Switzerland, France, Iran, Japan, Thailand) different countries operating in Hong-Kong	Survey questionnaire		PD	Centralization & formalization = f (PD)	Yes
					Centralization & formalization = f (UA)	Yes
					Structural differentiation = f (UA)	Yes

CD = Confucian Dynamism; ID = Individualism; M = Masculinity; PD = Power Distance; UA = Uncertainty Avoidance; ID/PD = The joint effects of ID and PD.
Note: *For a more detailed description see paper.

Merchant et al., 1995; O'Connor et al., 2004; Salter & Sharp, 2001; Sands & Pragasam, 1997; Schultz & Lopez, 2001; Tsui, 1996, 2001; Ueno et al., 1993; Van der Stede, 2003; Williams et al., 2001; Williams & Tower, 1998; Wong et al., 1994): ID is the most used explanatory variable, followed by Power Distance (PD), UA and CD. Masculinity (M) is used rather scarcely. The vast majority of studies use a combination of dimensions to examine potential correlations between control mechanisms and culture. Combinations of UA and ID, or PD and UA, or CD and ID dominate the literature. However, only a few studies explore the impact of a single dimension on control.

Ueno and Sekaran (1992) found a significant correlation between budget controllability and performance evaluation with ID. In addition, Ueno and Wu (Ueno et al., 1993) found a significant relation between ID and the control mechanisms of participative budgeting, controllable budgets, performance evaluation and budget slack. Salter and Sharp (2001) found a positive correlation between adverse selection behavior and ID. Finally, Van der Steede (2003) shows that nations which score high on ID also employ 'looser' budget systems than nations with low ID scores.

Only two studies which used PD as a single explanatory variable found significant relations between PD and control mechanisms employed: Chow (1996) found empirical evidence for the impact of PD on centralized directives and Wong (1994) showed that the higher a nation's PD score the higher the degree of formalization and centralization.

Concerning UA as a single independent variable, procedural controls (Chow et al., 1996), materiality estimates (Arnold, 2001), and warranty estimates (Schultz and Lopez, 2001) were found to be significantly positively correlated. None of the examined studies used CD or M/F as single explanatory variables.

Although there is evidence of some convergence for the effect of culture on MCS characteristics, the findings also show substantive disparities. In general, research findings on MCS with Hofstede's dimensions as explanatory variables brought rather contrasting results.

Cultural distance had a strong negative effect on IJV performance and profitability (Beard and Al-Rai, 1999; Li et al., 2002) (Negandhi & Baliga, 1979), which implies that establishing trust and control between partners with dissimilar norms and values seems to be especially challenging (Fryxell et al., 2003).

Given a world of 'global markets' and 'converging commonalities' (Levitt, 1983), we might cast doubts that culture does still matter. Nevertheless, a firm can be viewed as a social construction created by human beings (Berger & Luckmann, 1967). Within it each human being has his/her individual way of thinking about and understanding reality. The culture of the country in which an individual has been raised and lives and the education received determines a person's subjective logic (enculturation). In a business setting, the subjective economic logic as a pattern of rationality determines how employees actually interpret and understand management control and accounting tasks as well as the economic situation of the firm (Noerreklit et al., 2000). Nonetheless, Schein (1996) finds that culture is a missing concept in organization studies, and calls for more research on culture in organizations. Even Porter (1990) underscores the importance of nationality when he writes: 'It is tempting to conclude that the nation has lost its role in the international success of its firms. Companies, at first glance, seem to have transcended countries. Yet, what I have learned in this study contradicts this conclusion.'

In cross-cultural and comparative management studies, culture has been defined as 'the totality of man's products' (Berger et al., 1967), 'a set of control mechanisms for governing behavior' (Geertz, 1973), or as 'the way people in a society are collectively programmed' (Hofstede, 1980a). Western leadership and authority behavior can be examined using Weber's (1949) concept of rational authority and rational bureaucracy. These 'ideal types' of leadership and authority behavior as proposed by Weber and his intellectual heirs (e.g., Kluckhohn & Strodtbeck, 1961; Parsons, 1951) heavily influenced the thinking of management theorists, such as Trompenaars (1997), Hofstede (1980a) Shenkar (2001) and Omhae (1990), in their attempts to explain the emergence and the patterns of international management, globalization, industrialization and organizational behavior across cultures. Existing literature does not offer a clear consensus as to the role of culture on the magnitude of control a firm exerts over its overseas subsidiaries (Hamilton et al., 1999; Richards, 2000). Both national culture and differences among national cultures are found to be significant influences on managerial decision making and strategy (Tse, Lee, Vertinsky, & Wehrung, 1988), work values (Ralston, Holt, Terpstra, & Kai-Cheng, 1997), and patterns of negotiations and control (Hamilton et al., 1999). In general, it is argued that the greater the extent to which an MNC's HQ and subsidiaries are culturally distant, the more difficult it gets to effectively monitor and control the various units (Gomez-Mejia & Palich, 1997). Similarly, Roth and O'Donnell (1996) suggest that if HQ-subsidiary relationships are viewed from an agency theory perspective, agency costs will increase relative to cultural distance.

3.1.3.1 Country of origin effect

The literature on the importance of the country of origin effect builds on National Business Studies (Geppert et al., 2003; Lane, DiStefano, & Maznevski, 2003; Whitley, 2001; Whitley & Kristensen, 1996). Businesses are considered to derive enduring and distinctive features from their embedment in national institutional structures (Child et al., 2001; Doremus, Keller, Pauley, & Reich, 1998; Lam, 2003; Morgan, 2001; Pauly & Reich, 1997). It is argued that the nature and modes of operation of MNCs vary according to their national origins (Becker-Ritterspach, Lange, & Lohr, 2002; Beechler et al., 1994; Geppert et al., 2003; Kogut & Singh, 1988). Nationally specific characteristics are likely to influence the way in which MNCs manage and control their operations internationally (Ferner, 1997; Sands et al., 1997; Schultz et al., 2001).

For example, a multitude of studies (Bartlett et al., 1989; Gong, 2003; Harzing, 2003; Oliver & Wilkinson, 1992; Paik et al., 2004; Peterson, Napier, & Shim, 2000; Sohn, 1994) show that Japanese MNCs rely on close and frequent personal contact and supervision by expatriate managers as a key control mechanism. Thus, large Japanese MNCs rather rely on informal and implicit control mechanisms than on bureaucratic ones (Clark, 1979; Jaeger, 1983; Johnson et al., 1974; Negandhi et al., 1979; Ouchi & Jaeger, 1978). Human Resource Management (HRM) strategies of MNCs also affect the employment of expatriates. Japanese MNCs, for example, clearly protect the interests of core Japanese employees on international assignments given the exclusion of the local white collar managers from intra-organizational labor markets (Dedoussis, 1995). Although contrary to prior research, Chang and Taylor (1999) did not find a difference in output control between the United States and Japan on their Korean subsidiaries; their study also supports the prediction that Japanese investors exercise a higher level of staffing control in their Korean subsidiaries than their U.S. counterparts. Japanese and German MNCs are by far most likely to use expatriates as presidents or managing directors in their operations (Peterson et al., 2000). For example, the control structure of Japanese investments in the automotive industry in the United States shows an extensive use of Japanese expatriates in key positions in order to keep communication between JVs and HQ smooth (Beamish & Inkpen, 1998). Reasons for the overwhelming use of Japanese expatriates include the inability to communicate effectively with HQ, the preference for Greenfield investments, and language and cultural differences (Beamish et al., 1998). However, there is a definite trend of Japanese MNCs decreasing their use of expatriates over time (Beamish et al., 1998). Harzings (1999) empirical findings clearly show that Japan and Germany have a higher than average expatriate presence, while the Anglo-Saxon nations (United Kingdom and United States) score below average. Subsidiaries in Asian and Latin American countries showed higher levels of expatriate presence than their European and U.S. counterparts (Harzing, 1999).

Anglo-Saxon countries prefer impersonal control types and mechanisms (bureaucratic formalized control and output control) (Harzing, 1999). Nevertheless, U.K. MNCs also score high on personal centralized control (Ahrens, 1997). British accountants perceive their task as operationally linked to day-to-day operations and less formalized than, for example, their German counterparts (Ahrens, 1997). Case studies on U.K. MNCs generally display a pattern of formal controls (Ferner, 2000; Marginson, Armstrong, Edwards, Purcell, & Hubbard, 1993). Examining whether the nationality of the parent determines control preferences, a number of studies, for example Shetty (1979) Puxty (1979) and Erramilli (1996; 1993), found strong evidence that U.S. MNCs prefer ownership control. American MNCs appear to be most uncompromising in insisting on implementing detailed formal structures and accounting systems that match those of the home country (Bartlett et al., 1989; Firth, 1996). Geppert et al. (2003) found that the home-country effect together with ownership structure and pursued globalization strategy determine the extent and type of control exercised in MNCs. His findings also clearly show that subsidiaries of U.S. MNCs in Germany, for example, are characterized by highly formalized control systems and output control, while subsidiaries of Finnish MNCs in Germany display high levels of centralization. In both cases the chosen control mechanism reflects the home-country institutions (Geppert et al., 2003).

Given the U.S. MNCs preference for output control, U.S. multinationals are less likely to use expatriates than Japanese or European firms (Egelhoff, 1984). However, if U.S. MNCs do use expatriates as a means of control, cultural distance seems to be a decisive factor as they are more likely to put expatriates in charge of their Southeast Asian subsidiaries than of their U.K. ones (Richards, 2000). Richards (2000) found the level of autonomy given to U.S. subsidiaries in the United Kingdom to be much higher than in subsidiaries in Southeast Asia.

Studying the effects of ownership and institutional change on control in Hungarian enterprises, Whitely and Czaban (1998) found considerably different control patterns in SOEs as compared to private firms owned by MNCs. Enterprises owned by foreign investors displayed more centralized control structures and had more supervisors with substantial powers, resources and responsibilities than their privately owned Hungarian counterparts. Compared with similar studies in the United States and Japan (e.g., Lincoln and Kalleberg, 1990), employees studied by Whitley and Czaban (1998) reported a much greater sway on how they carried out tasks than did those in Japan or the United States.

A different picture of control emerges for German MNCs which tend to be high on both bureaucratic and personal forms of control compared to their Anglo-Saxon or Japanese counterparts (Ahrens, 1997; Ferner, 2000; Ferner & Varul, 2000; Harzing, 2003). In contrast to the United Kingdom, accounting information in German MNCs is not regarded as being able to capture reality but rather as a planning and controlling tool by German accountants and managers (Ahrens, 1997). Ahrens (1996) illustrates with an in-depth case study on British and German management accounting departments that interlocutors have very different views on which courses of action to take in specific situations, and on the role of management accountants. German controllers viewed themselves mainly as providers of information and had less direct influence in organizational processes of accountability compared with their British counterparts.

In general, Finnish and French subsidiaries experience rather low levels of formalized control (Harzing, 1999).

Central American managers view budgets as less critical than U.S. managers do (Mendoza et al., 1997). The authors see that as a result of the more volatile economic and political factors in Central America. Garcia-Sordo (1999) found that certain aspects of Central American national culture significantly affect the effectiveness of management control.

Also language differences play a role: Uncertainty expressions in International Accounting Standards are interpreted differently by German and U.S. accountants (Doupnik & Richter, 2003). Schultz and Lopez (2001) found by experiment that given similar economic facts and rules, judgments among French, German and U.S. accountants varied significantly. Some authors (e.g. Chaney and Martin, 1995; Noerreklit, 2000) even claim that problems related to the cross-cultural transfer of MCSs are actually communication problems, which might be overcome through more effective intercultural business communication.

Although the traditional institutional approach tends to predict organizational structure and strategy of MNCs on the basis of the national origins alone, Lam (2003) suggests that the dynamics of interaction between home-based institutions and the local context may also be relevant. Hence, institutional proximity between home and host-country environment may ease the cross-border transfer of management and control practices.

Nationality of the foreign partner was positively and significantly correlated to the extent of diffusion of management control techniques (Firth, 1996). JVs seem to be a good medium by which 'Western Management Control' styles can be transferred to foreign enterprises (Firth, 1996, p. 650). Interestingly, perceived national stereotypes indeed play a crucial role in IB partner selection (Cooper et al., 1998).

In sum, there is ample evidence that the country of origin of a parent is a decisive factor concerning the type of control exerted over subsidiaries (Geppert et al., 2003; Harzing & Sorge, 2003): Using Harzing's (1999; 2003) classification of control mechanisms we can compare the scope and extent of control preferences of MNCs headquartered in different nations. Our present findings are in line with Harzings (1999) findings. Table 3.5 gives an overview of preferred control mechanisms of MNC HQ stemming from different nations.

3.1.4 Moderators

The following variables were found to have a moderating effect on cultural distance and HQ-subsidiary relations: Expatriates, prior international experience of the parent, trust, and organizational culture. Table 3.6 below gives an overview on the analyzed articles and the moderators discussed.

Table 3.5 Parent nationality and management control type

	Use of control mechanisms in subsidiaries of MNCs headquartered in different countries	
Control mechanism	High use in subsidiaries of MNCs from:	Low use in subsidiaries of MNCs from:
Personal centralized control	Germany, UK, Japan	Switzerland, Sweden
Bureaucratic formalized control	UK, US (Germany)	Finland, Japan, Central America
Output control	UK, Germany (US)	Japan, Finland
Control by socialization and networks	Switzerland, Sweden, Central America	France, Japan

Source: Amended & updated based on Harzing (1999).

Table 3.6 Literature dealing with moderators

Moderators	
Authors	Moderator
Peterson (2003)	Expatriates
Peterson, Napier & Shim (2000)	Expatriates
Beamish & Inkpen (1998)	Expatriates
Björkman (2004)	Expatriates
Harzing (2001a; 2001b)	Expatriates
Ferner, Quintanilla & Varul (2001)	Expatriates
Paik & Sohn (2004)	Expatriates
Firth, M. (1996)	Expatriates
Whitley, Morgan & Sharpe (2003)	Expatriates
Dedoussis (1995)	Expatriates
Gong (2003)	Expatriates
Richards (2000)	Expatriates
Konopaske, Werner & Neupert (2002)	Expatriates
Fryxell, Dooley & Vryza (2003)	Trust
Tomkins (2001)	Trust
Luo, Y. (2002)	Trust
Gulati (1995)	Trust
Fisher (1996)	Personality
Whitley, Morgan & Sharpe (2003)	Experience
O'Connor, Chow & Wu (2004)	Experience
Robertson & Swan (2003)	Organizational culture
Björkman (2004)	Organizational culture & socialization

Source: Author.

3.1.4.1 Expatriates

MNC control requires detailed knowledge of context and circumstances. Such knowledge is easily accessed by the MNC parent if the key personnel running the operation are appointed by that parent (Wang et al., 1999). 'Staffing is an important vehicle for establishing and maintaining organizational control over international expansion activities' (Konopaske et al., 2002). Control by expatriates is a means to influence and transfer organizational culture, since expatriates can attempt to integrate host-country nationals by sharing information about the parent's norms, values, and behavioral prescriptions.

Edstrom's and Galbraith's (1977) seminal work identified three primary reasons for using expatriates: (i) technical expertise; (ii) management development; and (iii) organizational development. Further reasons include socialization of local management to corporate culture, control, and the creation of a verbal exchange network with corporate HQ (Kobrin, 1988). More recently, Harzing (2001a) sees expatriation as an informal coordination and control strategy through socialization and distinguishes three core functions of expatriates: First, expatriates as a means of formal direct control – 'bear', second, expatriates as a means for socialization – 'bumble-bee', and finally, expatriates as means for informal communication – 'spider'. Expatriates as socialization and network builders are more important in subsidiaries with a high degree of local responsiveness and/or a long-term relation between organizational units (Harzing, 2001b). Strong empirical evidence for the role of expatriates as a means of direct control in MNCs can be foremost found in wholly owned subsidiaries or Greenfield investments (Ferner, 2000; Harzing, 2001b). For example, Japanese MNCs with high levels of expatriates seem to maintain a similar level of control with lower equity positions than their counterparts with higher equity positions (Paik et al., 2004).

Moreover, empirical evidence accumulates that subsidiary performance, ownership structure, and expatriate presence are correlated: Wholly owned subsidiaries achieve better performance when expatriates are in place, while the opposite is true for jointly managed ventures (Ferner, 2000; Harzing, 2001b; Konopaske et al., 2002). These findings are in line with prior research (e.g., Tomlinson, 1970) which noticed a positive relationship between profitability of IJVs and more relaxed forms of parent control.

Based on agency theory and the resource based view, Gong (2003) found empirical support in Japanese MNCs that the use of expatriates is dependent on the degree of cultural distance and the length of operations. Cultural distance refers to the extent to which home and host-country cultures are different (Erez & Early, 1993; Kogut et al., 1988). The HQ-subsidiary relationship in MNCs has a principal-agent structure (Roth et al., 1996), thus the design of the optimal control mechanism makes agents behave in the principal's interest (Eisenhardt, 1989a). In managing culturally distant subsidiaries agency costs are greater due to information asymmetry. Expatriates (on all corporate levels from chief executive officer (CEO) to workforce level) who have already internalized the parent's values are a perfect means to ensure that subsidiaries act in accordance with the parent's strategic intent (Gong, 2003). The greater the cultural distance the greater the positive impact of expatriate staffing on subsidiary performance and control (Gong, 2003; Harzing, 1999). The length of the subsidiary interaction also interacts with cultural distance and affects the utilization of expatriates: The longer the duration of the operation the lower the proportion of expatriates as the subsidiary gradually learns and information asymmetry decreases (Gong, 2003; Peterson, 2003). Gong (2003) underlines the positive effect of expatriates on subsidiary performance since '[p]erformance generally becomes stronger as cultural distance increases, but weaker as years of operation increase'. Also Harzing (1999) found that expatriate presence in subsidiaries is positively related with subsidiary size and age. Entry mode also has a bearing on ethnocentric staffing, with Greenfield subsidiaries having a higher expatriate presence than acquisitions.

Beamish (1998) and Beard (1999) found that expatriate managers play a crucial role in representing and implementing the corporate objectives and structures of MNC HQ. They serve as an indirect control mechanism to assure that a subsidiary complies with corporate goals (Sohn, 1994; Sohn et al., 1996). However, Björkman (2004) found no support for the impact of expatriate managers on the extent of knowledge transfer from foreign subsidiaries to other MNC units.

Expatriates play a crucial role in both the communication and transfer of explicit and tacit knowledge of company practices and management approaches. Expatriates with the 'right' technical and personal skills can indeed reduce the 'friction' of cultural distance and trigger mutual learning processes (Gamble, 2003). Paik & Sohn (2004) underpin the importance of skill and sensibility of expatriates for their effectiveness, since only expatriates with a great amount of knowledge about the host culture can reduce the friction caused by cultural distance. Therefore, Paik and Sohn (2004) point to the crucial role of expatriate training. Studying the transfer of U.K. management practices to China, Gamble (2003) considers the presence of expatriates in key management roles as a key to a successful transfer of management practices. In sum, we conclude that the use of expatriates can have a moderating effect on cultural distance.

3.1.4.2 The role of trust

The pivotal role of trust in intra and inter-organizational relationships is virtually not present in current Management control research (Barney & Hansen, 1995; Knights, Noble, Vurdubakis, & Hugh, 2001; Tomkins, 2001; Zaheer, McEvily, & Perrone, 1998). Trust in its broadest sense is simply having confidence that one's expectations will be realized (Luhmann, 1979). Tomkins (2001) defines trust as 'The adoption of a belief by one party in a relationship that the other party will not act against his or her interests, where this belief is held without undue doubt or suspicion and in the absence of detailed information about the actions of that other party'. Trust is a fundamental factor in deciding what amount and type of information should be shared (Tomkins, 2001). According to Drucker (1990) trust is mutual understanding. Luhmann's (1995) revision of Parson's systems theory defines trust and distrust as equivalent strategies for dealing with the problem of 'double contingency': 'The core of the latter is that trust/distrust constitutes relevant responses to situations where one must enter into risks one cannot control in advance – or be forced to refuse participation' (Luhmann, 1995: 129). However, most studies have conceptualized trust along the lines of Rosseau et al. (1998) as willingness to make oneself vulnerable to the actions of another under conditions of risk, based on the characteristics or qualities of specific others, groups, or systems to be trusted.

Trust between organizations is an important variable of joint performance because it enhances cooperation, transaction cost savings, capability improvement, and strategic flexibility (Luo, Y., 2002, Gulati, 1995, Mayer et al., 1995, McAllister, 1995, Smith et al., 1995; [Mayer, Davies, & Schoorman, 1995; McAllister, 1995]. A positive link between trust and performance in the context of strategic alliances is validated by systematic research efforts [e.g., Inkpen & Curral, 1997; Saxton, 1997]).

Concerns of opportunism must be overcome as a prelude to creating effective norms and values that can reinforce confidence in international cooperation (Fryxell et al., 2003: 871). Ultimately, the efficacy of social control mechanisms will depend on the level of trust between the alliance partners (Das et al., 1998). Because social control does not rely on pro-specified behaviors or performance outcomes to influence behavior the level of perceived risk is increased.

In an empirical study of U.S.-based IJVs, Fryxell et al. (2003) found that social controls were positively related to IJV performance in the presence of trust. Cultural distance was negatively related to the level of trust which underlines the assumption that dissimilarity of cultural values would complicate the formation of trust (Fryxell et al., 2003). However, Luo (2002) empirically showed that once trust was established, the level of trust improved regardless of cultural distance. Gulati (1995) empirically shows that trust is a decisive factor in forming international alliances. Bijlsama-Frankema (2001) emphasizes that trust is the key to successful mergers and acquisitions and forms the basis for cultural integration.

The far reaching implications of bringing the variable of trust into the design of information and control systems might only be guessed. Based on the findings in the prevailing literature review trust does have a significant impact on the diffusion of management practices and control and is therefore seen as a moderator.

3.1.4.3 International experience of organizational units

Literature suggests that an MNC's degree of international experience has a significant impact on its various international activities (Erramilli, 1991; Fagre & Wells, 1982; Paik et al., 2004). The more experience an MNC gains in managing overseas ventures the less drastic are effects due to cultural distance and contextual complexities (Li et al., 2002).

Japanese car manufacturing MNCs, for example, invested considerable resources to transfer their distinctive way of managing complex production processes through the intensive use of expatriates. Whitley et al. (2003) noted a definite change in the straightforward transfer of the domestic recipe to foreign locations. Level and mode of central control of overseas units can change as firms become more willing to use foreign subsidiaries as a source of innovation and learning rather than as distribution channels only. Perceptions about core managerial skills and appropriate international structures (expensive expatriates!) started to change the more international experience an MNC gathered and the more trust was given to local managers (Whitley et al., 2003). Subsidiaries began to exchange ideas and practices between themselves, especially those in the United Kingdom and the United States, occasionally without direct control from Japan (Whitley et al., 2003). Those findings are consistent with previous research stating that the effect of cultural distance may disappear as firms gain more experience operating in foreign countries and only firms in their initial stage of expansion show preferences for investing in culturally similar countries (Li et al., 2002). We conclude that the level of international experience of an MNC moderates the effects of cultural distance.

3.1.4.4 Organization culture

Organizational culture is a subculture in the sense that 'it is a normative system of a group smaller than a society' (Yinger, 1960). Two strands of literature deal with organizational culture: First, the functionalist, unitary perspective of culture prevalent in the 1980 assumes a positive relationship between active management of culture and the promotion of normative control leading to improved organizational performance (Kilman, 1985; Schein, 1992; Trice & Beyer, 1984). Second, the more symbolic treatment of organizational culture (e.g., Alvesson, 1993; Filby & Willmott, 1988; Kunda, 1992; Martin & Meyerson, 1988; Meek, 1988; Willmott, 1993) underscores that 'meaning ascribed to a particular social situation subsequently guides individual behavior' (Robertson et al., 2003). This represents a more pluralist perspective since an individual interpretation of a given situation is not necessarily shared. This perspective ultimately questions whether management can actively create and sustain a strong culture that is 'shared by all' or a culture that will promote normative control, ensuring that workers will automatically work in the interest of the firm (Robertson et al., 2003).

Following the argumentation of the functionalist approach, it can be assumed that control needs to be based on strong consensual values (Kunda, 1992; Lowendahl, 1997; Mintzberg, 1979; Robertson et al., 2003). A strong organizational culture promotes normative control which serves to self-discipline and integrates individuals within organizational environments which are typically characterized by low levels of formalization and promotes a 'responsible autonomy' (Mintzberg, 1979). Knowledge intensive firms, for example, rely to a large extent on such forms of control (Robertson et al., 2003). Empirics show that an organizational culture that embraces ambiguity engenders a form of normative control whereby employees operate freely and willingly participate in the regulation of their own autonomy (Robertson et al., 2003). Some scholars, for example Jaeger (1983) even see organizational culture by itself as an effective governing mechanism.

Gamble (2003) found that 'above all specific firm level practices' expressed in organizational culture are a key for the cross-border transfer of management practices. Similarly, Björkman (2004) found that MNCs influence inter-organizational knowledge and practice transfer by utilizing organizational culture and social control mechanisms. We conclude that organizational culture has an important impact on the diffusion of management practices and can have a moderating effect on cultural distance. Since organizational culture is at the same time a component of management control we refrain from including it as a moderator in our comprehensive model.

3.1.4.5 Personality traits

The field of psychology is also relevant for understanding MCS and has attempted to shed some light on the interaction of individual characteristics such as personality and cognitive style and the reaction to different aspects of MCS (e.g., Brownell, 1981; Chenhall, 1986). For example, the relationship between the acceptance of reliance on accounting performance measures and environmental uncertainty may be moderated by an individual's tolerance for ambiguity (Fisher, 1996; Hartmann, 2000; Kenrick & Dantchik, 1983). Individual attributes can be combined with organizational context by determining the level of compatibility between individuals and their work situation, which has been referred to as the 'person-environment fit' (Deci, 1980) or 'person-organization fit' (Kristof, 1996). The extent to which individuals demand for financial, physical and psychological and task related resources fits with the supply of these attributes from the organization determines the degree of fit (Chenhall, 2003; Fisher, 1996).

Personality traits are not displayed explicitly in our model (Figure 3.4) since they eventually impact all elements of the organization were humans interact and are confronted with structures and decision making tasks.

3.1.5 Interaction of strategy, power and interdependence

3.1.5.1 MNC strategy

Bartlett & Ghoshal (1989) argue that subsidiaries require different coordination mechanisms according to their level of resources and the strategic importance of the local environment to the HQ. The extent to which subsidiaries are an integral part of the strategic plans of the parent and the degree to which the parent is dependent on the subsidiary has an impact on the transfer of managerial know-how (Beechler et al., 1994; Geppert et al., 2003). Different subsidiaries have distinctive powers to influence HQ decisions due to their different patterns of skills and competencies (Kristensen & Zeitlin, 2001). Research on different strategic roles of subsidiaries assigned by HQ (e.g., Birkinshaw, 1997; Birkinshaw & Morrison, 1995; Doz & Prahalad, 1991; Ghoshal & Bartlett, 1990; Martinez et al., 1991) leads to the conclusion that different strategic roles of subsidiaries have a substantial impact on the type of management control exerted. Different interactions lead to different rules, different institutions, different controls and different critical contingencies (Geppert et al., 2003; Weick, 1979). Basically, the higher the degree of local responsiveness of a subsidiary the lower is the extent of control exerted by the HQ. Subsidiaries with a limited role in non-strategic environments are likely to be coordinated by formal systems while strategically important subsidiaries tend to be managed by control through socialization and networks (Ferner, 2000).

3.1.5.2 Interdependence

According to Haspeslagh and Jemison (1991) interdependence is resource sharing between related businesses and transfers of functional skills or general management capacity. The tightness or looseness of the coupling between the HQ and its subsidiaries determines the level of interdependence (Calori et al., 1994). Three critical factors determine the dependence of a parent on its subsidiaries (Blau et al., 1963; Pfeffer et al., 1978; Thompson, 1967): First, the importance of the resource, and the extent to which the MNC HQ requires it for continued operation and survival. Second, the extent to which the subsidiary has discretion over the resource allocation and use, and third, the extent to which the resource can be substituted. More specifically, Thompson (1967) distinguishes three types of interdependencies within organizations: pooled, sequential and reciprocal. When organizational units share common resources but are otherwise quite independent Thompson (1967) speaks of pooled interdependence. Sequential interdependence exists where the output of one system is fed into another part of the system (Baliga et al., 1984). The most complex form of interdependence is the reciprocal one. Reciprocally interdependent organizational units feed their work back and force among themselves. Thus, reciprocal interdependence generates the maximum need for control, coordination, and consistency in decision making.

Another strand in the literature on control in MNCs is concerned with the evolution of different control patterns throughout different stages of MNC development (Ferner, 2000). A growing body of literature argues that hierarchically ordered MNCs with a clearly identifiable hub of power and authority become increasingly outdated, since the trend points towards more decentralized 'network'-based international operations, strategic alliances and JVs (Bartlett et al., 1989; Handy, 1992; Hedlund, 1986). Such 'loosely coupled' constellations are associated with less formal and more social types of control. There is empirical evidence that the scope and intensity of HQ control exercised is positively related to the level of interdependence (Harzing, 1999).

The extent of dependence of different organizational units on each other also determines the type of control employed. Empirical evidence (Baumler, 1971; Van de Ven et al., 1976) suggests that if there is little interdependence of organizational units, control can be handled by standardization (bureaucratic formalized control). Moderate levels of interdependence can be coordinated by plans or schedules (output control). Large amounts of interdependence, however, call for controls that enable mutual adjustment such as control by socialization and networks. Harzing (1999) found positive relationships between the level of interdependence between an HQ and subsidiaries and personal, centralized control structures and bureaucratic formalized controls exercised in subsidiaries. If subsidiaries were dependent on each other control by socialization and networks was found to be dominant (Harzing, 1999).

3.1.5.3 Power

Although control is undoubtedly linked with the notion of 'power' within organizations (e.g., Crozier, 1964; Doz et al., 1991; Otley, 1988; Pfeffer, 1981) relatively little has been said about the relationship of power between different corporate levels and actors with regard to management control. Doz and Prahalad (1991) stress that a better understanding of 'the processes of influence and power, of how the trade-offs between multiple stakeholders and multiple perspectives are made' is needed. HQ power might derive from formal systems such as investment approval procedures, or powers of recruitment and reward or through social control through the infiltration of shared understandings of implicit and/or tacit rules underlying bureaucratic control systems (Ferner, 2000). HQ power is confronted with the power of local units which can be based on their position in the local market and their know-how about country specifics.

Ferner (2000) shows by case studies on British and German MNCs that bureaucratic control systems depend on informal systems and power relations for their effective functioning. Thus, the distinction between bureaucratic formalized control and personal and social control can be questioned in the light of the underlying power relations. Yan & Grey's (1994) case study findings on Sino-U.S. IJVs clearly show that the bargaining power of the partners involved affects the type of MCS employed which in turn affects performance.

The element of power is certainly reflected in some of the organizational characteristics influencing the design and transfer of MCS, such as the ownership structure, size and interdependence; however, those factors might very well be only the peak of a much subtler concept of underlying power relations. Hence, in our model we define power as an interaction term between strategic intent and interdependence.

3.2 Discussion

There are basically two approaches found in the literature on international studies on management control: (i) research based on contingency theory, which considers contextual variables as major determinants of MCS and (ii) the culture based perspective, which sees culture as explaining international variations in management practices.

The following contingencies were identified as major influences on management control: uncertainty and complexity of the business environment, resources and ownership structure of MNCs, subsidiary size and age, and intra-unit interdependence. As there are plenty of studies examining context factors and their impact on management and control issues, identifying the studies relevant in an international context is challenging. Therefore, the selection of contingency studies used for this review is subject to criticism, as we consciously attempted to keep focused on international and cross-border topics of managerial control systems by all means.

Although there is evidence of some convergence for the effect of culture on MCS characteristics, the findings also show substantive disparities: The vast majority of research based on cultural theory has focused on Anglo-American vs. Asian societies, used Hofstede's taxonomy, and looked at differences in PD, ID and UA in particular. Since Anglo-American cluster nations score typically higher on ID and lower on PD, than their Asian counterparts, there has been a tendency to assume that ID and PD are equally important in these nations. However, 'the impact cultural values have is determined by their centrality within the value system of a cultural setting more than by their prevalence in this setting' (Lachman, Nedd, & Hinings, 1994). The more central the value, the stronger is its impact and the more sensitive it is towards managerial practices. Also, the more central values are, the more resistant to change they appear to be. It seems that the concept of core vs. peripheral values explains some of the disparities of findings in cultural studies in MCS, especially as the dimension UA seems to be virtually irrelevant in Asian cultures (Hofstede & Bond, 1988), and could guide further research (Harrison et al., 1999). Many studies selected only some cultural dimensions for their theoretical specifications while ignoring others. This is especially true for Hofstede (1980b) based studies. Since all dimensions are indeed present in the empirics, the choice to omit a dimension must be interpreted as this dimension being considered irrelevant.

Cultural studies show a tendency to treat culture simplistically as they restrict themselves to cultural dimensions and do not account for the depth, richness and complexity of culture (Harrison et al., 1999). Cross-cultural literature shows that the form and nature of cultural dimensions are quite different among, and even within, societies (Triandis, 1995). This means that findings made for one nation which scores high on PD are not automatically transferable to other nations which score high on PD. This approach would simply neglect that 'societal heterogeneity dramatically influences the viability of cross-national comparisons' (Enz, 1986: 187). The prevailing restriction to Hofstede's predefined value dimensions seems all the more problematic. Baskerville (2003) expresses her reservations against the continuation of accounting research utilizing Hofstede's cultural indices, by entitling her article 'Hofstede never studied culture'. There are several severe problems in using Hofstede as a theoretical basis for research: (i) the assumption of equating nations with culture; (ii) the difficulties of, and limitations on a quantification of culture represented by cultural dimensions and matrices; and (iii) the status of the observer outside the culture. See Baskerville (2003) for a detailed discussion of the above points.

Another target of critique on using Hofstede is the time element. Measures of pre-identified dimensions obtained from one study and applied to another face the risk of temporal anachronism, as cultural profiles are subject to change over time (Bhimani, 1999). Along those lines, the use of Hofstede's cultural dimensions, which are based on a study run in the 1960s and published 25 years ago, raises concern, given the salience of elements of a culture changing over time. More recent studies could avoid such criticism by referring to the findings of the Globe study (House, Hanges, Javidan, Dorfmann, & Gupta, 2004).

Studies on the 'country of origin effect' examining whether the nationality of the parent is decisive for the choice of control mechanisms show strong correlations throughout. We conclude that the nationality of the parent apparently does have a great impact on management control.

In order to understand why control systems vary across societies, Whitley (1999) posits that it is important to explore the nature of the processes connecting societal institutions, the constitution and behavior of interest groups, and the sorts of firms that coordinate economic activities. To search for direct correlations between 'cultural' predispositions as identified by survey questions and organizational control system characteristics isolated from these mediating and interconnected phenomena is to risk drawing rather superficial and misleading conclusions. In other words, context factors should be considered to a larger extent.

Studies based on either paradigm use predominantly quantitative methods to obtain data with the survey questionnaire being the most widely used method. Moreover, results are mainly interpreted using quantitative statistics. As data is collected from divergent sources, ranging from profit-center managers, manufacturing managers, to business students, comparability of results is limited. Given the complex nature of cross-cultural issues, it is indeed questionable if using a survey questionnaire is always the best approach to gather such sensitive data. Hence, a number of scholars (e.g., Geppert, 2003; Goddard, 1997; O'Connor, 2004) call for the adoption of qualitative methods in order to gain a better understanding of the cross-border diffusion of management practices.

We conclude that both perspectives single handedly have limited explanatory power by only focusing on some aspects of managerial control in MNCs. Neither culture nor contingencies can sufficiently explain differences in MCSs and little work has been done to test the validity of these approaches empirically (Beechler et al., 1994). Therefore, we apply a more comprehensive research design on international MCS in Central and Eastern Europe (CEE) considering both contextual and cultural factors, rather than only looking at either contingencies or cultural influences in isolation.

3.3 A comprehensive model of management control fit

In the following, all the factors and moderators identified in the literature are interconnected in a comprehensive framework displaying their mutual causes and effects and are briefly recapitulated.

1. Culture
   The cultural proximity or distance between organizational units of an MNC affects the applicability of management control and presents a major challenge to the diffusion of MCS. The effect of culture can be twofold: on the one hand it directly affects management thinking, styles and preferences through values; on the other hand it shapes HQ nature, structures and modes through the 'country of origin effect' arising through distinctive features in national institutional structures.

2. (a) Environment & (b) Organizational characteristics
   Research conducted under the contingency paradigm assumes that patterns of perception and preferences of organizational members are dictated by the environment and are therefore universal across borders. The following contingency factors relevant

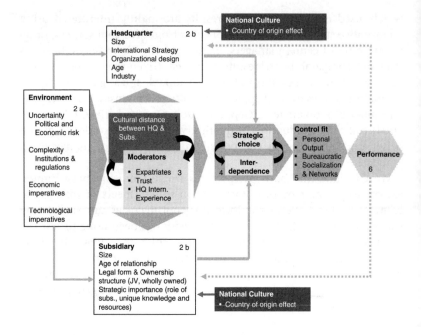

Figure 3.4 Comprehensive framework of dynamic fit.
Source: Author.

for management control in international contexts have been discussed here: age, size, interdependence, ownership structure, uncertainty, and heterogeneous environments including institutional differences, economic and technological imperatives. The presence, degree of intensity, and combination of those factors determine their magnitude on the diffusion process and the level of appropriateness and 'fit' of different control mechanisms.

3. Moderators

Moderating factors such as expatriates, organizational culture, trust and prior international HQ experience reduce the potential friction caused by cultural distance and play a crucial role in both, communicating and transferring control mechanisms across borders. For example, expatriates with the 'right' technical and personal skills can facilitate a common understanding between HQ and subsidiaries. Also trust acts as a key moderator for intra- and inter-organizational transfer of management control practices. Last but not least, international experience of

MNCs countervails effects of cultural distance and thereby facilitates the diffusion process. In a nutshell, the availability of one or more moderating factors counterbalances clashes caused by cultural distance.

4. Interaction of strategy & interdependence

    The mere existence of formal control systems whatever mechanism they might prescribe does not necessarily mean that they will be adequately adhered to in practice. Ultimately, power is required to activate formal systems. HQ power might derive from other formal systems such as investment approval procedures, majority ownership, recruitment and reward or through social control such as the infiltration of a shared understanding of implicit rules underlying bureaucratic control systems. Obviously, power interacts with the level of interdependence between HQ and subsidiaries, which in turn interacts with an MNC's strategic intent. Contingency factors, however powerful they might be, do not automatically change control structures unless they are enacted by management. Ultimately, it remains the choice of management how to react to exogenous challenges and decide on the strategy pursued. Therefore, strategic choice and interdependence are presented as an interaction term in the framework of the diffusion process of MCS.

5. Applicability and type of control mechanism 'fit'

    Both context and cultural factors determine the appropriateness and applicability of control mechanisms. However, the presence or absence of moderators also has a share in determining the level of fit between context factors, cultural distance and strategy. Given that some context factors rule out specific control types, and given all the potential interaction among those factors, and given the degree of cultural distance, and given the presence or absence of moderators, and given the interaction of strategic intent and interdependence, determining the 'right' control mechanism for a given scenario is extremely challenging. At any rate, there is no such thing as an 'ideal' control mechanism for a given scenario. Nevertheless, based on the literature analyzed, it is indeed possible to rule out some control types for a given combination of factors and to determine which types of controls are more suitable. For example, a highly unpredictable environment combined with a high degree of cultural distance and large size of a subsidiary does not go together with centralized control structures.

6. Performance

At large, empirics show that highly controlled subsidiaries tend to have poorer performance evaluations and tend to be more dissatisfied with their HQ. Nevertheless, empirical evidence on the performance of shared controlled IJVs as compared to dominantly controlled IJVs or fully owned subsidiaries is mixed. However, given that some control types are more effective in a specific cultural and contextual setting than others, we can safely assume that choosing the appropriate control type does also impact an MNC's performance.

The configuration of factors influencing the transfer of management practices and management control can change over time and space. MNCs also change national business systems not only by exerting economic power but also by introducing their distinctive way of doing things while at the same time learning from the environment. Therefore all the factors discussed above are integrated in a dynamic model. We conclude that neither cultural research alone nor looking at contingency factors only can explain the phenomenon of cross-border diffusion of managerial control sufficiently. Rather, both paradigms provide valuable insights and should not be looked at in isolation, since external and internal factors, institutional consequences, and the societal values of a culture influence the process that produces accounting values and control systems.

4
Cultural Research on Central and Eastern Europe

None of the investigated studies on MNC control dealt with the context of Central and Eastern Europe (CEE). Our empirical study will show whether or not the insights derived from the above literature review do also apply in a CEE context. We have shown that culture impacts the applicability of MNC control and will therefore briefly introduce the findings of existing cultural studies on CEE which might render explanations for cultural specifics as identified in the interviews.

Culture reflects the ideas, values, norms and meanings shared by members of a society and is perpetuated through families and communities (Hofstede, 1980b). The assumptions, beliefs and expectations that are ingrained in people through socialization shape their behavior and a nation's formal institutions (Lubatkin, Lane, Collin, & Very, 2005). Eastern Europe is by no means culturally homogenous. There are hundreds of different nationalities which vary in terms of language, culture and mentalities (Steinle & Lawa, 1996). Nevertheless, they share a common history of communism and a centrally planned economy, a one-party system, some Soviet influence, and are currently undergoing similar political and economic transition processes (Bakacsi, Takacs, Karacsonyi, & Imrek, 2002; Hickson & Pugh, 1995; Perlitz, Bufka, & Wagner, 1996). A centrally planned economy is defined as the economy being coordinated and governed by a central planning authority (Kleps, 1984).

Parts of CEE are still blind spots in empirical cultural research: CEE has not been studied much and is not found in fundamental studies such as Hofstede (1980a) (except for Yugoslavia) or Ronen and Shenkar (Ronen & Kraut 1977; 1985). (See Appendix for a short explanation of cultural dimensions developed by Hofstede [1980a]; House et al. [2004] and Trompenaars [1997; 2004]).

Trompenaars and Hampden-Turner (1997) included Bulgaria, Rumania, Serbia, Poland, Russia, the Czech Republic and Hungary in their study, which were found to be rather particularistic, scored medium to high on individualism, were mostly specific in their relations, clearly ascribed status based on family background and not on achievement, were outer-directed and had a polychronic (synchronous) perception of time.

More recently, the Globe study (Bakacsi et al., 2002; House et al., 2004) included Albania, Georgia, Greece, Hungary, Kazakhstan, Poland, Russia, and Slovenia in its database which form the Eastern European cluster (Gupta, Hanges, & Dorfman, 2002). This cluster differs in terms of language, ethnic backgrounds, religion and economics, but, – except for Greece – they all belonged to the Council for Mutual Economic Assistance (COMECON) and had a centrally planned economy for some 40 to 70 years (Bakacsi et al., 2002). The countries also differ in terms of economic development with Greece, Hungary, Poland and Slovenia dealing with the challenges of service and information economies while the rest of the cluster is still found in the industrialization stage.

The cluster's societal practices – 'as if' – are rated as high on group collectivism (5.53) and power distance (5.25). It has low ratings on Uncertainty Avoidance (UA) (3.57), future orientation (3.37), is relatively egalitarian (3.84) in terms of gender but assertive (3.58). The other cultural dimensions (humane orientation, performance orientation) are rated in the mid-range, around an average of 4 (Bakacsi et al., 2002). The countries within this cluster differ in values – 'should be' – such as assertiveness, performance orientation and Institutional Collectivism (IC) but rank very similar in terms of in power distance, UA, group and family collectivism, gender egalitarianism and future orientation. Although the 'should be' figures show that managers hope that their societies will become more future and performance oriented and less male-oriented and hierarchical, they also hope that the strong group collectivism will remain unchanged and high in the future. From a comparative standpoint with other Globe findings (House et al., 2004) this cluster stands out with a high group-orientation and a high power distance. Nations in this cluster have more tolerance in terms of uncertainty and are more egalitarian than the Globe average (House et al., 2004).

Many authors fail to explain the medium scores in 'as if' on IC of the Eastern European cluster with some countries, for example Hungary found among the most individualistic nations studied in Globe. In terms of values ('should be') the results of the Globe study show that an otherwise collectivist Russia and Georgia lead on the individualistic ranks. Fink & Lehmann (Fink & Lehmann, 2006; Fink, Holden, & Lehmann, 2007) render an explanation for the relatively high scores in individualism in the Eastern European cluster by analyzing the functioning of the former socialist economic and political system and the behavior of the people living within it in depth: People under socialist regimes found ways to keep the state intrusions at bay with the workplace being the center of dissent. The communist party assumed that workers cannot be trusted and ensured that they were under permanent pressure to conform by the means of a control method named 'socialist discipline' (Fink et al., 2006). At the workplace the latter was called 'cadre' who could be found in every organization to make sure that the will of the state was carried out. In response people developed 'a very self-conscious form of individualism to get the best out of the system' and some sort of 'subversive privacy' at the workplace (Fink et al., 2007). Small groups of people pooled together as 'informal collectives' at the work place and created their own communication channels based on shared tacit knowledge undermining official authorities and control mechanisms. As Fink & Lehmann (2006) explain, Lenin's model of revolution was a mixture of a corporate view of society and a bureaucratic view of the organization. Since he found economy and politics, and organizations and society to be identical, he invented a 'total institution'. Given his understanding of organization, he needed control. Fink and Lehman (2006) argue that Lenin's 'New Economic Policy' can be seen as an adaptation of Taylor's scientific management since it used cadre politics as a regulative. Both, Lenin and Taylor were suspicious of the workers, and Lenin attempted to control them by the means of bureaucracy and terror. Consequently, the primary principle for workers to undermine bureaucratic control was to keep a low profile and never stick out. On the surface, individuals showed organizational loyalty but at the same time maintained their social networks which aimed at undermining organizational control hidden from observation. Since the best way to generate loyalty was to establish tight friendships with their co-workers the frontiers between private and professional life became blurred. Centrally planned targets could not be met without loyal and obedient subordinates (For a detailed description of subversive behavior in communist regimes see Fink 2006). Since it was neither in the interest of the workers nor in the interest of the superiors to have demanding plan targets, plan figures were changed frequently and were more often than not inconsistent (Fink, 1971, 1987).

After the collapse of the communist system people's abilities to effectively subvert communist authorities became meaningless. Social group networking and subversion lost its reference and did not work confronted with Western management techniques. The fall of communism entailed not only the destruction of institutional entities but also radically challenged fundamental values, beliefs and assumptions held by society (Roth et al., 2003). Johnson et al. (2000) conclude, that 'cognitive processes must be put in place that are the reverse of those that led to institutionalization in the first place'. The first wave of enthusiasm following the collapse of the communist regime gave way to tremendous confusion, anxiety and uncertainty caused by a culture shock, and a huge gap between people's desire for stability and the slow development of new institutions and the economic turmoil (Bakacsi et al., 2002). People who grew up in socialist societies usually avoided taking on responsibility and rather depended on their superiors, and expected their superiors to take care of them. Now there is a widespread feeling and attitude of inefficiency, unfairness, 'learned helplessness', workplace anxiety and favoritism (Pearce & Branyiczki, 1994).

The transition process might render an explanation for some scores in the Eastern European cluster: In contrast to Hofstede (1993) who points to the passive uncertainty avoiding Russian cultural heritage, the Globe scores show a rather high uncertainty bearing in Eastern Europe (House et al., 2004). In the Globe findings, Russia scores lowest on the UA 'as if' rankings, closely followed by Hungary while Georgia, Kazakhstan, Poland and Slovenia can be found in the last third. However, the results for 'should be' scores differ with an average of 4.93 (Bakacsi et al., 2002).

Following the culture standard method of Alexander Thomas (Thomas, 2003) culture standards of the Czech Republic (Fink, Novy, & Schroll-Machl, 2000; Novy & Schroll-Machl, 2003), Russia (Lyskov-Strewe & Schroll-Machl, 2003), Hungary (Meierewert & Topcu, 1999), Poland (Boski, 2003) and other CEE countries were established yielding insights in a bi-cultural comparison with Germanic countries (Germany and Austria).

Since most parent companies in the present study belong to the Germanic cluster, a comparison between the Germanic and the Eastern European clusters might shed some light on cross-cultural HQ-subsidiary relations between those two (see Figure 4.1). In general, the Germanic cluster in 'as if' terms is characterized by a stronger tendency for standardization and rules, higher levels of assertiveness and more gender inequality (Szabo et al., 2002) (These findings correspond with Hofstede's (1980a) results, which found high UA for Austria (Uncertainty

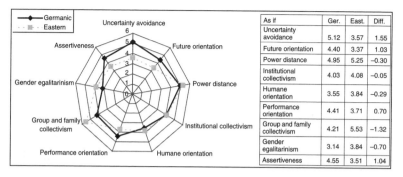

Figure 4.1 Differences in 'as if' scores: Germanic versus Eastern European cluster.
Source: Based on data from (Bakacsi et al., 2002; Szabo et al., 2002).

Avoidance Index [UAI] = 70 on a scale between 8 and 112), Germany (UAI = 65), and Switzerland (UAI = 58). Hofstede's masculinity dimension (uniting gender differentiation, gender discrimination and a tough-gender component) also places Austria (masculinity index Management Accounting System [MAS] = 79 on a scale between 5 and 95), Germany (MAS = 66), and Switzerland (MAS = 70) among the masculine countries (Szabo et al., 2002).)

A comparison of the Globe 'as if' scores between the Germanic and the Eastern European cluster shows that the two clusters differ most in terms of UA with the Eastern European cluster scoring 1.55 lower than the Germanic cluster (see Figure 4.2). Eastern Europe shows by 1.32 higher scores on group and family collectivism than the Germanic cluster. Regarding future orientation the scores for Eastern Europe are by 1.03 lower than the ones for the Germanic cluster. Eastern Europe is more gender egalitarian (difference 0.70) and less performance oriented (difference 0.70) than Germanic nations.

Figure 4.2 compares the 'should be' scores for the Germanic and the Eastern European cluster. The scores for 'should be' show a reverse result for UA as compared to the 'as if' scores, with the Germanic cluster wishing for less UA and the Eastern European cluster wishing for more UA, resulting in a difference of 1.47 between the two clusters. Apart from a difference in assertiveness of 0.81, the two clusters score rather similar in 'should be' figures.

Leadership profiles might also add some explanatory power for HQ control since they shape the expectations of CEE subsidiary personnel towards their Western HQ. Figure 4.3 below compares leadership scores of the Eastern European and the Germanic cluster.

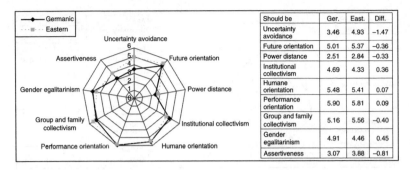

Figure 4.2 Differences in 'should be' scores: Germanic versus Eastern European cluster.
Source: Based on data from (Bakacsi et al., 2002; Szabo et al., 2002).

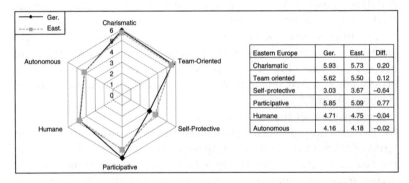

Figure 4.3 Differences in Eastern European and Germanic leadership-profile scores.
Source: Data based on (Bakacsi et al., 2002; Szabo et al., 2002).

The Globe findings point to team oriented (5.87), transformational-charismatic (5.73) and participative leadership (5.08) as the most successful leadership styles within the Eastern European cluster. According to Bakacsi (2002) participation can be explained historically, since traditionally large consultative bodies practiced a somewhat paternalistic, but officially participative leadership style. During socialism the 'cadres' practiced a team oriented leadership based on participation (Fink et al., 2007). Maybe the low scores on autonomous leaders can be explained as a conscious rejection of the widely practiced autonomous leadership style of the past (Bakacsi, 1999). However, those findings should be handled with care, since there are remarkable differences among the countries within the cluster. For example, Greece, Hungary, and Albania stand out from an otherwise relatively homogeneous picture.

4.1 The aftermath of communism

After 1989 the institutions and the logic of central planning were abandoned resulting in a vacuum. 'New values and norms were slow to develop, as were the political, legal, and financial institutions that are legitimated by underlying values and norms' (Newman, 2000). The post-communism changes undertaken in most countries of CEE are clear examples of institutional upheaval (Roth et al., 2003). The key characteristic of the transition is a fundamental change in the norms, values, and assumptions underlying economic activity. Communism was abandoned with astounding speed but is only slowly being replaced with new norms, values, and assumptions that are more consistent with democracy and a market-based economy. New capabilities such as efficiency orientation, strategic thinking, entrepreneurial initiative and proneness to take risk are required, but those develop only slowly (Newman, 2000). Our findings underline an upheaval in values since we found a substantial rift in prevailing values among different generations.

5
Method

As identified in our literature review, empirical studies on international management control have predominantly used quantitative methods to obtain data, which might have yielded to a lower level of understanding of the underlying phenomena than required. The majority of studies on the international transfer of Management Practices in general are based upon rather large-scale surveys based on questionnaires (Gamble, 2003). Quantitative research generally tests theoretical propositions with hypothesis derived from theory and relies on large sample sizes (Ongwuegbuzie, 2003). However, using standardized measures implies that varying perspectives and experiences of people fit into a limited number of predetermined response categories. Consequently, comparison and statistical aggregation of data is facilitated, leading to a generalizable set of findings, with the validity of findings being dependent on the careful construction of the instruments used (Patton, 2002).

A number of scholars (e.g., Geppert et al., 2003; Goddard, 1997; O'Connor et al., 2004) call for the adoption of qualitative methods in order to gain a better understanding of the dynamic process of cross-border diffusion of management practices and its cultural interplays. Questionnaires are often inadequate instruments for the complex issues of international business, 'some of the most provocative work of researchers [...] has come from those who have plumbed in depth the behavior of individual firms [...]' (Vernon, 1994). Andersen and Skaates (2004) found that a mere 10 percent of articles published in six leading international business journals in the 1991–2001 period used qualitative research techniques. Qualitative Research attempts to generate theories and new hypotheses based on empirical data

(Bewely, 2002; Froschauer & Lueger, 1992; Kölbl, 2001). Qualitative research is of explorative nature as it aims to explain social reality and to identify causal relations and phenomena by describing the complexity of a social setting based on empirical data (Flick, 2002a). Going in the field without being preoccupied by predetermined categories of analysis allows for depth, openness and detail of the qualitative inquiry (Patton, 2002). Qualitative research methods typically produce a wealth of in-depth information about a much smaller number of people and cases in a specific context, thus, generalization is reduced (Marschan-Piekkari & Welch, 2004a). It goes beyond the 'what' – the measurement of observable behavior – and strives to understand the 'how' and 'why' – the meaning underlying the action (Buckley & Chapman, 1996; Marschan-Piekkari, 2004; Morgan & Smircich, 1980).

Given the diverse and sometimes even contrasting findings on the effects of culture on the design and management of HQ control, and given the novelty of exploring management control in a Central and Eastern Europe (CEE) context we decided to use a qualitative method. We conducted an exploratory study in order to analyze the current state of management control of Austrian based MNCs in CEE and how control mechanisms are transferred across borders.

The research design for this study therefore comprises four stages:

- desk research: literature review, identification of important issues and development of interview guide
- field research: semi-structured interviews
- data analysis: qualitative content analysis
- development of propositions

First, based on our literature review on management control in MNCs we developed an interview guide which allowed us to identify the type and extent of control exerted by Austrian based HQ in CEE. Second, the salience of context and cultural factors impacting transfer of management practices was tested by a qualitative research design, using the technique of the semi-structured interview. Our interviewees were parent managers and controllers in charge of managing foreign subsidiaries and joint ventures in CEE. Third, interview data was analyzed with qualitative content analysis (Mayring, 2002b). Finally, propositions regarding MNC control in CEE were drawn based on the analysis of the interviews. The individual stages are discussed in some detail below.

5.1 Semi-structured interview

> When in doubt, observe and ask questions. When certain, observe at length and ask many more questions.
>
> George S. Patton U.S. general (1885–1945) from Halcom's Laws of Inquiry (Patton, 2002)

The data was collected through semi-structured personal interviews that lasted about one hour on average. All interviews were conducted by the same researcher. 65 percent of the interviewees were among the top five top executives of the regional HQ (including 30 percent CEOs) while the remaining 25 percent respondents were middle managers. The format of the semi-structured interview and the open nature of inquiry allowed us to draw-up causal and other relations between the single variables. Those relations form an essential part of the findings and allowed us to put up propositions.

Based on extensive literature review on the issue investigated, a set of topics was established to be explored with each respondent (Bortz & Döring, 2002; Mayring, 2002b). Although it might be highly useful to examine instruments others have used in successful studies on related topics, published articles rarely include copies of the questionnaires (Daniels & Cannice, 2004). A basic checklist, the interview guide (see Appendix 2 for the complete interview guide), was developed to ensure that we covered all relevant topics and that the same line of inquiry was pursued with each person interviewed (Mayring, 2002a; Patton, 2002). To answer our research questions three sets of variables were included in the interview guide based on our findings from the literature review.

The first set of questions centered on the *organizational characteristics* which were found to have an impact on control types, such as market entry mode (Greenfield vs. Acquisition vs. International Joint Venture [IJVs]), size, and importance of CEE subsidiaries in terms of sales and profit for the MNC.

The second set of questions was designed to capture the *nature and extent of control mechanisms* identified as relevant for MNCs in the literature. Based on Harzing (Harzing, 1999; Martinez et al., 1991) information on the extent and scope of *explicit control* mechanisms, including the degree of centralization, formalization, planning, output control and personal control was collected. Data on the extent and scope of *implicit control mechanisms,* including control by lateral relations, network building, international management training and organizational culture was collected. Questions following this line of inquiry allowed us to identify how HQ manage and control their CEE subsidiaries. Furthermore, the *implementation and transfer* of management control systems into CEE subsidiaries was a subject of inquiry.

The third set of questions was kept very open and focused on *perceptions of cultural differences* and their potential influences on the design, applicability and functioning of control and coordination systems in CEE subsidiaries and the mode HQ-subsidiary relationships.

The semi-structured interview was chosen because it allows for maximum flexibility by using different types of questions and by dealing effectively with theory based assumptions. There is an openness to changes of sequence and forms of questions in order to follow up answers given and stories told by the respondents (Kvale, 1996). Collecting short stories and examples about events enabled us to analyze those events and convert collected experiences of the interviewees into knowledge. We were free to explore, probe and ask questions, and build conversations within subject areas, in order to elucidate the subject in question (Patton, 2002). At the same time, the interview guide ensured that interviewing a number of people was done systematically and comprehensively by confining beforehand the topics to be explored. The principle of openness is imminent in the process of the interview dialogue, by making the interviewee's position more explicit, and by using different questions and approaches (Flick, 2002b; Hoffmann-Riem, 1980). The interviewee has a complex stock of both explicit and implicit knowledge about the topic under study (Scheele & Groeben, 1988). Explicit knowledge can be accessed by answering open questions while implicit assumptions are more difficult to reveal. In order to do so we used methodological aids, namely different types of questions designed to reconstruct the interviewee's subjective theory about the issue under study (Flick, 2002a). The semi-structured interview is a good way of revealing existing – and often implicit – knowledge in the form of verbal answers and making it accessible for interpretation (Flick, 2002a).

Most people like to talk about themselves and the semi-structured interview makes use of this proneness by including open-ended questions (Bewely, 2002). During our data collection we often experienced that the time frame of an hour agreed upon before the interview was extended because interviewees actually enjoyed talking about their work. Moreover, what is said in a relaxed frame of mind is usually more consistent with the overall logic of what is said and reflects views more accurately then simply ticking off questions on a list (Bewely, 2002). A consistent use of the interview guide adds to the comparability and structure of the gathered data (Flick, 2002a).

Interviews may allow researchers to develop a deep rapport with informants which enables them to gain honest and accurate responses and to add insights that lay groundwork for larger follow-up studies (Daniels et al., 2004). By properly managing interview studies researchers can develop a network of new data, insights and referrals, which may be even more important in cross-border contexts (Richards, 1995).

By trying to secure relevant information and subjective perspectives some issues arise in the course of the semi-structured interview: The interviewer has to constantly mediate between the input of the interview guide, the aim of the research question, and the interviewee's style of presentation (Flick, 2002a). During the interview the interviewer must decide ad hoc on the question sequence. The interviewer decides spontaneously when to inquire in greater detail, when to support the respondent in venturing into seemingly far-fetched, yet potentially research-relevant fields which might yield new insights into the topic, and when to return to the interview guide. The term 'semi-structured' already reflects the element of choice during the actual interview, a choice between sticking to the guide and at the same time keeping open to other topics relevant to the respondent (Flick, 2002a). Such decisions not only require a great deal of overview regarding the course of the interview by mentally checking off questions that have been answered and sensitivity towards the interviewee, but also in-depth knowledge of the research topic. Sticking too bureaucratically to the interview guide restricts the benefit of gaining additional information (Hopf, 1978). On the other hand, the more the interviewer allows the interview to extravagate outside the guide the less comparable the data might get. The interviewer needs to keep track of what has been covered already, and which topics might fit in next, while at the same time paying close attention to what is said at the moment. Permanent mediation between the course of the interview, the interview outline and the time requires some experience and management to effectively handle the situation.

A crucial point was to create willingness on the side of potential interviewees to participate in such an interview and to report relevant events freely (Fink & Meierewert, 2001; Hermanovicz, 2002). Creating a convenient atmosphere and a good relation between the interviewee and the interviewer as well as the ability of the interviewer to stimulate the memory of the interviewee, contributed vitally to the success of the interview process (Fink et al., 2001; Fink, Kölling, Meierewert, & Neyer,

2004a; Hermanovicz, 2002). It is up to the interviewer to create an atmosphere that allows the interaction to go beyond a merely polite exchange of ideas while at the same time avoiding direct answers (Kvale, 1996). At the beginning of the interview, after exchanging business cards, a few minutes spent on unrelated 'small talk' – such as how the trip to the office was – helped to put the informant at ease (Daniels et al., 2004). Then the study was explained briefly and confidentiality assured once more. The interviewer has to keep in mind that he defines the situation and steers the course of the interview, thus, there is a definite asymmetry of power. This aspect has to be handled with care when interviewing high ranking executives which are used to direct conversations. To improve the interview technique it is essential for the interviewer to reflect on his/her experiences after every single interview. We found interview training helpful and performed four pretest interviews.

Before recording an interview, we sought for agreement. Although transcribing the interview was extremely time intensive, recording not only guaranteed that the data is not distorted but also facilitated the conduct of an interview distinctively. However, some informants tended to be more guarded when being taped (Daniels et al., 2004). The knack of a good interviewer is to get the respondent so involved that he/she forgets about the interview situation. Concentration and a good memory are essential for obtaining valuable information. We found that paying undivided attention to the informant and showing that we followed closely of what had been said by summing up parts and going deeper into the field worked astonishingly well.

Interviewing business people was challenging in so far as they have a busy timetable, thus we found it vital to sustain their interest in the subject. Since maintaining eye-contact helped, we had to memorize the key questions to be covered and avoid looking down at the interview guide. A good way of renewing interest and at the same time covering potentially interesting issues was to invite the informant to bring up new aspects of the topic. For example, 'Is there something I should have asked and have neglected?' (Bewely, 2002)

5.1.1 Potential sources of bias and ways of dealing with it

> Simply observing and interviewing do not ensure that the research is qualitative; the qualitative researcher must also interpret the beliefs and behaviors of participants.
>
> (Janesick, 2000)

Context plays a major role in qualitative research. Context can be defined as 'the surroundings associated with phenomena which help to illustrate that phenomena' (Capelli & Sherer, 1991). Marschan-Piekkari et al. (2004) go even further by defining context as 'both, the environment of the phenomenon under study and the setting within which research is conducted'. Figure 5.1 depicts various layers of contexts in an interview setting: Bias is 'any tendency causing a person consistently to give different responses to test items than he would when the same content is presented in a different form' (Cronbach, 1946). Any attempt to eliminate or correct errors provokes further reaction effects and prevents maximization of validity (Esser, 1977).

In the following the four different layers of context are discussed in some detail:

The *interview context* encompasses all situational factors of the interview: setting, mood of the participants, number of interruptions, time pressure, and so on. In the course of the interview both participants generate a shared context where meaning, ideas and experiences are exchanged (Kvale, 1996; Marschan-Piekkari et al., 2004b). Interviews are by nature 'social encounters where speakers collaborate in producing retrospective (and prospective) accounts or versions of their past (or future) actions, experiences, feelings and thoughts' (Rapley, 2004). Therefore, interviews are interactional events, since both speakers mutually monitor each other's speech and non-verbal expressions, creating meaning collaboratively (Froschauer et al., 1992). The quality of the gathered information depends largely on the interviewer (Foddy, 1995; Patton, 2002).

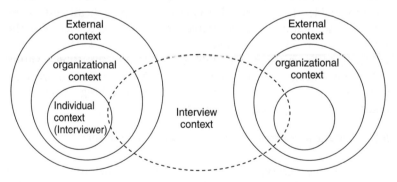

Figure 5.1 Four contextual levels of the research Interview in international business.
Source: Marschan-Piekkari (2004b).

Interviewed persons are careful not to lose face in the course of the interview or even give socially accepted answers (Bewely, 2002; Esser, 1975). Interviewers might very well surrender objectivity by aligning themselves with the interests of senior managers in the organizations they are studying (Fletcher, 2002; Macdonald & Hellgren, 2004), since they must up to a certain degree please powerful people to retain access.

The *individual context* refers to the context of the interviewer and the respondent in terms of external influences such as profession, gender, age, culture, education, social networks, organizational affiliation and countries in which they have worked. The degree to which those differ has an impact on the dynamics of the interview. Thus, the researcher should reflect how those things might affect the data (Prasad, 2002).

There seems to be a tendency in international business research to focus on elite interviewees (Ghoshal, Szulanski, & Korine, 1994; Macdonald et al., 2004). Scholars often reason that the more senior the interviewee the more he/she knows about the organization (Macdonald et al., 2004). It is not uncommon that researchers measure the success of an interview not in terms of the information obtained but rather in terms of the importance of the person interviewed. However, both empirics and theory provide different evidence: Top management does not necessarily know most about what's going on in an organization; indeed middle management seems to be better informed (Johanson & Mattsson, 1998). Moreover, senior managers tend to share a transnational elite culture which transcends national and cultural boundaries, therefore having convergent views (Welch, Marschan-Piekkari, Penttinnen, & Tahvanainen, 2002). Consequently, we also interviewed people from lower-ranking positions. Expatriates seem to form a special category by being able to switch from the HQ point of view to the one of the local unit and back (Marschan-Piekkari et al., 2004b).

The *organizational context* includes the type of organization under study, its size, structure, culture, division and history and is also affected by the researcher's organizational context, which is the academic institution (Marschan-Piekkari et al., 2004b). Even if the research question is not directly related by the organizational characteristics they are very likely to shape the research process (Capelli et al., 1991).

The ways MNCs coordinate and integrate their far-flung units are an enduring theme in international business research. Sampling often becomes a multi-staged process where not only the organizations are to be selected but also the number and types of units to be included. Over time the unit of analysis has changed from headquarter–subsidiary relationship to the subsidiary and the individuals inside them (Gupta et al., 1991; Marschan-Piekkari et al., 2004b). Yeung (1995) criticizes that MNC research is often 'methodologically separated' by either focusing on HQ or subsidiaries but not on both. Since HQ cannot be assumed to be the ultimate source of truth, triangulation of HQ responses with subsidiary views might be useful (Holm, Johanson, & Thilenius, 1995; Mezias, Chen, & Murphy, 1999). This adds a new dimension of triangulation namely 'unit triangulation' (Denzin, 1989; Patton, 1990). When both units of analysis – subsidiaries and HQ – are included in a study the researcher may get more insight into internal power plays (Marschan-Piekkari et al., 2004b). In four out of forty MNCs investigated we had respondents from both the subsidiary and the HQ level.

Research in organizations is constrained by the fact that it is always done 'by permission', thus access is a major challenge (Buckley et al., 1996; Welch et al., 2002; Yeung, 1995). The researcher needs to generate a win-win situation where the organization receives something in exchange for their time and trust. We promised all our interviewees to share our findings with them. Furthermore, it is vital that confidentiality is provided by the researcher.

People tend to be more cooperative and willing to give an interview if the name of a trusted third party comes into play (Bewely, 2002). Obviously, such names are gained through networking using and following a chain of personal contacts. Ideally, a domino effect is created by asking an interviewee for further informants after the interview. However, it is important to approach different people from several industries to avoid getting trapped with people who think along the same lines. Our sample consists of a variety of industries and we can almost exclude convenience sampling in our study, since we contacted most interviewees independently from each other.

The *external context* comprises national cultural, political, economic, and industry environments in which organizations are embedded (Pettigrew, 1985). Research findings cannot be separated from the context in which data collection and analysis takes place (Eckhardt, 2004; Michailova, 2004; Punnet & Shenkar, 1994).

Interviewer bias is often amplified in cross-cultural contexts (Brislin, Cushner, Cherrie, & Yong, 1986). Conducting interviews in a foreign language has an impact on the flow of conduct, trust building and on the actual content (Adler, 1984; Morrison, Conaway, & Borden, 1994). For a comprehensive literature review of methodological issues in cross-cultural research refer to Cavusgila and Das (1997). In order to keep the interviewer bias as low as possible both the interviewer and the interviewee should share the same cultural background. Since our sample consisted mostly of Austrians, and some Germans and Swiss, a cross-cultural bias is not likely.

The four contextual levels are intricately interwoven and mutually influenced by each other (Marschan-Piekkari et al., 2004b). While 'pure science' holds that research objects can and must be 'abstracted from their context' to allow for accurate measuring (Morgan et al., 1980) it seems worthwhile in qualitative research to argue that the meaning of a phenomenon cannot be understood in isolation from the social processes ('wider reality') through which that meaning is constructed since reality is ultimately situational (Marschan-Piekkari et al., 2004b; Morgan et al., 1980). There are a growing number of scholars among organizational theorists which call for context to be taken into consideration in both conceptual and methodological terms (Alvesson & Deetz, 2000; Cassell & Symon, 1994; Johns, 2001; Marschan-Piekkari et al., 2004a; Rousseau & Fried, 2001; Symon & Cassell, 1998).

5.2 Qualitative content analysis

> It wasn't curiosity that killed the cat. It was trying to make sense of all the data curiosity generated.
>
> From Halcom's Laws of Inquiry (Patton, 2002)

Recorded data was transcribed to enable interpretation (Kowall & O'Connell, 2002). Each transcribed interview was also linked to the characteristics of the interviewed person, such as gender, age, experience, position, and so on, which might have an impact on the interview setting and could be taken into account (Kuckartz, 1999). 'Interviews yield so much and such diverse information that even simple aggregation presents problems' (Macdonald et al., 2004). The transcriptions – so-called primary documents – were analyzed by using the qualitative content analysis developed by Mayring (2000b; 2002b; Mayring, 2003). 'Qualitative content analysis [...] is an approach of empirical, methodological controlled analysis of texts within their context of communication, following content analytical rules and step by step models, without rash quantification' (Mayring, 2000a). It comprises categorization along two methods:

1. **inductive categorization**, which means that the categories, themes and patterns emerge out of the interview material itself (Bernard, 2000; Patton, 2002); and

2. **deductive categorization**, which means that categories will be built based on prior studies and existing frameworks (Fink et al., 2004a, Mayring, 1999, Mayring, 2000).

Figure 5.2 below depicts the steps of analysis in inductive and deductive category development:

According to Mayring (1999, 2000) content analysis comprises three steps: summarizing, explicating and structuring (Lamnek, 1995). First, the text was broken down to its core content by selecting, bundling, omitting, integrating and generalizing (*summarizing*). In order to make sense of those parts of the text which cannot be easily interpreted due to wording, terminology or incomplete formulation, additional material, such as the relevant scientific literature, was consulted (*explication*). The final step was twofold, since it comprised an inductive and a deductive process (*structuring*):

First, the characteristics of a piece of text or phrase were defined in order for that text to be included in a specific category. Basically, the challenge was to figure out what things fit together by looking for recurring regularities in the data (Guba, 1978; Patton, 2002). Categories

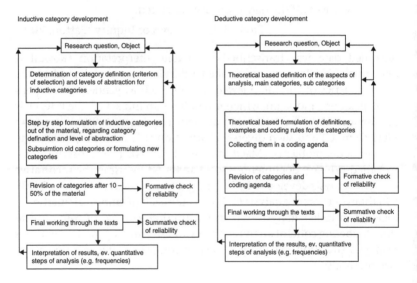

Figure 5.2 Step model of inductive and deductive category development.
Source: Mayring (2000a).

or codes are specific characteristics of a text generated inductively by the researcher while analyzing the transcripts (Kuckartz, 1999; Lamnek, 1995). 'How categories are defined [...] is an art. Little is written about it' (Krippendorff, 1980). Developing categories is the core of the qualitative content analysis since it allows for breaking down massive amounts of data to its quintessence (Atteslander, 2000; Mayring, 2000b; Mayring, 2003). This process is often called 'open-coding' in order to emphasize the importance of being open to the data (Strauss & Corbin, 1998). The term 'grounded theory' applies, which underlines 'being grounded' as becoming immersed in the data in order to discover embedded meanings and relationships (Glaser, 2001; Glaser & Strauss, 1967; Strauss et al., 1998). We identified, defined and elucidated categories developed by people studied to focus analysis. Anthropologists call this emic analysis and distinguish it from ethic analysis, which refers to labels imposed by the researcher itself (Patton, 2002). Categories were judged by two criteria: *internal homogeneity* – the extent to which data belonging to a category 'fit' together in a meaningful way – and *external heterogeneity* – the extent to which differences among categories were bold and clear (Guba, 1978; Patton, 2002). Then we worked back and force between the classification system and the data in order to verify meaningfulness and accuracy of categories and placement of data. Once a category was identified it was further differentiated by breaking it down into subcategories (Strauss et al., 1998). Finally, the category system was tested for completeness along the following criteria (Atteslander, 2000; Merten, 1995; Patton, 2002):

- External and internal plausibility: Categories should be internally consistent and comprise at the same time the whole picture when viewed externally.
- Independence and exclusiveness: Categories should be clearly distinguished from each other and not overlap (internal homogeneity and external heterogeneity).
- Completeness: All data should be assigned to the established categories.
- Reproducibility: Any other competent judge should be able to come up with the same set of categories.
- Credibility: The set should be credible to the persons who provided the information (Guba, 1978).

Once the patterns, themes or categories were established by inductive analysis, the deductive element of the analysis came into play by complementing the inductively derived categories with matching categories derived from the relevant literature. Studies analyzed in the literature review were used for deductive categorization. In addition, culture dimension studies (Hall & Hall, 2000; Hofstede, 1980a; House et al., 2004; Kluckhohn et al., 1961), studies on culture standards (Thomas, 2003), and studies on personality traits (Black, Mendenhall, & Oddou, 1991; Caligiuri, 2000; Gudykunst, Hammer, & Wiseman, 1978), were also resorted to. Generating propositions from data is considered to be a deductive process (Strauss et al., 1998). Grounded theorizing involved both inductive and deductive elements: 'At the heart of theorizing lies the interplay of making inductions (deriving concepts, their properties, and dimensions from the data) and deductions (hypothesizing about the relationships between concepts)' (Strauss et al., 1998).

For this study, Atlas.ti Version 5 was used which has proven to be helpful for qualitative content analysis (Mayring, 2000a). Although software facilitates the drudgery of data storage, coding, retrieval, comparing and linking, analysis is still left for the human brain (Durkin, 1997; Kelle, 1995; Kuckartz, 1999; Patton, 2002). The use of Atlas.ti was highly helpful for 'quantifying' our qualitative analysis: Every code based on interview quotations is displayed with the number of quotations it is based on and the number of links made from it to other codes. Atlas.ti allowed us to easily draw network views which visualize underlying relations for our assigned codes grounded on our data. Groundedness and density of assigned interview codes are always displayed. The code 'development stage' (9/11), for example, means that this code is grounded on 9 quotations ('grounded') in the interview text while 11 stands for the number of links made to other codes ('density'). Links to other codes were established based on the interview material.

5.2.1 Validity and reliability

The measurement validity is the core quality indicator in qualitative research (Bortz et al., 2002). Validity of qualitative findings is based on six factors (Mayring, 1999; Mayring, 2002a, 2003):

- Documentation of the method: The choice of a particular analysis tool, the data collection process and the data analysis has to be made

transparent and documented to allow others to retrace the data collection.
- Argumentative coverage of the interpretation: Coherent and logical interpretation of data and line of thought.
- Adherence to method rules: Following the single analysis steps closely and systematically is crucial to obtain high quality data.
- Closeness to the subject: Going into the field to gather information within the natural environment of the interviewee is crucial.
- Communicative validity: For example. discussing and jointly interpreting results with research participants. In order to avoid being subject to bias as much as possible the constant comparative method was used by integrating feedback loops during and after the interview. Furthermore, the same topics are covered with semantically different questions to ensure internal consistency of answers (Fink et al., 2001; Fink et al., 2003).
- Triangulation: Results were compared with different methods and studies. For example, company strategy statements and performance figures were compared with information given in the interview.

5.2.1.1 Validity and reliability check in the present study

All six criteria were closely adhered to in the data collection and analysis process: Data sources were triangulated to validate answers and impressions on the interview script wherever possible. Sometimes several respondents in a single corporation were interviewed allowing for checking internal consistency while taking into account each informant's responsibility and position within the organization. In some cases, data was triangulated by collecting both the view of the HQ and the subsidiary. Interview data was compared with public company reports and press releases and other coverage available. Moreover, some quantitative analysis was made. By combining information from different companies tendencies can be revealed for example, what percentage of interviewees in which positions consider a certain factor as being important. During transcription and coding sometimes unexpected information was found which was coded as 'new insights'.

5.3 Rationale for chosen methodology

As this study is designed as an exploratory study in an emerging research field, the method of the semi-structured interview was chosen to increase the ability to capture the phenomenon (O'Connor et al., 2004). The interviews are intended to serve two purposes: On the one hand, they provide insights into the MNCs management control practices as such. The advantage of the interview approach is that it permits following up 'why' and 'how' questions (Yin, 1994) and to 'map novel, dynamic, and/or complex phenomena ignored or inadequately explained by existing theories' (Daniels et al., 2004; Keating, 1995). Ticking off apparently transferred elements on a list overlooks the likelihood of transferred elements being interpreted very differently in novel contexts (Ferner et al., 2000). So far relatively little attempt has been made to either analyze the mechanisms of transfer or to compare the actual content of transferred management control practices. In-depth case studies or interviews best explore the intricacies involved in such undertakings (Gamble, 2003). Detailed qualitative interviews provide the opportunity to investigate hypotheses developed in larger survey-type studies and to 'follow through complex linkages, explore processes, and uncover how decisions are really made' (Ferner, 1997). Therefore, interview-based studies are particularly well suited for exploratory and theory building studies (Eisenhardt, 1989b; Parkhe, 1993) when there is little theory out there or when there is 'too much to learn for a survey questionnaire to do justice' (Daniels et al., 2004). Also, for the purpose of promoting change, it is important to gain insights into such questions as 'How do various factors, for example, Austrian management norms or training, affect the extent of change and its course' (O'Connor et al., 2004). Lastly, interview-based research is a good option when there is a small population of possible respondents (Daniels et al., 2004).

Our interviews can inform the development of a survey instrument by which hypotheses based on existing literature and on insights gained by the interviews will be tested as a follow-up project after the dissertation. As compared to the interview approach, surveys do not effectively produce in-depth findings (Daniels et al., 2004). Therefore, an increasing number of scholars (Birnberg, Shields, & Young, 1990; O'Connor et al., 2004) recommend the use of a multi-methods approach.

We conclude with the words of one of the interviewees, who had participated in a number of studies on international Management and Control before and felt that the chosen method of the semi-structured interview was the right format of analysis for the topic in question:

> I need to compliment you on the choice and design of your questions and the manner they were introduced [...] I have been talking to a

great many people about that topic also with consultants who tried to analyze us but none of their questionnaires were so openly formulated and looked at that great many facts. [...] I think we really covered everything now there is nothing we left out I could think of. (P2: 111)

Time is not an issue! I'm actually enjoying this! It's really great to be able to talk about how it really is instead of ticking off some questions on a questionnaire [...] questionnaires hardly capture reality [...] We have now spent 10 minutes on exploring our motives of using so many expatriates, now you know what's up. [...] Forget about knowledge transfer, we need them to control our subsidiaries (P5: 94)

6
Sample

Semi-structured interviews were conducted with 46 interviewees on a sample of 40 MNCs having their international or regional HQ for Central and Eastern Europe (CEE) located in Austria. The companies were selected following a non-probabilistic method from an identified population of approximately 200. Hence, the sample represents some 20 percent of the population.

Data was gathered by the means of semi-structured interviews with MNC managers and controllers in charge of controlling and governing foreign subsidiaries and/or joint ventures in CEE during January and June 2005. An interview lasted about one and a half hours on average. All interviews were conducted by the same researcher. Ideally, interviews were made with senior and functional managers in order to cover both managerial levels because controls applicable or applied to each may differ (O'Connor et al., 2004). Moreover, obtaining data from more than one source also facilitated triangulation.

With 91 percent of all interviewees being male and a mere 9 percent being female, our sample distribution mirrors the real distribution of females in senior positions in Management and Control in Austria. 30 percent of respondents were fluent in at least one language used in CEE and the great majority (70 percent) did not speak any native CEE language. On average respondents had been working for 10 years at their current corporation. All of them had some experience with CEE by either having worked directly in CEE for an extended period of time ranging from one to ten years and/or working regularly in CEE.

The vast majority of informants hold a university degree or even a postgraduate degree mostly in business but also in science and only 9 percent do not hold a university degree. The age mean of respondents is

40 years, ranging from 30 to 63 years. 83 percent of the interviewees were Austrians, 10 percent Germans, 4 percent are of 'double' nationality being Austrians but rooted in CEE and 2 percent were Swiss.

While 65 percent of the interviewees can be regarded as 'senior' filling positions such as Chief Executive Officer (CEO), Chief Financial Officer (CFO), or head of corporate control, approximately 25 percent of the interviewees hold a position in middle management such as being responsible for management control of several countries. The remaining 10 percent of the interviewee sample are ranked as 'junior' occupying positions such as business unit controllers and the like. Table 6.1 provides an overview of all respondents.

In order to control for extraneous variation across industry sectors, firms were selected from various industries likely to differ on factors affecting the motivation to adopt more formal and transparent management control systems (e.g., market competition and technological dependence on foreign investment). The companies in the sample include the following industries: financial intermediation (5), exploitation and manufacturing, construction and mechanical and electrical engineering (5), chemical industry (3), manufacture (8), Wholesale (3), Sales (3) (Automotive; Electronics, agricultural material), Software Consultancy and Supply (2), Consulting (3), Telecommunication (1), Chemical and Pharmaceutical industry (2), Exploitation and Manufacturing (1), other business activities (1).

In all companies the ownership percentage of the CEE-subsidiaries was at least 50 percent, and in most companies this percentage was 100 percent. All HQ had at least two subsidiaries and/or joint ventures in CEE, ranging from two to forty. The size of the companies ranges from 600 to more than 100,000 employees worldwide with the majority of companies having between 10,000 and 40,000 employees. The investigated international or regional HQ were of Austrian (47 percent), German (40 percent), Japanese (5 percent), American (2.5 percent), Swiss (2.5 percent) and Danish (2.5 percent) ownership. All HQ were located in Austria and relied mostly on Austrian and German personnel. In addition, these firms have had to be in place for a minimum time of five years in order to have a history of operating data.

A widespread criticism of interview-based studies centers around sample sizes, claiming that findings are not generalizable due to too-small samples (Kvale, 1996). The attitude of some scholars seems to be that the more interviews conducted the better the research (Ghoshal & Westney, 1991; Marcus, 1988; Pettigrew, 1990; Simons, 1991). The use of effective sample sizes 'qualitizes' qualitative empirical data by enabling

Table 6.1 Interviewee sample

#	HQ/SUB	Position	Rank	Years employment At firm	Years foreign CEE stay	Age	Education	Sex	Nationality	Language CEE
1	HQ	Chief executive CEE	Senior	29	reg	57	University	m	A	
2	HQ	Country controller	Middle	13	reg	37	University	m	A	
3	HQ	CEE control	Middle	9	3	37	University	f	A	
4	HQ	Group control	Middle	2	reg	31	University	m	A	
5	HQ	Strategic control	Junior	5	10	31	University	f	A & HU	Hungarian & Russian
6	HQ	Business unit controller CEE	Middle	3	reg	33	University	m	A	
7	HQ	Head of group control	Senior	5	reg	40	University	m	G	
8	HQ	CEO	Senior	6	10	40	University	m	A	
9	HQ	Controlling	Junior	1	reg	29	University	m	A	
10	HQ	Country control	Junior	6	reg	26	University	m	A	Slovak
11	HQ & SUB	CEO	Senior	16	6	38	University	m	A	Czech
12	HQ	CFO	Senior	3	reg	36	University	m	A	

13	HQ	Corporate controlling	Senior	3	reg	41	University	m	A	
14	HQ	Head of corporate control	Senior	5	reg	42	University	m	A	
15	HQ	Controller	Middle	15	reg	41	Business school	m	A	Rumanian
16	HQ	CEO	Senior	12	reg	42	University	m	CH	
17	HQ	Partner	Senior	11	reg	36	University	m	A	
18	HQ	Investment controller	Middle	13	reg	29	University	m	A	
19	HQ	Head of corporate control	Senior	14	reg	36	University	m	A	
20	HQ	Head of CEE control	Senior	13	reg	38	University	m	A	Russian
21	HQ	Head of group control	Middle	6	reg	34	University	m	A	
22	HQ	Manager	Junior	3	reg	33	University	m	A	
23	HQ	CEO	Senior	30	reg	59	University	m	A	
24	HQ	CEO	Senior	10	reg	52	University	m	A	
25	HQ	CEO	Senior	8	5	41	University	m	A	Polish
26	HQ	Head of corporate control	Senior	4	reg	42	University	m	A	

Continued

Table 6.1 Continued

#	HQ/SUB	Position	Rank	Years employment At firm	Years foreign CEE stay	Age	Education	Sex	Nationality	Language CEE
27	HQ	Head of corporate control	Middle	2	reg	30	University	m	A	
28	HQ	CEO	Senior	9	10	63	University	m	A	Russian
29	HQ	CFO	Senior	4	reg	33	University	m	A	
30	HQ	CEO	Senior	8	reg	38	University	m	G	
31	HQ	Head of corporate control	Middle	8	reg	31	University	m	A	
32	HQ	Head of corporate control	Middle	11	reg	36	University	f	A	Russian
33	HQ	CEO	Senior	34	reg	59	Apprenticeship	m	A	
34	HQ	CEO	Senior	12	reg	58	University	m	A	Russian
35	HQ	Head of corporate control	Senior	2	reg	29	University	m	A	
36	HQ & SUB	CEO	Senior	4	reg	46	University	m	A	Polish
37	HQ	General manager finance and controlling	Middle	6	reg	36	University	m	A	

ID	Unit	Position	Level			Age	Education	Sex	A/G	Language
38	HQ	Controller	Junior	2	reg	32	University	m	A	
39	HQ	Chief executive CEE	Senior	22	6	40	University	m	G	Serbo-Croatian
40	HQ	Head of corporate control	Middle	4	reg	39	Business school	m	A	
41	HQ	Chairman CEE	Senior	21	reg	59	High school	m	A	
42	HQ	Chief executive CEE	Senior	31	reg	58	University	m	G	
43	SUB	Business unit controller	Junior	1	1	30	University	m	A	Croatian
44	SUB	CEO sub	Senior	5	5	31	University	f	A	Czech, Russian, Slovak
45	HQ	CFO	Senior	5	reg	35	University	m	A & Serbia	Serbo-Croatian, Croatian, Russian, Czech
46	SUB	CFO	Senior	2	reg	33	University	m	G	

analysts to determine the size of the observed effect (Ongwuegbuzie, 2003). The point of saturation in qualitative interviews tends to be around 15 +–10 interviews (Kvale, 1996). In sum, 46 interviews were conducted on a sample of 40 MNCs from an identified population of approximately 200, representing some 20 percent of the underlying population.

7
Empirical Results: Western Management Control in CEE

To answer our research questions three sets of variables derived from the literature review were covered in the interviews: First, information on organizational characteristics such as size and market entry mode was collected. The second set of questions was designed to capture the coordination and control mechanisms used by the HQ to govern their foreign ventures. The third set of questions was intended to identify cultural differences perceived by HQ employees and effective ways of dealing with them. The presentation of our empirical results follows our line of inquiry:

7.1 Strategic choice: market entry strategy

Our literature review revealed that strategic choice – especially regarding market entry – seems to have an impact on management control in MNCs. Therefore we asked our respondents how and why they entered the Central and Eastern Europe (CEE) market.

7.1.1 Motives for market entry

The internationalization of multinational corporations in the context of CEE has been intensifying since the start of transition in the region from central planning to market led in 1989. One of the most important modes of penetrating the CEE market has been through Foreign Direct Investment (FDI) (Marinov, Marinova, & Morita, 2003). Western European MNCs were the major investors in CEE. Germany has been the major player, followed by MNCs from the United States (Culpan and Kumar 1994; Jain and Tucker 1994; Marinov and Marinova 2001; Peng 2000). The present study identified the growth potential and a possible first mover advantage as major motives for market entrance by Western MNCs in CEE.

7.1.1.1 Growth potential

41 out of 46 interviewees described the potential for growth as a major driver for market entry. In the words of an executive:

> We could **increase our turnover in CEE 10 times since 1989** and we are experiencing **growth rates in the double digit range each year** [...] we grow by some 100 million Euros per year in CEE in terms of sales [...] While growth rates in Western Europe and Austria remain static we generate major growth rates in CEE. (P4: 41)

While growth rates in Western Europe have fallen short for the last couple of years, the CEE region pulled in many investors with growth rates in the double digit range (Gigouline et al., 2001). Hence, most respondents of the present study pointed out that market entry in CEE was driven by the potential for profit and growth. Two forces in particular drive the inflow of investments into the CEE region: First, there is a need to 'catch-up', since notable capital investment in the CEE region was not possible before the 1990s, resulting in a strong need for capital due to much needed technological and infrastructural development (Spitz, 1995). Second, the transformation process itself triggers Eastern European markets to conform to Western standards rendering the engagement of private foreign capital possible (Protsenko et al., 1999).

7.1.1.2 Early birds and first movers

Although we did not ask specifically for it, 23 of firms in the sample were reported to benefit from first mover advantages. Many corporations are indeed pioneers in CEE as they have been operating in the market even before the fall of the Iron Curtain. Being early in the markets is paramount thus attention shifts from already established CEE nations eastwards. An executive explains:

> [w]hen we founded our first subsidiary in Hungary in 1986 nobody even remotely thought that the Iron Curtain would fall sometimes [...] Today we have an established network of 15 subsidiaries in CEE with more than 900 branches. In a way we anticipated the European integration process; therefore, we perceive ourselves as a **pioneer in CEE**. (P44: 10)

> A major strategic success factor in CEE was that **we were damn fast**, in a way we consolidated the whole industry there. [...] We acquired everything we could get in order to increase our market share fast. (P24: 57)

7.1.2 Market entry mode

With 55 percent of MNCs setting up Greenfield operations, this is the prevailing form of market entry in CEE based on our sample. Some 38 percent of MNCs pursue a mixed entry strategy, which comprises combinations of acquisitions and/or Greenfields and/or Joint Ventures (JVs). Only 10 percent entered the market exclusively via acquisitions. Opportunity costs and pace of growth were decisive factors for market entry decisions. In the words of an executive:

> [m]arket entry decisions – Greenfield versus Acquisition – are based on considerations on opportunity costs and utility [...] and on **how fast we can grow**. [...] Consequently, we entered the market via Greenfield operations in Serbia, Croatia, Poland and Slovenia and bought the rest. (P6: 43)

In terms of ownership, most HQ prefer fully owned subsidiaries. However, sometimes legal constraints prevent companies from acquiring 100 percent stakes. As an executive explains:

> We always bought state-owned enterprises; that's why we entered into JV-agreements. We would have preferred to buy 100 percent stakes immediately but that was not always possible due to local legal requirements. [...] We were forced into JV-agreements by local laws. (P4: 33)

Harzing (2002) found a correlation between market entry mode and MNC strategy: Greenfields are the preferred entry mode for firms pursuing a global strategy and acquisitions are prioritized in case of multi-domestic strategies. Quinn (1980) and Mintzberg (1979) point out that most strategic change is the result of a step by step process and carefully planned out grand strategic designs rarely work. The firms in the present study are no exception: Mixed entry modes were often triggered by emergent strategies as a result of jumping at chances. In fact, 21 out of 40 companies 'had a try at markets', starting off step by step with very little risk and capital involved and gradually invested more if the initial investment paid off. A revolving pattern in our data was to start off with export agents, founding a representative office and finally setting up a subsidiary:

> We pursue a gradualist policy. In Russia, e.g. we have two representatives [...]. We use representatives to screen the **markets and figure out the market potential**. [...] If we see that we should go directly in the country via FDI, we do so. But we do not have a great strategy for it. (P29: 33)

Basically, we pursue the same strategy in every country: **First we found a representative office with only a few people.** [...] We try to identify the major player in the market and the market potential for our products. [...] **After some 2 to 3 years we have gathered enough experience to think about further steps and founding a company.**

Such cautious entry mode strategies are also a consequence of the prevailing economic and political risks in CEE:

We face an **increased political risk in CEE** although the risk differs considerably from country to country. [...] Every election is risky, because not only politicians are exchanged but more or less everything. The new government replaces all the key economic players as well. Nothing remains as it was. That means you have to start from scratch. (P18: 102)

Much of CEE business was induced by other foreign direct investments, as a result of following clients on their Eastward expansion. In the words of a Chief Executive Officer (CEO):

Most of our market entries were project induced [...] **we followed our Western European clients** [...] if they entered a new CEE country we accompanied them. (P11: 45)

Other factors reported to determine 'found or acquire' decisions are the pace of market entry, the degree of local market preferences, the cost of due-diligence and restructuring and tax reasons. 20 percent of respondents mentioned the faster pace of growth as a major motivation for acquisitions. As outlined by executives:

[t]o found 100 branches in a country takes up to four years. [...] If we acquire an existing bank which already has some 400 branches, we have to close down approximately 100 but then we have 300 branches up and running within a very short time. (P7: 93)

If we wanted to **speed up our regional growth pace we acquired** existing firms. [...] to acquire is much faster than entering a country via Greenfields. (P44: 13)

Some 22 percent of respondents underlined the importance of local market preferences and know-how as an argument for acquiring; Buying existing local brands, for example, can serve as a key to market success:

It is **very important to acquire the local brand rights** because people want to keep buying established local brands which they have bought for decades. [...] Even 15 years after our market entry local brands have a larger market share than our international brands. (P4: 35)

Last but not least, two interviewees indicated that tax advantages make acquisitions rather appealing. Explained by an executive:

> Given the latest change in IRS a firm's goodwill is no longer needed to be depreciated over a given period of time, but is subject to a fair-value assessment [...] an acquisition seems very charming from a tax point of view. (P7: 92)

7.2 Management control types in MNC headquarters

Based on Harzing (1999) and Martinez (1991) we developed the following categorization of control mechanisms. This categorization comprises all subcategories of Harzing's classification and also allows us to group the control mechanisms into Harzing's broader categories of Personalized Centralized Control (PCC), Bureaucratic Formalized Control (BFC), Output Control (OC) and Control by Socialization and Networks (CSN).

Explicit control mechanisms
- *Extent of centralization*: The extent to which decision making takes place at the HQ. A high centralization implies that decision making is largely centralized at the HQ and subsidiaries do not have a large amount of autonomy to decide on their own strategies and policies.
- *Extent of standardization*: The extent to which all subsidiaries are supposed to operate in more or less the same way.
- *Extent of formalization*: The extent to which an MNC has written rules and procedures for everything and employees are expected to follow these procedures accurately.
- *Extent of output & performance control*: The extent to which an MNC exerts output control by the means of a continuous evaluation of the results of subsidiaries. It comprises three elements:
  - Extent of planning (top-down, bottom-up)
  - Extent of output control
  - Extent of evaluation-reward systems
- *Extent of expatriate control*: The extent to which expatriates are assigned to subsidiaries to ensure that headquarters' policies are carried out.

Implicit control mechanisms by socialization and networks
- *Control by lateral relations* cuts across the vertical structure and includes permanent or temporary teams, task forces, integrative

departments, task-related direct contacts between managers from different units, and so forth (Galbraith, 1973; Galbraith et al., 1986; Lawrence et al., 1967).
- *Control by informal communication and personal intra-group networks* comprise intra-group networks based on informal communication and personal relations among managers from different units of a company, supplementing formal communication channels.
- *Control by socialization via organizational culture:* MNCs attach a lot of value to a strong 'corporate culture' and try to ensure that all subsidiaries share the main values of the firm. Thus, values and objectives are communicated by socialization (Martinez et al., 1991).
- *International management training*: MNCs make extensive use of international (as opposed to purely national) management training programs. In these programs executives from different subsidiaries and the HQ follow courses that deal mostly with the transfer of company-specific knowledge (Harzing, 2003).

In the following the findings on the different types of control are presented:

7.2.1 Explicit MNC control

7.2.1.1 Extent of centralization

More than 90 percent of the interviewees indicated that their CEE subsidiaries are controlled centrally by the HQ or the regional HQ. Therefore, important decisions such as investment and finance decisions are usually made at the HQ level. Centralized control means that the control locus is situated at the higher levels of the command chain (Galbraith et al., 1986; Lawrence et al., 1967; Pugh et al., 1968). Decision making is largely centralized at the HQ and subsidiaries do not have a large amount of autonomy to decide on their own strategies and policies (Harzing, 1999). Our empirical findings clearly show that management control is a very centralized task in MNCs operating in CEE (see Figure 7.1). 60 percent of the MNCs are reported to have a rather low level of operational autonomy in their CEE subsidiaries. The remaining 40 percent are reported to have a substantial amount of autonomy on the operational level, although strategic decisions are usually made at the HQ level. Important decisions concerning investment and finance, and human resources, such as the appointment of subsidiary CEOs and Chief Financial Officer (CFOs), are almost always taken by the HQ or regional HQ. Often there are times when the HQ even has a say on deciding on second-line subsidiary personnel.

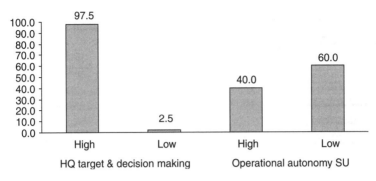

Figure 7.1 HQ decision making and subsidiary autonomy.
Source: Data analysis.

These rather high levels of HQ control might increase even further in the future: According to the interviewees, 62 percent of the MNCs in our sample will see even more centralized forms of managerial control and only 8 percent will have more decentralized structures in the future. In some 30 percent of MNCs no trend regarding centralization or decentralization in decision making was noted.

46 Quotations of executives underpin the importance of centralized structures and a clear trend towards more centralization. As explicated by executives:

> The **degree of autonomy of the subsidiaries changed considerably over time**. [...] Five years ago, our CEE subsidiaries had a lot of autonomy but now we govern them very centrally from our HQ. [...] We have very **stringent rules now**, without the HQ consent local subsidiaries cannot decide on important issues. (P1: 134)

> There is a **clear trend towards more centralization and centralized structures** in governing our CEE subsidiaries. We used to have subsidiaries in the single countries but now we are converting them into mere branches [...] otherwise we cannot handle them. [...] It is also a question of costs, but primarily, it is a question of manageability. [...] I cannot fly to every office every month and check everything, that's simply not possible. [...] Therefore, we decided to cut down the room for maneuver for CEE subsidiaries. (P14: 56)

The following network view visualizes underlying relations for centralized control grounded on our data. Groundedness and density of

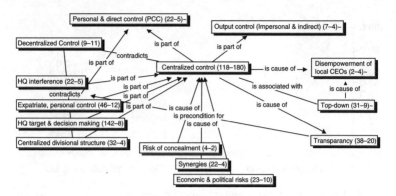

Figure 7.2 Network view on centralized control.
Source: Data analysis.

assigned interview codes are displayed, for example (38–20) means that a code is grounded on 38 quotations ('groundedness') in the interview text and 20 stands for the number of links made to other codes ('density') based on the interview texts. The following causal relations were identified based on the interview material.

Centralized control is characterized by a high level of HQ target and decision making combined with high levels of HQ interference if subsidiaries do not perform as well as planned. Furthermore, centralized control is marked by high levels of personal expatriate control. Often a centralized divisional structure is found in foreign subsidiaries. Top-down planning is also associated with centralized control.

Centralized control ensures transparency and reduces the risk of concealment and malpractice in offshore ventures. Moreover, HQ responds to high economic and political risk with centralized structures and controls. Last but not least, centralized control facilitates achieving group-wide synergies. As explained by a CEO:

> All those countries are **still in a state of transition** that implies that there is some **instability and element of risk involved**, especially in Russia and the Ukraine. I would not say that Hungary, the Czech Republic or Poland is not stable, but they are still not up to Austrian or German standards. Just look at the development of the Hungarian Forint. That's the reason why we manage our CEE subsidiaries centrally. (P17: 70)

More centralization and pooling of functions enhance the discretion and influence of HQ and pull autonomy away from local subsidiaries. There might be no need for local subsidiary CEOs in the future. However, centralizing functions does not necessarily mean that all functions must be under the HQ roof. Rather, in order to exploit cheap resources, for example low labor costs and/or qualified CEOs at the subsidiary level, HQ increasingly establish 'shared service centers' or 'competence centers' wherever the cost-quality ratio is best. This means making use of the most favorable conditions, and at the same time, maintaining attractive jobs at foreign locations. As one executive explicates:

> Frankly speaking, the **increasing trend towards centralization raises the question of the necessity of subsidiary CEOs.** For now we have a CEO at every subsidiary, who is responsible for communicating our goals and ensuring that certain targets are reached. [...] If I think further, however, I can simply set a retail target for the Czech Republic and I only need to communicate that target to the [subsidiary] board member who is in charge for retail. That implies that **I do not need a CEO for a subsidiary any more**, which is the best paid and most exiting job at the moment. [...] That coordination and goal setting function is done directly by the HQ. (P12: 76)
>
> For now the subsidiary autonomy is rather high, but that's a problem for a streamlined centralized management control. **We have rather powerful local CEOs**, powerful because we consciously recruited 'strong and tough' people for those jobs. [...] **Well, if we [the HQ] now deprive those people of their power by pooling decision making at the HQ those people might just leave.** [...] Since we want to keep them our group steering committee decided that centralization does not mean centralization of functions at the HQ location [in Austria]. [...] Who says that Austria is the best place? We could as well have our centralized competence center for retail in Prague or elsewhere. (P12: 63)

On the other hand, strong centralization tendencies might endanger the future of regional CEE HQ since CEE subsidiaries might be managed directly by the international HQ in the future. For example a German MNC with a regional HQ for CEE situated in Austria might very well decide to streamline its structures and govern its CEE ventures directly from its international HQ in Germany. Some interviewees indeed raised the issue of the future necessity of regional headquarters:

> Formerly [the regional HQ in] Vienna had a say on important issues, but this is changing [...] due to an increasing regionalization and verticalization. [...] **Regionalization implies that single countries are grouped into regional clusters and verticalization basically means a more direct and centralized control by our international HQ** which is based in Germany [...] There will be one person in Germany who is in charge for CEE and one regional sales manager per country who is responsible for the planning. Vienna [the regional HQ] will not have any authority on CEE matters in the future any more [...] rather each division will deal with CEE directly. (P26: 55)

Based on the data analysis the following propositions can be made:

P (1) Centralized control causes transparency thereby decreasing the risk of malpractice and concealment at the subsidiary level
P (2) Centralized HQ control will increase in the future.
P (3) Centralized control is used in case of high economic and political risk
P (4) Centralized control facilitates achieving group-wide synergies and the creation of group-competence centers.

7.2.1.2 Extent of standardization

Standardization implies that all subsidiaries are supposed to operate in the same way using standardized reporting systems, IT, etc. (Harzing, 1999). As depicted in Figure 7.3 below, 97.5 percent of companies are reported to have high levels of group-wide standardization. 115

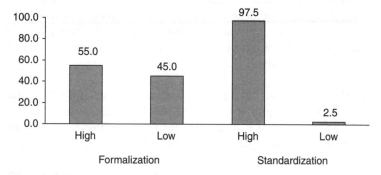

Figure 7.3 Levels of standardization and formalization.
Source: Data analysis.

quotations throughout 46 interviews underline the importance attached to standardization. In the words of two executives:

> I would say **we are about 80% standardized**. To achieve 100% standardization we would need to have identical organizational processes which is not a matter of management control but a political one. (P12: 21)

> We have about **90% standardization**. All our costing schemes and mechanisms are the same, our organizational structure is virtually identical everywhere. [...] Our reporting is completely standardized. (P29: 60)

Based on the interview material the following relations regarding standardization were established, which will be explained in some detail (see Figure 7.4).

Market entry mode is decisive for the level of standardization: Greenfield operations allow for implementing the same standards up front and have generally more standardized processes and structures than acquisitions.

> By entering the market via **Greenfield operations** [...] we had the chance to introduce our standards from the very beginning [...] in

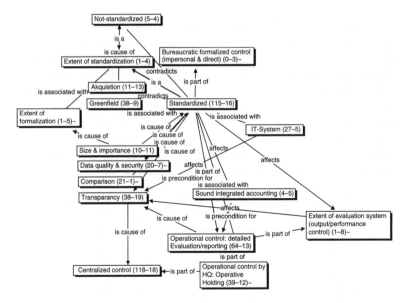

Figure 7.4 Network view on standardization.
Source: Data analysis.

fact **we set the standard**. Every person we hired had to act according our standards, there was no discussion. (P1: 81)

Our philosophy to set up **Greenfields automatically** brought about that we **have the same systems** in all our subsidiaries. [...] We have a standardized general ledger system and a standardized management control system. (P7: 68)

Standardization and integrated IT systems are essential for achieving sound data quality and group-wide synergies. As a CFO outlines:

> [t]he **software must be standardized throughout the whole group**. The HQ has to set the standards and the subsidiaries simply have to apply the alleged systems. By doing so, we **achieve data security and reliability** which is substantially better [than in case of not standardized systems] and we achieve a **reliable and secure integrated system**. It is much easier to set up management control instruments based on integrated systems. Granted, such systems cost much more but they guarantee a much higher data security and reliability. [...] To save on data security is saving on the wrong end. [...] Integrated reliable systems are crucial. (P1: 123)

An integrated IT system ensures a high level of transparency and is an important feature of centralized control, since the most current figures of foreign subsidiaries are displayed at the HQ within no time. Therefore, corrective action from the HQ can be taken immediately or with very little delay. Some 48 percent of the corporations use SAP (Systems, Applications and Products in the area of data processing), 18 percent rely exclusively on Excel, 15 percent use Hyperion and the rest uses other systems. Interestingly, almost all respondents no matter what reporting and control system they use indicated that Excel is still very important for management control purposes and heavily used because of its flexibility. However, the current IT landscape in CEE subsidiaries still leaves room for improvement. In the words of two executives:

> We use Mumex for our CEE subsidiaries. [...] Let me do a live demonstration of what I can do with that system: [...] Here, **I can see all our subsidiaries in detail, I can virtually see everything**. Here we see Hungary, e.g., they booked these figures, this is the general ledger, and these are the leasing rates displayed in the local currency. The main server is located here [at the HQ]. I can create any report I want from any subsidiary directly here at the HQ. We do not do the accounting ourselves [the subsidiary does it] but we can see all entries

immediately here. We also consolidate all subsidiaries here and we see any deviance from the plan immediately. (P20: 47)

By pressing a single button I can see automatically within one minute after the accounting entry all figures from all subsidiaries. Formerly it took weeks or even months to get that information. [...] That **enables me to spot problems and high performers immediately. I can display any data on any subsidiary in great detail without delay.** If I spot here, e.g. a minus of EUR 20,000, I can track from here how that figure emerged without having to call somebody. (P3: 86)

50 percent of the interviewees indicated that data quality and security is crucial for successfully managing subsidiaries in CEE. Therefore, time and effort spent on integrated and standardized systems pays off in the long run. As described by two executives:

The **major difficulty** in CEE has always been **data security** in the [management information] systems. That's why **we had to design integrated systems** for our CEE subsidiaries to ensure that we have closed circuits wherever possible. **Only integrated management control and information systems are the basis for data security.** In the past we repeatedly found that single and ad hoc reports were not plausible. [...] we have to make sure that data only comes out of integrated systems. We devoted much time and effort to create reliable and standardized group-wide systems. (P1: 45)

When I started here five years ago, the firm relied on accounting information on the one hand, and a separate control system on the other, which were not interlinked. People calculated wildly with diffuse calculatory figures which never matched the accounting figures. [...] **Throughout the year figures were looking OK and at the end of the year came the great light-bulb moment and nobody knew why.** We badly needed integrated systems. (P13: 127)

Standardized management control and information systems enable group-wide comparisons, benchmarks and transparency, which are essential for achieving synergies and transferring best practices. Standardization prepares the ground for a sound, integrated reporting and accounting system, which in turn forms the basis for detailed and operational HQ control. Two executives explain:

The all-dominant thing for effective management control is a **standardized reporting**. [...] Management control ensures transparency within a group [...] In order to generate transparency we created integrated IT systems. **Only group-wide transparency based on standardized reports and management information systems enable the management to make sound decisions.** Gut feeling is not enough; we need a sound institutionalized management information system in order to make substantiated decisions. (P33: 95)

A **standardized** reporting system allows us to **benchmark** subsidiaries. We can **compare** them in terms of cost and return. (P1: 128)

Central control and administration of standardized controlling and reporting systems is essential to ensure sound data quality and prevent malpractice.

We have one group-wide standard which is only rarely adapted to local requirements. **Standardization is the key to success for an efficient management control** [...] otherwise we compare apples and oranges. Standardization **requires effective systems and SAP is such a system.** Granted SAP is very complex and people require some experience for effective handling but once it is up and running the information output can be trusted, especially if you hold the administrator rights in your hands. [laugh] [...] We **govern SAP centrally** from the HQ; we decide on creating and changing accounts [...] and establish a single standardized table of accounts. [...] (P27: 98)

In order to achieve a certain standard, however, certain rules must be formulated. Hence, standardization automatically leads to a certain degree of formalization as well.

We prescribe **one reporting scheme for all countries.** In the beginning we granted some degrees of freedom in reporting [...] but we need detailed guidelines [...] **in order to manage our subsidiaries effectively.** That's why we established rules and templates. [...] Now we can benchmark our subsidiaries. (P15: 67)

In addition, subsidiary size was found to go hand in hand with standardization. The larger and more important a foreign venture is, the higher its degree of standardization. For some companies it is not efficient to introduce standardized systems, such as SAP, into small ventures. However, the trend is to also integrate small ventures in the prevailing structure in the long run. As explicated by an interviewee:

Reporting is **completely standardized.** All subsidiaries use the same SAP-system – they all use SAP R3 – except for a few small countries which do not yet have SAP. [...] The Business Warehouse system is a main instrument for **group steering** [...] since it enables us to operate based on one standardized database. [...] We [HQ] can see everything what happens in the countries and can **intervene easily**. (P33: 47)

In sum, the following propositions on standardization can be drawn based on the interviews:

P (5) Group-wide standards and standardized IT systems are essential for achieving synergies. Standardization and integrated IT systems guarantee data quality and security.
P (6) Greenfield operations have a higher degree of standardization than acquisitions.
P (7) A high degree of standardization allows for inter-unit comparisons, benchmarks and adds to group-wide transparency.
P (8) There is a positive relation between size and importance of a subsidiary and the degree of standardization.

7.2.1.3 Extent of formalization

The level of formalization is the extent to which policies, rules, etc. are written down in manuals or other documents, which usually leads to standardized procedures (Lawrence et al., 1967; Martinez et al., 1991). Employees are expected to follow these procedures accurately (Harzing, 2003). 55 percent of corporations were reported to be rather formalized while 45 percent rank rather low on formalization. Figure 7.5 depicts the relations on formalization identified in our data analysis.

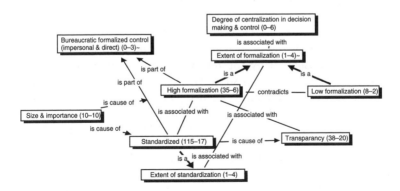

Figure 7.5 A network view on formalization.
Source: Data analysis.

Our findings regarding size and formalization are in line with the results of the literature review. Our data clearly shows that the level of formalization increases in proportion to subsidiary size and perceived importance of the subsidiary. Executives explain the relation between subsidiary size and the degree of formalization as follows:

> At the beginning when we operated in only 6 countries [subsidiaries] we tried to generate synergies by having 2 or 3 people traveling regularly to the single subsidiaries. [...] **Now we are operating in 21 countries**, we have a great number of employees and **we needed some formalization**. [...] Therefore, we developed group-wide guidelines and rules. (P13: 72)
>
> **We needed more guidelines, rules and regulations the more we grew**. We needed to copy more things down. In the beginning, when we were small, we could handle things more informally. But the larger we get, the more employee fluctuation we have [...] and we need a manual or some sort of documentation that we can present to every new employee to give him some idea of how to do his or her job. [...] We [as a HQ] need to provide some rules. (P14: 86)

Furthermore, a high degree of specified rules and regulations add to transparency. As already mentioned above, the degree of standardization and formalization is related.

P (9)   The levels of standardization and formalization are positively correlated.

P (10)   The larger the size and the perceived importance of a subsidiary the higher the degree of formalization

7.2.1.4   Extent of output & performance control

Output control focuses on realized outputs and results which are usually made transparent by the means of continuous monitoring and evaluation of the results of subsidiaries. MNCs which rely on output control typically have a rather detailed planning, goal setting and budgeting system, that includes clear-cut (often quantitative) objectives to be achieved at both strategic and operational levels (Harzing, 2003).

Extent of planning.   Planning refers to systems and processes such as strategic planning, budgeting, establishment of schedules, top-down vs. bottom-up planning, and detailed budgeting. Figure 7.6 depicts the distribution of planning types of the investigated MNCs. More than 60

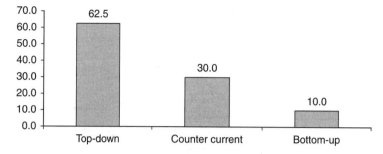

Figure 7.6 Type of planning.
Source: Data analysis.

percent of MNCs are found to use top-down planning, some 40 percent use counter-current planning and a mere 10 percent use bottom-up planning in their CEE subsidiaries.

Given the high degree of centralized HQ decision making, the overwhelming use of top-down planning does hardly come as a surprise.

Extent of output control. The extent of output control is based on the frequency and scope of evaluation of files, records and reports of subsidiaries submitted to HQ management (Martinez et al., 1991). In our sample, 90 percent of MNCs exert a high degree of output control, by means of a continuous IT-based evaluation of the results of subsidiaries. As two executives explicate:

> I can see each turnover, ratio or whatever figure from each subsidiary in great detail. [...] **I can see every little detail** because all entries concerning all transactions are registered in SAP and the server is located here at the HQ. [...] **CEE is a glass region.** Our subsidiary managers often speak of me as **Mr. XX with his x-ray machine who sees everything.** [...] (P3: 82)
>
> We have a very extensive monthly and quarterly reporting. [...] **Regular reports** on budgets and plan deviations are required and we [the HQ] look at the figures closely. [...] We do govern our subsidiaries based on performance figures. (P6: 65)

Figure 7.7 depicts how a detailed output control by the HQ based on continuous evaluation and reporting is linked with organizational

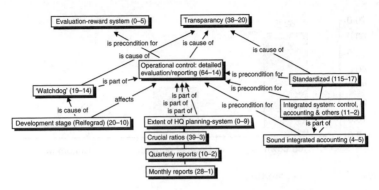

Figure 7.7 Network view on detailed control and evaluation.
Source: Data analysis.

structures and procedures and impacted by the development stage of subsidiaries.

Our data analysis clearly shows that a detailed output evaluation and reporting system adds to transparency of foreign ventures. It relies on integrated control and accounting systems which require a high degree of group-wide standardization. More specifically, it consists of detailed and frequent reports to the HQ and a number of crucial performance ratios. The key ratios used differ according to the industry, but the most named ratios include Earnings Before Interest and Taxes (EBIT), Earnings Before Interest, Taxes, Depreciation and Amortization (EBITDA), Return On Capital Employed (ROCE), Free Cash FloW (FCF), Return On Sales (ROS), and order backlog. In addition, expatriates are often strategically placed in subsidiaries to ensure that certain standards of data quality are met. The quality of reports and analyses is affected by the stage of development of the subsidiaries. In the words of a CFO:

> Our Vienna based HQ is responsible for 29 countries. [...] Each legal entity in each country consists of four divisions which are further divided into more than 100 products and 1000 articles. Given that complexity we [the HQ] have to **painstakingly audit all performance figures. The number and variety of data is legion** and we [the HQ CFO] must be constantly informed of the key figures and ratios. (P4: 91)

The scope and intensity of control exercised by the HQ is higher in CEE subsidiaries than in other Western subsidiaries. This suggests that development stage and scope of control exercised might be correlated. A CEO explains:

> The intensity and scope of management control in our CEE subsidiaries is considerably higher than in our domestic subsidiaries. The latter we control only rudimentary. (P1: 33)

Evaluation-reward system. 'Pay schemes orient executives toward different aspects of their organization and environment, influence risk preferences, and can act as agency control devices' (Luo, 2005). Performance-based pay therefore is the most output oriented form of control. Without exception all MNCs in our sample use performance-based pay systems. Thus, goal achievement by managers and employees is rewarded and shortcomings are penalized. In 13 percent of the investigated MNCs the proportion of variable salaries is considerably higher in CEE than in other Western European or overseas ventures.

> We use **performance-based pay** to a different degree in each country [...] In general, the variable component is **much higher in CEE** [and the fixed component much lower] as compared to Austria. (P2: 109)

> The **variable fraction of the salary is much higher in** CEE than in other [Western] European countries. We even work with performance-based pay schemes in CEE which are completely performance based; I mean they do not include a fix component. (P16: 82)

In general, performance-based pay schemes are relatively well received in CEE. At first, introducing the idea of variable compensation caused mixed feelings. In the meantime, however, performance-based wages are commonplace and particularly well received by the younger generation.

> [w]e need to make profit and we need to create that understanding throughout our firm down to the last white-collar employee. That requires that our employees are able to interpret P&Ls correctly and they need to see that they personally benefit from variable pay schemes. [...] We need to generate that understanding in the transition economies. Many people there are coming from a **culture where performance did not matter**; hence, we need to familiarize them with entrepreneurial thinking patterns and the importance of performance. (P19: 76)

> Some people in CEE are **'hot' and extremely performance oriented**, that's why we also use wage compensation models which are entirely performance-based with no fixed elements. People accept that they

earn lots of money if they are successful and earn nothing if they are not. (P16: 83)

Propositions. Figure 7.8 below depicts a network view on output and evaluation control, planning and the evaluation-reward system as discussed above.

In sum, the extent of evaluation control is affected by the extent of the planning system, some MNCs use a very detailed budgeting and planning process, others only have strategic, less detailed plans for their foreign subsidiaries. Based on our data, the following propositions are made:

P (11) A high degree of centralization in control and decision making at HQ level is reflected by top-down planning approaches.
P (12) Detailed output evaluation requires a high degree of standardization and integrated accounting and control mechanisms.
P (13) The presence of expatriates enhances compliance with group-standards and the quality of data.
P (14) Data quality is a function of time and maturity: The longer a subsidiary belongs to a group the better is the quality of data.
P (15) Performance-based pay is widely used in CEE-subsidiaries. Acceptance for performance-based pay schemes is high especially among the younger generation in CEE.

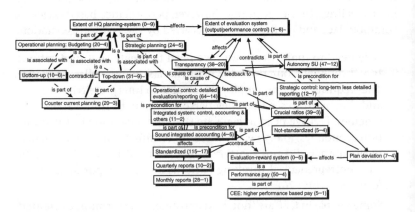

Figure 7.8 Network view on the extent of evaluation control, planning and evaluation-reward system.

Source: Data analysis.

7.2.1.5 Extent of expatriate control

Expatriate control is based on direct personal surveillance of subordinates' behavior. Parent-Country Nationals (PCNs) are assigned to subsidiaries to ensure that HQ policies are carried out (Harzing, 2003). Three quarters of the HQ rely to a great extent on expatriates as a means to control foreign subsidiaries. The positions of the CEO and the CFO are more often than not awarded to PCNs. Only a quarter of the investigated MNCs do rely on Host-Country Nationals (HCNs) for running their foreign operations. The following quotations illustrate the importance placed on expatriates by the HQ and the rationale for appointing PCNs in key subsidiary positions:

> We use **parent-country nationals** to a great extent in our subsidiaries to **guarantee that our way of thinking is lived in CEE.** [...] At least one top-position in each subsidiary is taken by an expatriate; mostly it is the CEO or the CFO, or both. [...] The CEO and the CFO are expatriates; that's the rule. (P40: 34)

> If we have an expatriate in charge in our subsidiaries we encounter far less difficulties in implementing our structures and processes. [...] **It makes all the difference if there is somebody on the spot who is loyal to the parent and bears the group-interests in mind or not.** (P40: 37)

> The **CFO and the Head of corporate control are both expatriates.** Always in each subsidiary [...] that's a rule. (P7: 34)

Although 76 percent of the analyzed HQ rely to a great extent on personal control in the form of expatriates, this does not imply that the CEO is automatically an expatriate, although the great majority of CEOs (60 percent) are indeed expatriates. After all, HCNs have local market and cultural expertise and are crucial for market success. Often, the executive board consists of a mix of home and HCNs, with financial positions often being taken by PCNs and sales positions by locals. In the words of an HQ CEO:

> If the CEO [of the subsidiary] is a host-country national, at least the **CFO is a parent-country national**. Somewhere somebody from the parent has to be in charge and **finances are fundamental**, that's why it is crucial to somebody from the parent in charge for finance. (P1: 63)

Reasons for using expatriates in subsidiaries. The following reasons for the use of expatriates were identified in the interview data: Know-how transfer, control, trust, size and importance of the subsidiary, qualification and HQ career decisions. Table 7.1 gives an overview on reasons given by the

Table 7.1 Reasons for using expatriates

Reasons coded	Grounded	Density	% interviewees
Know-how transfer	58: total 80	15	75%
Sub-code: 'development aid'/	18	2	25%
coaching	4	1	10%
Sub-code: specific company knowledge			
Control: expatriate, personal control	46	11	70%
Integrative function	18 total: 57	9	35%
Sub-code: network building	39	8	55%
Trust key positions	16 total: 20	4	33%
Sub-code: 'elite know how circles'	4	5	10%
Size & importance of subsidiary	10	10	22%
Qualification & fill in for 'unwanted people'	8	3	19.5%
Career: job enrichment for HQ people	3	1	7.5%

Source: Data analysis.

interviewees. 'Grounded' stands for the number of quotations for each code and 'density' shows the number of links established between single codes in the course of the analysis. Moreover, the percentage of interviewees per coded reason is given to indicate the perceived salience of the matter.

In the following the reasons are discussed in some detail.

Know-how transfer. Know-how transfer is mentioned by an overwhelming 75 percent of interviewees as a reason for using expatriates. Some executives were pretty outspoken about the state of former state-owned enterprises and the lack of management know-how in CEE:

> We use Expatriates to transfer knowledge and to **speed up the transfer of knowledge**. At the time we acquired the Czech subsidiary it was an old and incrusted state-owned enterprise. They had no strategy, no service quality absolutely no risk-management let alone management control systems. There was absolutely nothing whatsoever. In such a situation you have to have some key people who take the Czechs by the hand and show them how things are done in Austria. And then you can start to slowly developing processes. (P2: 74)

> For an effective know-how transfer it is indeed essential that we have parent-country nationals in all subsidiaries. That presence builds the ground for effective know-how transfer. You have to keep in mind that 'management control' and 'customer service' were foreign words there. (P6: 109)
>
> Management control was nonexistent when we took over the firm. That means training people has priority in the beginning, therefore **we need expatriates, to show them what controlling is and coach them in the process.** That is a long term process ... (P4: 77)

These findings are in line with past and current research on expatriates at both HQ and subsidiary levels which also identified knowledge transfer as the most prominent reason for expatriation superseding the control function to second place (e.g., Edstrom et al., 1977; Harzing, 2001a; Hocking, Brown, & Harzing, 2004; Riusala & Suutari, 2004).

The number of expatriates employed depends on the development and maturity of the subsidiaries. In CEE, the only acquisition options available were state-run enterprises with very little, if any, Western managerial know-how; hence, the intensity of expatriate use is usually higher in the beginning of the operations. Expatriates are primarily used to coach personnel in CEE subsidiaries. Only a quarter of the respondents indicated that the number of PCNs used decreased over time. Key positions, however, are permanently held by PCNs. In the words of the executives:

> In the **beginning** [...] we used **a lot of expatriates** approx. 60–80 people in the Czech republic alone [...] now there are no more than 20–30 remaining [...] Once things run smoothly it is no longer necessary to have so many expensive expatriates on the spot [...] thus, **we draw off people and only leave some expatriates in key positions.** [...] It depends on the majority stage of the subsidiary. (P2: 77)
>
> [a]t the outset we **need expatriates to set up the local management team over time** [...] we had to do some development aid and lot's of coaching. (P11: 31)

Another vital aspect for knowledge transfer is that expatriates have specific knowledge about the corporation and the right connections within the group to essentially transfer their unique knowledge to offshore subsidiaries. As explained by two executives:

> Usually we send out expatriates to transfer our organizational culture, to control local employees, and to lay the ground for our organizational

processes and structures. Those are all things which are parent-specific therefore only somebody who worked at the parent for a long time is able to perform those functions. (P3: 49)

Well, the main reason for relying on expatriates is that **they are well connected within the group** and they have the required **specific knowledge about the group** and know the right contact persons. [...] A newly hired person would be at a loss. (P32: 57)

Control function. Expatriate control entails that the behavior of subsidiary personnel is monitored closely and that somebody from the HQ is directly on the spot to be able to execute what the HQ pleases. 70 percent of the HQ rely to a great extent on expatriates as a means to control foreign subsidiaries. The positions of the CEO and the CFO are more often than not in the hands of PCNs. Only a quarter of MNCs investigated do rely on HCNs running their foreign operations. Some respondents explicitly state that expatriates are used to clearly show that the HQ sets the agenda and structure for foreign ventures. The following quotations illustrate the importance placed on expatriates by HQ:

We exclusively rely on Austrian nationals as CEOs, not only to have a better connection to the parent, but also to **clearly show that the parent sets the agenda and structure**. In addition, also for know-how purposes. That principle of having Austrian CEOs is adhered to in every single country no matter what. (P29: 57)

The reasons for using expatriates to control CEE ventures are all motivated by reducing risk: Political and legal risks and a general mistrust that important things might be disguised by local subsidiary personnel trigger HQ to rely on expatriates.

Another reason for putting expatriates in charge is the Croatian mentality [...] many **persons there are not free from corruption** and we try to avoid engaging in corrupt behavior. (P39: 34)

The higher the HQ investment in the subsidiary the more likely expatriates are used for control purposes. Expatriates are used in the early stages of subsidiary development, thus, know-how transfer and control go hand in hand. Mistrust towards local managers is also mentioned as a major trigger for using expatriates. Key personnel have to be trustworthy and must therefore come directly from the HQ. Last but not least, cultural differences induce HQ to rather rely on expatriates than on locals. Key functions such as the CEO and the CFO in particular are often held by PCNs.

These findings are in line with prior empirical studies, for example (Harzing, 1999, 2003; Ondrack, 1985; Paik et al., 2004; Vance & Paik, 2005), which identified control as a major reason for expatriate assignments. As already distinguished by Edström and Galbraith (1977) and Harzing (1999), the control function of expatriates can differ in terms of directness. PCNs can be used to execute control explicitly or rather implicitly. Grounded on the interview data two different forms of expatriate control can be clearly distinguished: Expatriates who execute direct surveillance over subsidiaries and work as 'watchdogs' for the parent, and expatriates who work as 'social butterflies' by gaining insights and ensuring transparency in delicate and sophisticated ways, working their magic through intricate networks and social contacts. The following quotes taken from the interviews underline the function of expatriates as HQ watchdogs, or to put in Harzing's (2001b) terminology, as 'bears':

> The second thing, and let me put it bluntly, you do need a watchdog for certain things. If you let things slide in the subsidiaries you are bound to experience some nasty surprises. Basically, things in CEE are not like here in Austria. The frontiers between what we see as legally justifiable and what is not justifiable any more are blurred. You have to be guarded, keep a close look and establish a stringent regime. (P6: 93)

> We need to have expatriates **directly on the spot because** it is impossible to see control and manage a subsidiary effectively from the HQ only. **We simply cannot see everything from here** [...] From the HQ we have no chance [...] even if subsidiaries are working with BSC and CRM essentially **they could enter any information and we would have very little chance to validate that information.** (P28: 69)

> [m]onitoring is an essential part of management control [by expatriates]. We need to check the records and to **spread the feeling of 'being controlled'** in the subsidiaries. (P38: 38)

Another vital aspect of expatriation is to discover 'soft' or embedded information which cannot be spotted by looking at figures or reports but entails being directly on the spot. In order to extract such delicate information expatriates need to establish trust. This can only be achieved via socialization, thus, apart from being 'watchdogs' expatriates are also used in more delicate ways and fulfill their control function via socialization and waving informal communication networks by being 'social butterflies'. No support could be found for Harzing's (2001b) further subdivision of the social control function of PCNs into bumble-bees – socialization – and spiders – network creation. Instead, our interview data calls for a new category which we label 'social butterflies' which fulfills both functions at the same time by establishing trust through socialization and prepares the ground for effective informal communication networks which cut across vertical structures and organizational units within an MNC. The term 'social butterfly' was chosen because it stands for a person whose strength lies in social interaction, creating and fostering personal relations and creating networks among employees. One CFO explicates the importance of the social control function of expatriates as follows:

> You **can only learn so much from looking at and analyzing figures**, to round off the picture you also need **'soft information'** embedded in the incidents and stories behind the figures and the guesswork involved. Such things, which are nevertheless essential, are not written down. You have to extract that information by conducting conversations or by phoning or e-mailing somebody, but phone or e-mail can never replace a personal encounter. **Being personally at the spot is the best**. I send my people out there at a regular basis or have the locals flown in, or even better have my country controllers directly on the spot. **They need to go out with the locals have dinner with them and socialize. Only by doing so they are able to get access to the really important information and get a complete picture. The key to get access to soft information is to establish trust.** Trust building takes time and once you've earned trust, you must never abuse it. Trust is like a plant, which you foster and look after and one day it's big and that is of tremendous importance to us. (P4: 65)

Moreover, social control by expatriates has a positive impact on integration and interest alignment in MNCs. They transfer the organizational culture into the subsidiaries and at the same time weave networks across the whole organization. For example one executive noted that

> [i]t is a fact that the organizational culture in the subsidiaries is very similar to the one of the parent if expatriates fill key positions. (P21: 30)

Both, the 'watchdog' and the 'social butterfly' function allow for transparency which is much needed for operational control. Table 7.2 gives an overview on how the different functions of expatriates help to align interests and reduce information asymmetry between HQ and subsidiaries.

Trusted key positions. Often key positions such as the CFO or the CEO are permanently held by HQ expatriates in order to have somebody in charge that 'can be trusted'. The risk of concealing relevant information was mentioned as a major reason for putting expatriates in charge. Ultimately, the efficacy of social control mechanisms will depend on

Table 7.2 The impact of expatriate control on headquarter-subsidiary relationships

Functions of expatriate control	Headquarter-subsidiary relationship	
	Reduce goal conflict	**Reduce information asymmetry**
Watchdogs	*Reduce goal conflict by* • Enforcing parent goals in subsidiaries • Conveying the impression of 'being watched' • Key positions held by trusted expatriates	*Reduce information asymmetry by* • Closely monitoring behavior of subsidiary personnel • Enhancing information processing capacity of subsidiary boards
Social butterflies	*Reduce goal conflict by* • Establishing trust • Integrating & network building through socialization • Establishing a common organizational culture • Communicating common goals	*Reduce information asymmetry by* • Extracting soft and embedded information by building trust • Facilitating knowledge transfer from subsidiary to HQ by informal intra-group communication networks • Enhancing information processing capacity of subsidiary boards

Source: Brenner & Reus (2006).

the level of trust between parent and subsidiary partners (Das et al., 1998; Zaheer et al., 1998). The central role of trust is even more pronounced in CEE since private and business spheres tend to overlap in CEE culture. Establishing close ties between expatriates and local employees and building long-term relations between the HQ and the subsidiary is of utmost importance for aligning parent and subsidiary interests. One CFO explicates the importance of personal social control as follows:

> **Somebody from the parent is a confidant**; that means he belongs to the **inner circle of trust** within the group. Apart from management and technical expertise it is the human element which rules. That means **I only send out people who I trust and of whom I can be sure that they inform me openly and immediately if something is not right.** That is a major problem in using locals, because their job depends on the performance of the subsidiary and in case of problems local people tend to disguise them rather than report to me because they automatically assume that their jobs are jeopardized. We experienced that people covered up things as long as possible and that is indeed a real danger. When I started here 5 years ago our Eastern subsidiaries tended to cover up things massively. Until we debunked all that it was already very late for corrective action and restructuring. (P1: 69)

> **Finances are always a delicate issue** and Controlling even more delicate than finance since it enables very **deep insights** into the corporation. That's why such positions are always held by PCN. (P9: 15)

Having had a great deal of prior experience in the parent is another case in point. People who worked for the parent for some time and have proven to be successful and reliable in the past are an optimal choice for filling satellite positions. An executive remarked that:

> Control by the parent is simply a lot easier if we employ parent-country nationals as CEOs, which have a lot of prior experience within the group. [...] All our CEOs do come directly from the Headquarter and had been working there for a long time. That means that the parent knows those people very well and can rely on them to a 100%. It is not easy to rely on somebody in an outpost. (P30: 31)

An expatriate is perceived to act less opportunistic than a local subsidiary manager since his employment and future career lies with the HQ and is not entirely dependent on the subsidiary. Therefore, a profound reason for relying on expatriates instead of locals is that they bear the interest of the group as a whole in mind and not just the performance of a single subsidiary since subsidiary and group interests do not necessarily always match:

> Expatriates bear the **group-interest in mind** [...] and not just the interests of a single subsidiary. [...] Additionally, expatriates have **excellent networks and connections** within the parent which is essential for effective communication and integration. [...] It helps to **speed up decision making**. (P40: 40)

In line with the literature on the 'country of origin effect' (e.g., Sohn & Paik 1994) our data also points to the nationality of the parent company affecting the degree of personal control used. However, given our limited sample of HQ nationalities, our findings on this point have to be handled with care.

> [taken from a Japanese multinational] Japanese people do **hold top positions** but they also hold other positions, because up-and-coming junior managers are sent to Europe for a last finishing touch or to get additional know-how and information and to **transfer this know-how back** to Japan. (P17: 58)

Integrative function and transfer of organizational culture. Working with expatriates has a big impact on integration. Expatriates transfer the organizational culture of the parent into the subsidiaries and at the same time establish links and weave informal intra-group communication networks across the whole organization. Some 55 percent of respondents underline the important role of expatriates in establishing intra-group networks and 35 percent mentioned their role in group-wide integration of foreign units in spreading a common organizational culture. For example one executive noted that:

> It is a fact that the organizational culture in the subsidiaries is very similar to the one of the parent if expatriates fill key positions at the very top but also in middle management. However, where expatriates are only a minority in the board such as in our recent Polish acquisition the organizational culture differs considerably. (P9: 57)

> We try to have our [PCN] people on the spot as much as possible. That is done for a reason: It **is very helpful to** have Austrians or Germans as CEOs or CFOs at the spot to – how shall I put it – **maintain a good relation to the home base and to integrate** the single subsidiaries. (P1: 150)

Subsidiary size and importance. The intensity of expatriate control is positively correlated with size and importance of subsidiaries. Some 22 percent of interviewees indicated that the larger and more important a subsidiary is, the more expatriates are in charge.

> The **number of expatriates is determined by the size** of the foreign subsidiary. The larger and more important the subsidiary, the more expatriates are used. It's as simple as that. (P2: 76)

Job enrichment. Expatriation is also used as job enrichment for high-flying HQ personnel whose careers hit a ceiling in the HQ. In the words of two executives:

> Three quarters of our CEOs in CEE are Austrian nationals we see that as some sort of **job-enrichment**. Strategically important employees are given a chance to climb up the career ladder. Frankly, what job can I give to somebody who hits **the ceiling here at the Headquarter** there is only a certain number of jobs here. A position as a **managing director at a CEE subsidiary is a good alternative**. After a couple of years there, people can come back here or go to the international HQ in Germany. Well, actually, that makes me think, I guess that job-enrichment factor is prevailing at the moment here. (P4: 49)

> [taken from a Japanese multinational] Japanese people do **hold top positions** but they also hold other positions, because **up-and-coming junior managers are sent to Europe for a last finishing** [...] and to **transfer this know-how back** to Japan. (P17: 58)

Qualification and replacing 'unwanted' persons. Sometimes expatriates are used if positions cannot be filled with appropriate and qualified local people. A CEO explains:

> Well, what if I find out that I cannot work with somebody because he has deceived me and I kick a local CEO out? [...] I search internally here at the parent for qualified people who are interested in doing the job. [...] This way, we have somebody who is excellently qualified and who can broaden his horizon with a new task. We do actively and consciously send our people all over the place to foster mutual learning. As a side effect we create an excellent network. (P4: 51)

Propositions. Based on the interview findings the following propositions regarding expatriates can be made:

P (16) Expatriates are used to transfer knowledge from headquarters to subsidiaries.
P (17) Expatriates are used to control foreign subsidiaries and execute HQ policies.
P (18) Key positions such as CEOs and CFOs are mostly held by expatriates; hence, mistrust towards locals is major reason for using expatriates.
P (19) Expatriates are used to transfer organizational culture to subsidiaries.
P (20) The more important the subsidiary is the more likely expatriates are employed.
P (21) The more political and economic risk in the host country, the more likely is the use of expatriates.

7.2.1.6 Reasons for using Host-Country Nationals (HCN)

MNCs do not exclusively rely on expatriates in key positions. For example, often board members in charge of sales are of host-country nationality. Some MNCs even use HCNs exclusively in their CEE ventures. Access to local market knowledge and the need to be linked up locally are the most prominent drivers for using locals. In order to get a more complete picture on the use of HCNs see Table 7.3 below provides an overview over reasons coded for HCN use.

In the following the single reasons are explained in some more detail.

Table 7.3 Drivers for using host-country nationals in top positions

Local use reasons	Grounded	Density	% of interviewees
Local market & cultural know	29	5	45%
Well-known 'pioneers'	22	2	40%
Local linking up	20	9	33%
Mutual know-how transfer between subsidiary and HQ	11	5	25%
Language capabilities	33	7	20%
Subsidiary size & importance	10	10	18%
Legal constraints	17	7	10%
Use low labor cost	1	1	2%

Source: Data analysis.

Local market and cultural know-how. The knowledge about local market preferences and specifics is the main reason for employing locals in key positions, as 45 percent of the interviewees indicate. Local and cultural know how of HCNs are reported to be a key success factor in CEE markets. Some insights on HCNs as illustrated by executives:

> Our slogan is **think global and act local**. We think that a **Czech person can do business with Czech persons far more successful than e.g. an Austrian**. At the same time, we try to implement the HQ strategy at the subsidiary level. [...] Act local therefore implies that our [HQ] global strategy is enacted in the subsidiary by locals. (P10: 52)

> An **understanding for local specifics is crucial** [...] without trying to understand the issues of a specific country we are at a loss [...] when implementing our structures and processes. **Once we understand the how business is done locally we can introduce our systems far more effectively.** (P24: 96)

Mutual know-how transfer. A combination of local know-how and HQ global strategic know-how builds the ground for a unique competitive advantage and success in CEE markets. 25 percent of very successful MNCs specifically underpin the importance of combining local know-how from HCN with HQ expertise and strategy. Executives explicate that point as follows:

> We are market leader in the Balkan region [...] our success in grounded in combining Western knowledge with local knowledge with enables us to create a unique mixture. (P42: 74)

> We transfer our know-how within the group [...] the local business is run by **locals who know their region, business environments, markets, business conduct and cultural specific best.** Only somebody with expertise in local markets and cultures can run be successful. [...] we call that 'glocal' [...] **A local CEO who is rooted and well connected in the region can never be matched by an expatriate.** (P42: 38)

> You should never enter a country and with an 'I know it all' attitude. Only if both sides [HQ and subsidiary] are willing to learn from each other, appreciate each other's expertise, and are devoted to a common goal, we are successful. [...] **Locals know their markets best** [...] far better than we do. (P16: 113)

Local linking up. Local linking up is crucial for success in CEE. In order to establish necessary connections outside the firm 33 percent of MNCs rely on HCNs. Successful MNCs in CEE do not only need to establish efficient intra-group networks, but also need to be well networked with the business and regulatory environment. Only locals have the necessary cultural and language background to nurse existing and foster new business relations on the spot. This knowledge is paramount when it comes to handling local authorities and competing for public tenders. (In the culture section the importance placed on personal relationships in CEE culture is discussed in detail.) As some executives elucidate:

> He [the Polish CEO] knows how to do business in Poland. **He has excellent connections** [...] he was in a high ranking management position even before the Iron Curtain fell and **he has still very good networks including connections to the authorities** [...] **and also to our clients.** [...] Relations rule in Poland. [...] **He knows best how to deal with the people there and how to win market share.** (P34: 42)
>
> [...] in order to be successful **in CEE you need connections and networks** [...] only local have access to those networks. (P44: 20)
>
> [...] **locals are crucial in dealing with local authorities**, that's one of the reasons why we always have locals in our management team. It is virtually impossible for a foreigner to penetrate public sector people. That's not about bribes and stuff but an outsider cannot establish the essential networks and connections. (P10: 97)

Language proficiency. Although language is a major reason for using HCNs, the opinions concerning the importance of speaking a local language differs substantially among interviewees: While some find it crucial to speak the local language, others maintain that the importance of being able to communicate in the native tongue is overestimated. Interestingly, the estimation whether or not language proficiency is important depends on the language proficiency of the respondent: those who are able to speak the local language consider that capability as important, while those who do not master it, think of it as little important. However, it seems that the capability to speak the native tongue facilitates relation and trust building. In any case, interviewees are in complete agreement as to the importance of language when it comes to hiring locals. The words of executives giving account of the importance of language.

> [w]e need people with regional competence and **most importantly language capabilities**. English alone does not get us far [...] e.g. in Rumania. (P37: 62)
>
> Speaking the local tongue is essential in a lot of ways. [...] e.g. when it comes to reading contracts [...] being able to communicate in the local language enabled me **to build up relationships much faster**. [...] You can be the best educated business man but without being able to communicate well with locals you are at a loss. [...] People appreciate it when their boss speaks their language. (P43: 66)
>
> **Locals are** essential because they are not only well-connected but also **able to communicate with our clients in their mother tongue**. (P27: 59)

Well-known pioneers/trust.   40 percent of HCNs in top-positions are very well-known employees who are pioneers in the sense that they have been with the group from the very scratch of market entry and often succeed expatriates after they returned to their home base. Thus, they proved to be reliable and loyal and enjoy the HQ trust.

> We always have host-country nationals in charge of our profit centers. **As a general rule the first employee we recruited in a country eight or ten years ago is now in charge of the profit center.** [...] Most of our local CEOs or board members have been with us from the very beginning. (P5: 55)
>
> We try to use local CEOs after some time [...] Basically **we prefer to put people in charge who we have known for some time and who we can trust**. [...] (P11: 48)
>
> **I know my regional CEO in Rumania for some 20 years now, I trust him**. I do not need to have an eye on him [...] he runs the organizations correctly, I simply know he does. If he happens to make a mistake I might have made the same mistake too. (P13: 100)

Legal constraints.   Legal regulations sometimes require local nationals in the board, or they do ensure that local nationals are employed by more intricate rules. Therefore, legal considerations also lead to appointing HCNs. Some executives explain:

> We have a local board member, because we were **forced into a JV agreement**. [...] We would have preferred to buy 100 percent immediately but the local laws prevented that. [...] That's why we have locals [...] otherwise we would rely on our own people. (P4: 33)

It was important to speak the local Polish tongue because **the Polish law requires that the CEO has to speak the local language.** That's not an EU law [laughs] but a Polish law anyway. (P6: 76)

Size and importance of subsidiary. As already noted, 18 percent of interviewees outline that the smaller the size and the importance of a subsidiary, the more likely HCNs are employed. In the words of the executives:

In the smaller countries we rely on host-country nationals as CEOs. (P1: 61)

The number of expatriates used depends on the size of the subsidiary: If the subsidiary is large we have more expatriates in charge. (P2: 76)

Low labor costs. Only one informant mentioned low labor costs as a specific reason for appointing HCNs.

We want to exploit the low labor costs in CEE [...] therefore we try to employ as many locals as possible. [...] also in management. (P13: 60)

Propositions
P (22) Access to local knowledge, language abilities, and networks are primary reasons for employing HCNs.
P (23) Combining local know-how with HQ know-how lays the ground for competitive advantage.
P (24) The smaller the size and importance of a subsidiary the more likely HCNs are employed.
P (25) HCN in top positions are well-known pioneers who have been with the corporation for some time.

7.2.2 Implicit MNC control

Implicit controls are of rather informal nature and not necessarily consciously designed. Rather, control mechanisms are *informal, subtle and sophisticated* (Harzing, 1999) and often derive from organizational culture. Implicit controls comprise intense lateral relations, informal communication and personal networks between HQ and subsidiaries and between subsidiaries, international management training, and the cross-border transfer of organizational culture. More than half of the MNCs in our sample make rather high use of one or more forms of control by socialization and networks, while the others do not use social control to a great extent. In the following the findings on the social control mechanisms are presented in some more detail.

7.2.2.1 Control by lateral relations

The variable lateral relations – mentioned 55 times in 36 interviews – comprises temporary or permanent task forces that cut across vertical structures of different units within an MNC in order to resolve problems and tap into group-wide synergies. Such interactions between the HQ and subsidiaries and subsidiaries among each other create informal intra-group communication and personal networks as a spin-off. Group-wide task forces are a form of implicit control since they add to the transparency within the MNC and lay the ground for effective management control. As described by executives:

> We have a lot of **projects where employees from the HQ and the subsidiary work together**, e.g. in the form of group-wide project teams. At the moment we are working jointly on the realization of a shared-service center. [...] **As a side effect our employees learn how to deal with foreign cultures** and multinational composed teams. We have permanently about five to ten such teams. (P20: 64)

> We **foster exchanging people across countries**. [...] Often times **we [in the HQ] tell staff in new subsidiaries to turn to other subsidiaries to look for solutions**. For example, if I [head office] am asked for a specific problem [...] by the Slovenian subsidiary and I know that the Czech subsidiary already effectively tackled a similar difficulty **I tell the Slovenian subsidiary to contact the Czechs**. That way they [the subsidiaries] can learn from each other plus at the same time create cross-national networks [...]. **That way a network is created among our subsidiaries.** (P9: 61)

The need for integration of international units and for tapping into group-wide synergies, the spreading of group-wide best practices, causes the formation of international teams and task forces cutting through vertical and legal organizational structures. The nature of FDI-induced business leads to the creation of lateral relations. Figure 7.9 provides an overview on the causes and effects of lateral relations.

In the following, the causes and effects of lateral relations are briefly discussed. First, the need for integration is a major driver for establishing lateral relations and network structures in MNCs. As an executive explains:

> We have a number of committees, e.g. our group strategic support, where all board members of the major subsidiaries meet four times a

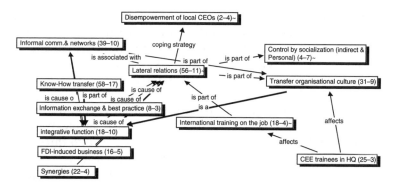

Figure 7.9 Network view on lateral relations.
Source: Data analysis.

year to decide on major strategic issues for the whole group. [...] Surely, the single votes are weighed [...] and the HQ CEO has a voice over others [...] but in any case there is a discussion. [...] There is a federalist element in our decision making. (P22: 49)

We have **regular workshops on specific topics** every two months where **all persons in charge of the countries meet in Vienna for three or four days**. [...] We could as well meet elsewhere but Vienna has the best flight infrastructure for CEE. [...] **regular meetings automatically generate group-wide networks**. (P20: 55)

Making use of synergies is another case in point for lateral relations since group-wide synergies can only be achieved by group-wide linkages. In the words of an executive:

Sure thing that we want **to create synergies** [...] group-wide coordination requires that people from different subsidiaries work together [...] this way we create lateral relations. [...] If we already have a great system set up and running in Croatia there is no need to reinvent the wheel in Slovenia. Rather we put the subsidiaries in touch with each other to share solutions. (P15: 50)

By establishing **shared-service centers we pool resources** [...] e.g. IT systems are designed for the whole region not just for single countries, that way we save costs and have a standardized rollout to each country. [...] Therefore, we need some sort of intra-group coordination by international task forces. (P18: 91)

Another important case for the creation of a global network structure marked by lateral relations lies in the nature of business: Much of the CEE business is FDI-induced by following clients on their international expansion. Thus, to serve their customers best a close cooperation between different international units is essential.

> [w]e **basically followed our Western-European clients into CEE.** [...] Most of our business consists of projects from big Western European MNCs, and if such a customer [...] enters into three new countries he lets us know that he wants us to be present in those new markets as well. [...] Serving such a client efficiently requires quite some intra-group coordination on our side. (P14: 31)

> We need to have **efficient networks between** our single subsidiaries because we have many key-accounts which are operating all over Europe. [...] Our key-account managers in the single subsidiaries need to cooperate closely. We need to effectively communicate. (P16: 104)

Last but not least, lateral relations are essential for information and knowledge exchange and serve as a platform for developing and spreading best practices:

> Communication between the parent and the subsidiaries is rather intense. [...] Mostly we exchange best-practices. (P2: 104)

> [b]y intensive communication and exchange between the HQ and the subsidiaries we discover potential for further improvement. [...] If that is the case we usually hold a workshop to define group-wide best practices. [...] It **is essential to meet face to face** from time to time to exchange ideas and discuss. [...] Light-bulb moments are guaranteed almost every time at such meetings. (P20: 53)

Lateral task-forces are vital for building group-consciousness and commitment to a common goal. At the same time, international network structures foster the transfer of organizational culture to CEE subsidiaries. The following quotations illustrate the importance of the integrative impact of lateral relations:

> We need to create a **common identity based** on our regional success rather than subdividing our performance to single nations. The whole CEE region needs to be our first priority. [...] We need to think in terms of the region as a whole [...] egoistic national thinking of

single subsidiaries is contra-productive [...] Therefore it is crucial to create a lot of links between our subsidiaries and exchange people across borders. (P18: 98)

Our HQ investment controllers are directly on the spot regularly [...] at least 4 days per months, often also much longer than that. [...] A **major success factor** regarding regional expansions is to build bridges to the people in the countries and to create a common identity as a group among subsidiaries. [...] We need to communicate that our strength lies in a common identity and mission. (P33: 61)

At the same time, task induced interaction between employees from different international units adds to cross-cultural understanding. An executive remarks:

We have many projects on which **people from the parent and people from subsidiaries work together in teams**. [...] Our employees learn automatically how to effectively deal with foreign cultures in those multicultural teams. (P20: 64)

We are working with **international teams** in a lot of areas, e.g. when we perform a due diligence in order to acquire a new subsidiary we use an international team consisting of people from all over group. By doing so, managers from different units can **exchange experiences and best-practices which generates a common basis for mutual understanding**. [...] We have been fostering group-wide network building over the last couple of years. (P2: 101)

The increasing centralization of tasks in regional HQ entails that subsidiary managers have less discretionary power. Establishing group-wide networks by lateral relations and task forces means that pooled competence centers may be located at subsidiaries. Putting a subsidiary in charge for a group-wide project or service center is an effective strategy to keep highly qualified subsidiary managers in the group even if the power of the subsidiary manager is decreased due to more centralized decision making. By network structures the job of the subsidiary manager can be upgraded and high potentials are more willing to work at local subsidiaries, since they lead important group-wide projects.

It is not uncommon that a **Czech [at the subsidiary level] has the lead for procurement for an area**. That does not mean that he needs not to consult with the HQ or the other subsidiaries but he is in charge. Involving people in committees and shifting responsibility, is a good method to keep highly able and ambitious persons in our subsidiaries. (P12: 71)

We try to **weave networks among our subsidiaries.** [...] And we cluster single countries into sub-regions, e.g. our Czech CEO – which is one of our most experienced managers – is also in charge for Poland, the Slovak Republic and Hungary. [...] Network structures are becoming increasingly important. (P10: 70)

Based on the interview findings the following propositions regarding lateral relations can be made:

P (26) Integration and establishing group-wide synergies and spreading best practices are major drivers for lateral relations.
P (27) The greater the amount of FDI-induced business and global clients, the more likely lateral relations are created.
P (28) Establishing lateral relations is a way to spread organizational culture.

7.2.2.2 Control by informal communication and personal intra-group networks

Control by informal communication and personal intra-group networks differs from lateral relations in that it is not focused on a specific task and is therefore of an even more informal and indirect nature (Martinez et al., 1991). Informal intra-group networks are found to be of great value for governing CEE subsidiaries. As an executive expounds:

We foster mutual and multi-faceted learning [...] If people tackle differing tasks in various countries and settings we learn and we create a great intra-group network. (P4: 52)

We foster the **exchange of people across countries.** [...] If we recruit new people for Rumania, e.g., we send them to Croatia to get some experience. That's common practice. [...] This way we create a network at the same time, because people get to know each other (P9: 60)

We have some rollout projects such as SAP where teams were working together till late every day. [...] That **creates some sort of 'togetherness'.** [...] When a group-goal is reached our board invited all teams who contributed to the success to a mountain hut [...] such **social happenings** are important for creating a **common identity.** (P24: 81)

Informal communication supplements formal communication and leads to network building. Informal communication includes informal and personal contacts between managers from different units in the form of meetings and conferences, management trips, personal visits, international transfers and the like (Das et al., 1998; Edstrom et al., 1977; Ferner, 2000; Fryxell et al., 2003; Harzing, 1999; Martinez et al., 1991). According to 30 percent of the interviewees, informal communication flows add to group-wide transparency and are needed to complement formal communication channels. In the words of the executives:

> **Communication between the HQ and the subsidiaries is rather informal** and very cooperative. I keep telling my people that it all depends on how you are personally perceived by your people. [...] The most **important characteristic of a 'controller' is to be able to communicate well and a certain social competence**. [...] Different mentalities need to be taken into account [...] Creating a good relations and goodwill among the people is vital. [...] short and informal communication whenever necessary helps. (P36: 68)

> We **communicate very openly based on a network structure**; sure we have some hierarchies, nevertheless, we are very network-like organized. Information flows in all directions which is very productive. [...] We do not rely on formal communication only. (P35: 53)

Based on the interviews the following relations for network building are identified. Figure 7.10 shows the relations for network building based on the interviews.

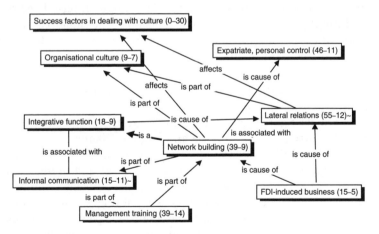

Figure 7.10 Network view on network building.
Source: Data analysis.

Intra-group network building is an essential part of informal communication. It is vital for FDI-induced business in order to coordinate the needs of global clients. Intra-group network formation often builds the underlying motivation for international management training or is at least a welcome side-effect. The creation of networks is often caused by establishing lateral relations across units as people get in touch in order to tackle certain tasks and keep using those connections for other purposes as well. The importance placed on networks, their formation and the extent to which they are used, depends on the organizational culture of the group. Establishing networks is also associated with expatriate control, since placing parent-country personnel in foreign units facilitates the creation of connections between the HQ and its offshore units. Both informal communication and the creation of networks between HQ and subsidiaries prepare the ground for successful integration and create a common identity and commitment to common goals:

> We see to it that we **do not only send people from the HQ to CEE but also vice versa**. [...] Having people from CEE at the HQ creates appreciation for the countries among HQ personnel. At the same time, **we infect the people from the subsidiaries with our spirit and create commitment to group-goals**. We have an intense exchange between HQ and subsidiaries not only institutionalized but also via informal channels. (P33: 36)
>
> In every country where we rely on a CEO who has **internalized our philosophy and values** and passes them on to the employees we are successful. Whenever this is not the case we do not achieve the same turnover and motivation. (P28: 72)

Figure 7.11 shows the how integration is achieved in MNCs of our sample.

As the above figure shows, integration is greatly facilitated by direct personal contact, thus an intense and ongoing communication flow between HQ and subsidiaries is essential. Ideally, communication entails a great amount of direct personal contact and mutual visits between HQ and subsidiaries. Additionally, management training on an international scale serves not only as a training ground for future management elites, but also fosters close relations between units. Our data shows that intense personal relations are vital to establish trust

Empirical Results 157

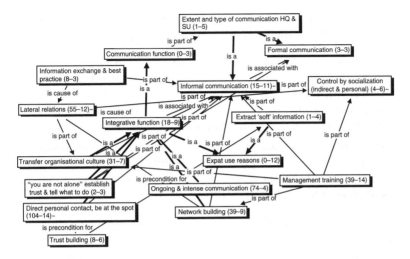

Figure 7.11 Network view on integrative function.
Source: Data analysis.

between managers and employees from different units and nations. A high level of trust is needed in order to gain insights into crucial information which cannot be gained by relying exclusively on formal reports. MNC controllers are aware of the duality of their profession by being trustworthy consultants and controllers at the same time:

> We have to communicate to the local subsidiary managers that they cannot act on their own but are part of the group. [...] We try to **integrate** them from a human point of view by **developing a basis of trust** and by **trying to be confidants to whom they can talk to.** [...] That means that we [HQ-control] are having a **dual function by being consultants** for the local subsidiary managers to whom they can turn to with their questions and discuss solutions. At the same time, however, **we are the ones who point out difficulties and risks.** (P28: 72)

7.2.2.3 *Control by international management training*

Classic management training. An important driver of management training is the more or less subtle infiltration with a company's organizational culture, value and 'way of doing things'. In the following, executives explain how trainees get brainwashed with organizational culture or to put in their words 'infected with HQ culture':

> The reason why we train our future subsidiary managers at the HQ for three to four months is **to infiltrate them with our organizational culture**. They get the XY injection and get infected with our spirit and culture. [...] That way we ensure that those people will pass on our spirit and motivation into the subsidiaries. (P28: 71)

> High potentials for top-management positions in CEE are invited to our premises for training purposes. We group them all together for a month in a training program. [...] The **underlying idea is to spread our spirit and culture** among them. (P24: 78)

All MNCs investigated have management training programs. Since qualified personnel are often hard to find in CEE some MNCs pursue a long-term personnel strategy by establishing tailored programs to create a human resource basis.

> We are about to set up **a training program for our future management elite on an international scale**. [...] It is open to potentials from all subsidiaries and countries. (P2: 103)

> Since we have been growing very fast we needed to **pursue a long-term HR strategy** [...] we set up a 'junior sales manager program'. That program is targeted towards young CEE university graduates. It is a **comprehensive training program which lasts for one and half years and includes training at the HQ**, and intense language and management training. (P5: 84)

Management training is not necessarily institutionalized, rather, an important aspect of management training is 'training on the job'. Young potentials are not only sent to the HQ for training purposes but also to other subsidiaries ensuring know-how and information flows in all directions.

> **I bring young employees with me on each of my business trips for learning purposes**. [...] Experience needs to be passed on and that's a good way to do so. (P6: 104)

> [w]e focus on **training on the job** [...] we invest in employees in who we have a strategic long term interest. We rotate them in our subsidiaries [...] that gives them a chance to have a **hands-on learning experience** [...] they accumulate important knowledge and work at the same time. (P30: 45)

International job-rotation for training purposes bears not only a learning effect for subsidiary personnel but also transfers valuable knowledge from subsidiaries to the HQ or/and other units. Apparently, corporations are increasingly becoming aware of the value of local know-how and are trying to tap into that potential not only by sending their trainees to foreign subsidiaries for learning purposes but also by establishing shared service centers in subsidiaries. These findings are in line with Vance (2005) who underpins the importance of HCNs as promoters of effective knowledge generation and transfer. An executive gets to the point:

> We offer plenty of training opportunities including **extended stays in foreign subsidiaries** [...] within the CEE region people are exchanged among subsidiaries to a great extent. **That exchange enables us [HQ] to learn from subsidiary staff as well.** [...] That's a good thing. (P26: 47)

Naturally, training aims at fostering promising employees and creating a group-wide 'best breed' thus some groups have sophisticated long-term human resource strategies. Often special emphasis is put on up-and-coming CEE locals:

> We **train our people on a global scale** [...] we invest years to train our people. [...] We strive to **generate a 'best breed' in the long term** [...] rather than simply hire and fire. [...] One management program – our executive program – is specifically targeted towards board members. Our board members in CEE are much younger than the ones in our Western European subsidiaries; e.g. our CEO in Russia looks like 16, he is actually 32, but he is doing a superb job. (P42: 87)

Interestingly, trainee programs are not limited to training at the HQ premises only, rather, people are being sent to other subsidiaries for learning purpose. As outlined by an executive:

> Fostering exchange is very important to us. [...] **new colleagues e.g. are sent to Croatia for learning purposes.** [...] They come to us [HQ] first for a couple of months but then they go to a subsidiary for further learning before they are ready to do their actual job at another subsidiary. (P9: 62)

Another side-effect of exchanging people for learning purposes is to foster appreciation for different nationalities:

> We see to it that we not **only send out people from the HQ to CEE but also bring in CEE people to the HQ**. [...] Doing so fosters mutual understanding for different cultures. (P33: 37)

A welcome side-effect of training is to create close personal ties between employees from HQ and subsidiaries. Furthermore, through a common training, networks between different subsidiaries are created. In the words of an executive:

> [m]anagement training on an international scale enables the participants from different subsidiaries and countries **to get to know each other**. [...] That aspect is **at least as important as the training itself**. (P23: 54)

Depending on the nationality of the HQ, management training did also serve other purposes. The interviewees of two Japanese regional HQ for CEE, for example, all mentioned that the senior management training program in Japan was some kind of silk ribbon of excellence and a sign of entering 'the inner circle of important people'.

> [taken from a Japanese MNC] we have a senior management training in Japan for people who have been with us for more than five years and who are considered to be important. The training content itself is not very special but it brings people together and the president of the group himself is present. Forgive me the expression but I would compare it with a 'B- public servant exam' in Austria [...] it's more like **a ritual that one belongs to a higher illustrious hierarchy now**. People in or mother in Japan keep score of it [...] Ahh... that's Mister XY from country XY and he has completed the senior training program. (P17: 88)

Inpatriates: An emerging form of control by socialization. An increasing number of companies strike new paths by using inpatriates to control subsidiaries. Adler (2002) defines inpatriates as 'managers different from the parent country brought into the home country on assignments designed to help them learn about the HQ organizational culture and ways of doing business. The HQ then returns the inpatriates back to their local culture to manage local operations.' While Peterson (2003) found that the number of inpatriates from CEE countries during the

1991–1994 period was quite small, the present study found that inpatriates as management trainees in the parent country are common practice used by 43 percent of MNCs.

> **Trainees from CEE subsidiaries are here [at the HQ] all the time** [...] they are here for six months before being sent back to their subsidiaries. [...] For future leaders and top-managers we have an **international assessment center** and an international management program where those people undergo training at the HQ and various subsidiaries. (P6: 102)
>
> Ten years ago, a Russian employee **was not used to take on responsibility**. [...] we needed to train them to take on responsibly. [...] We brought them all to Vienna for some three to six months for training purposes. That way they **learning how we handle things and got to know their future contact persons face-to-face**. (P25: 64)
>
> We **select high potentials from CEE subsidiaries and bring them into the HQ for one or two years**. They run through all our divisions and functions [...] and are then sent back with all that know-how into their subsidiary to take on a management position. (P33: 37)
>
> Our colleagues **from CEE are here [at the HQ] for approximately a year** and **work jointly with us** on all kinds of projects. [...] That way they get **acquainted with our tools, and structures, and values**, and ways of doing things. (P11: 66)

A major driver of inpatriation is to infiltrate subsidiaries with the MNC's organizational culture, values and the HQ 'way of doing things'. In the words of an executive:

> We **rotate those** [promising people from subsidiaries] **internationally throughout our network** of subsidiaries this way they are learning by doing. At the same time, best-practices are spread group-wide. (P8: 112)

Moreover, inpatriates are highly successful in promoting mutual knowledge exchange between HQ and subsidiaries. For all those reasons, we find that inpatriates have a positive impact on interest alignment between HQ and subsidiary by fostering mutual understanding and spreading a common organizational culture. Additionally, they reduce information asymmetry between HQ and subsidiaries by mutual know-how transfer and network building. Table 7.4 gives an overview on how different forms of management training impact HQ-subsidiary relations.

Table 7.4 The impact of management training & socialization on headquarter-subsidiary relations

Control by socialization & training	Headquarter-subsidiary relationship	
	Goal conflict reduction	Information asymmetry reduction
Classic Management training	*Reduce goal conflict by* • Creating links between HQ and subsidiaries and among single subsidiaries through common training sessions • Transferring organizational culture • Fostering group-wide 'best breed'	*Reduce information asymmetry by* • Establishing a common ground of understanding • Enabling knowledge exchange between HQ and subsidiary • Creating links between subsidiaries through 'training on the job' by international job-rotation • Fostering cross-cultural competence
Inpatriates	*Reduce goal conflict by* • Transferring HQ values and organizational practices to subsidiaries • Enhancing commitment to HQ goals. • Fostering close personal ties between HQ and subsidiaries • Creating informal networks between HQ and subsidiary	*Reduce information asymmetry by* • Enabling mutual knowledge transfer between HQ and subsidiaries • Increasing mutual understanding between subsidiary and HQ

Source: Author.

The following network view on management training provides an overview of all aspects discussed and displays the groundedness and density of the single variables. In sum, control by management training is caused by the need to pass on an MNC's international experience, to fill in potential lack of management knowledge of less mature subsidiaries in CEE, and to improve the qualifications of subsidiary personnel. It comprises classical forms of management training and more state-of-the-art forms such as inpatriates. At the same time, management training has an impact on MNC control by transferring organizational culture and creating informal networks across borders and organizational units.

Empirical Results 163

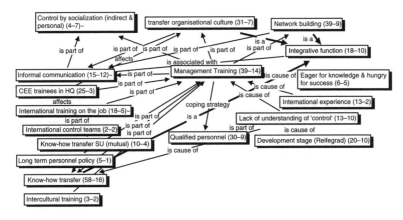

Figure 7.12 Network view on management training.
Source: Author.

Based on our data the following propositions regarding management training can be made:

P (29) Management training in all forms (classic, trainees, inpatriates, international training on job) is a means to transfer organizational culture and a catalyst for knowledge exchange between HQ and subsidiary and subsidiaries

P (30) Exchanging people across borders for learning purposes fosters not only task-related learning but also understanding and appreciation for cultural differences.

7.2.2.4 Control by organizational culture

Control by organizational culture depends on developing identification with and commitment to the values and objectives of the corporation (Child, 1984), and transferring the 'way of doing things' (Martinez et al., 1991; Pfeffer, 1982). In our sample, 25 out of 40 corporations transfer their organizational culture into their CEE ventures. Based on the interviews, management training, inpatriates, network building activities, lateral relations, using expatriates and a great degree of informal communication are means of transferring organizational culture and management styles and practices. Figure 7.13 below gives an overview on the means of transferring organizational culture.

Three quarters of the MNCs make use of expatriates and are convinced that expatriates automatically spread HQ culture into subsidiaries. As already discussed at length, management training is another case in point as training often serves to infiltrate subsidiary staff with

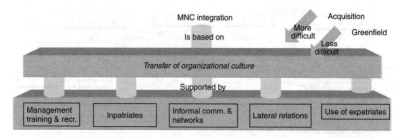

Figure 7.13 Pillars of intra-organizational transfer of organizational culture.
Source: Author.

a company's spirit. Also, using inpatriates is a widespread practice to establish HQ culture in CEE subsidiaries. In addition, the creation of intra-group networks and lateral relations automatically transfers organizational culture and practices. The more intense and informal information flows between single units the more easily a 'common culture' is created. Since the transfer of organizational culture has already been discussed in the context of management training, inpatriates, network building, lateral relations, informal communication and expatriates, only a brief overview on the role of the various pillars supporting the transfer of organizational culture is given. Table 7.5 illustrates the single means of organizational culture transfer with exemplary quotes.

An alternative way to ensure a common culture is to select employees who 'fit in' with the existing organizational culture. Whether or not a potential new employee 'fits' into the existing corporate culture is checked during the recruitment process. Since key persons are almost always selected by HQ, recruitment already prepares the ground for a common organizational culture:

> Ultimately we **only recruit people who are comfortable with our organizational style and culture**. If they are at ease with our culture or not can be easily spotted at the recruitment process. [...] We only employ people who fit into our culture. (P29: 77)
>
> Our HR department sees to it that we **recruit the 'right' people**. The selection process is crucial. [...] We need to have a good working atmosphere and therefore we need the 'right' people. (P19: 79)

Transfer of organizational culture is also affected by market entry choices (Harzing, 2002). Interviewees indicated that organizational culture is transferred more easily to Greenfield operations than to acquired

Table 7.5 Pillars of organizational culture transfer

Pillar of organizational transfer	Exemplary quotes for organizational transfer
Use of expatriates	'It is a fact that the organizational culture in the subsidiaries is very similar to the one of the parent if expatriates fill key positions at the very top but also in middle management. However, where expatriates are only a minority [...] the organizational culture differs considerably.' (P9: 57)
Management training and	Transfer of organizational culture into our subsidiaries just happens [...] First, we have lots of trainees and inpatriates from our subsidiaries at the HQ. That's an important first step for a true internationalization [...] and it helps to foster group-wide mutual understanding. [...] When people return to their subsidiaries they automatically bring 'our ways of doing things' with them. (P2: 100)
Inpatriates	'We select high potentials from CEE subsidiaries and bring them into the HQ for one or two years. They run through all our divisions and functions [...] and are then sent back with all that know-how into their subsidiary to take on a management position.' (P33: 37)
Lateral relations	'We work with international teams [...] People from all units work together on a permanent basis [...] that creates a basis for a common understanding. [...] We have been fostering group-wide lateral relations among employees from all units. [...] That way a 'shared organizational culture' was developed.' (P2: 126)
	'It just happens naturally that we transfer our organizational culture and management style into our subsidiaries. [...] Our structure requires permanent interaction of subsidiary personnel with HQ personnel [...] our culture is automatically passed on to our foreign units.' (P23: 49)
Informal communication & network building	Our world can already be identified by our office furniture, no matter if you enter a branch in Warschau, Budapest or London; you can spot our style at first sight. We interact with our subsidiaries permanently and we carry our spirit into our subsidiaries. E.g. our open door policy and transparent office structures are the same worldwide. [...] And that style how we design our offices reflects or management style. (P16: 98)

Source: Data analysis.

firms, who already have an existing, however different, culture. The following quotations illustrate that phenomenon:

> Part of the **reason why we did not acquire was that we wanted to create our own organizational spirit and culture** in our subsidiaries. If you take over an existing firm you have to deal with an existing culture which often hinders successful integration. That's why **we only entered the market via Greenfields** [...] that enabled us to bring in our own ideas, structures and processes [...] (P15: 95)
>
> Greenfields allowed us to build a subsidiary a 100% according to scheme. [...] **If we merged or took over firms we had to deal with an existing organizational culture and structure** and had to gradually adapt those to our own organizational culture. [...] That's a process. (P8: 19)

Industry might be another determinant of organizational culture. For example the telecommunications industry in general seems to be dominated by a more informal communication style and flat hierarchies than other industries.

> We automatically transfer our organizational culture into our subsidiaries. All our board members use the informal 'you' no matter which unit they communicate with. [...] I guess our informal ways, and **organizational culture, and flat hierarchies are a general characteristic of the industry we are working in.** (P22: 77)

Nationality of the parent company might also play a decisive role on the type of an MNC's organizational culture and the manner of how it is spread in international ventures. The CEO of the regional HQ for CEE of a Scandinavian MNC explains his encounter with Scandinavian management culture and how he in turn passes this culture on to their CEE subsidiaries:

> Let me illustrate that with an example: When I started here in 1971 [...] I was used to very hierarchical, formal and conservative structures [...] **When I came to our international HQ in Denmark for the first time** [...] **I met the CEO who was not dressed formally, greeted me informally and addressed me by my first name.** [...] That was a shock for me at first. [...] I tried to implement that Scandinavian management style and open **door policy into Austria and later into our CEE subsidiaries.** [...] Sure enough that style

caused some sort of shock in CEE. [...] People there were used to sit behind closed doors and did not appreciate being interrupted in their isolated private-ness. [....] It was quite a challenge to introduce flat hierarchies there and encourage employees to address me directly whenever they need advice. (P19: 81)

7.2.3 Communication HQ-subsidiary

7.2.3.1 Intensity of communication

The frequency of contact between HQ and subsidiaries sheds light on the nature of HQ-subsidiary relations and helps to determine the extent of HQ interference. 39 out of 40 MNC HQ entertain an intense and ongoing communication with their subsidiaries. The following quotations illustrate the importance attached to communication:

> **Opinions between us and our subsidiaries are exchanged permanently.** Subsidiary managers consult with us [the HQ] on a regular basis. [...] Clearly, the HQ interfaces to the subsidiaries pool knowledge which we are eager to share with the subsidiaries. [...] Although our CEE managers have lot of operational experience they still need administrative support. (P3: 54)

> The **intensity of communication with our subsidiaries is very high** [...] we e-mail, phone or visit them directly very often. Additionally, our CEE colleagues come here at least every half a year. [...] Ongoing and intense contact is crucial. (P5: 76)

> We need to see our subsidiaries not just once a year [...] the **key to success is to be there personally not just once a year, but at least every three to four weeks.** Face-to-face interaction and close personal contact is of utmost importance. Apart from my frequent visits **I need to call my colleagues [in the subsidiary] at least once a week.** (P6: 89)

> Statistically spoken I spend most of my time in plane somewhere above Hungary. (P14: 70)

Some 38 percent of interviewees underline the importance of informal communication channels between HQ and subsidiaries:

> **Informal communication channels** between HQ and subsidiaries are **almost more important than the formal ones.** Basically, informal telephone calls form our main communication basis. [...] It's fast and efficient and informal. (P31: 53)

We are in **daily contact** with our subsidiaries [...] we have many joint projects and coach subsidiary staff permanently. [...] A quick telephone call here, an e-mail there. (P18: 84)

7.2.3.2 Group language

Concerning group language the following was noted: 43 percent of corporations use both English and German, 42 percent use English, and 15 percent of MNCs use German as a group language. The use of German as a group language seems to decline; however, some companies still insist that their top-managers learn German. As one executive explains:

> **People who strive for a management position in our subsidiaries need to learn German.** [...] We offer both, German and English courses for all our staff on a voluntary basis. But people who want to reach a management position need to master the German language [...] all our managers speak German. (P27: 72)

7.2.3.3 Communication functions

Communication between HQ and subsidiaries takes place in both ways, formally by the means of reports and informally by personal and/or impersonal contacts. Communication lays the ground for integration of HQ and subsidiaries. Moreover, ongoing communication fosters information exchange and group-wide spreading of best practices and it is a way to control subsidiaries. Table 7.6 gives an overview over communication functions illustrated with exemplary quotes and indicates the percentage of interviewees per function.

7.2.4 Conclusion: extent and types of control classified

The above analysis provides an answer to our first research question:

Which Management Control Systems (MCS) do MNCs use to coordinate and control their foreign subsidiaries in CEE?

In the following, the frequency of control types in our sample and the extent of control exerted by the HQ are given:

7.2.4.1 Frequency of control types

The layout of our interview guide allowed us to account for the frequency of control types as distinguished by Harzing (1999). Using Harzing's (1999) terminology 35 of the investigated HQ conduct

Table 7.6 Communication functions

Communication functions	Exemplary quotes	%
Integration	Our controllers are directly on the spot [in the subsidiaries] at least once a month for a couple of days, sometimes even longer. E.g. I just came back from Turkey yesterday […] Personal presence is important to ensure that our systems are working properly, you need to talk to people and encourage them to ask questions. The key to success in our Eastward expansion is to create a feeling of belonging to the group. (P33: 62)	50
Information exchange & best practice transfer	'Intense communication between single subsidiaries and the HQ is important for sharing and spreading best practices group-wide.' (P2: 104) Face-to-face interaction is crucial for successfully exchanging ideas and discussing new solutions. […] Almost every time we experience some 'light-bulb' moments of how we can improve processes. […] ongoing communication and meetings are vital. […] Conversing in a second language is tough, and if both are doing so, misunderstanding are commonplace. By personal interaction we make sure that we talk about the same thing [laughs]. (P20: 66)	18
Control (by socialization & networks)	'We communicate very openly based on a network structure, sure we have some hierarchies; nevertheless, we are very network-like organized. Information flows in all directions which is very productive. […] We do not rely on formal communication only.' (P35: 53)	50

Source: Data analysis.

Personal Centralized Control (PCC), 20 pursue Bureaucratic Formalized Control (BFC), another 23 score high on Control by Socialization and Networks (CSN) and 32 score high on Output Control (OC). In line with the literature, we found that MNCs usually combine two or more forms of control and do not rely on one control type exclusively. Figure 7.14 below depicts the frequency of control types used in our sample.

7.2.4.2 Combinations of control types

Having described the single control mechanisms and its perceived effects by headquarters, we attempt to identify how various headquarters

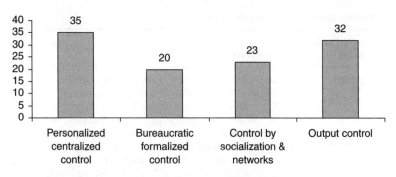

Figure 7.14 Distribution of Harzing's control typology.
Source: Data analysis.

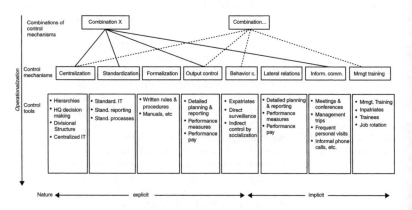

Figure 7.15 Configurations of control mechanisms.
Source: Author.

combine and use single mechanisms. As shown in Figure 7.15, the combination of control mechanisms employed by an MNC is only the macro-level of management control. Each combination is made out of any variety of control mechanisms, which form the mezzo level in a hierarchical view on control. Each mechanism is made out of a number of tools which enforce various control mechanisms on a more operational level.

The intensity of use of single mechanisms is based on the assessment of the executives, by asking them, once they had indicated that they use a specific type of control, to what extent on a scale from 1 to 10 they use single mechanisms. Out of the 40 analyzed MNCs, we find that companies which have a high level of centralization (35) also rank high on standardization (29) and output evaluation (32) (see Figure 7.14). Our data clearly shows that firms who use centralized decision making to a large extent also rely on standardized systems (Figure 7.16, graph A) and output control (graph B). Top-down planning is not necessarily combined with centralization, although 25 of the 35 firms ranking high on centralization resort to top-down planning, while 12 use a countercurrent approach. No relations could be found for the use of social control and output control (graph C).

Some 22 out of 40 MNCs are reported to make high use of formalization in the form of written policies, rules, job descriptions and the like. We found two clusters of firms which rank high on centralization with regards to formalization (graph D): First, a number of MNCs rank high on both formalization and centralization. The second cluster includes MNCs which rank high on centralization and low on formalization. A closer look at the relation between formalization and behavior control shows that behavior control can be used as a substitute for formalization, since a number of firms which do not use formalization to a great extent do use high levels of behavior control (graph E). At the same time, combining high levels of formalization with high levels of behavior control is also common (graph E). No relations can be found between formalization and social control (graph F).

Three quarters of our sample make a high use of direct behavior control by assigning key positions to expatriates. However, as our interviews reveal, not all the expatriates do perform a direct control function, some are clearly used in more subtle and informal ways in order to create networks and socialize with local employees. The great majority of companies (29) which are marked by high levels of centralization also use expatriates (graph G). The two outliers in graph G are companies which are rather decentrally organized and rely on network structures. The sometimes dual function of expatriates as means of direct behavior control and social control is shown in graph (H): Most firms which use expatriates to a great extent also rank rather high on social control. The same two outliers who do not use centralization also refrain from using direct behavior control.

Three quarters of the investigated MNCs have a rather high use of informal control mechanisms by either fostering lateral relations across international units, and/or informal communication by personal contacts and/or international management training or by using

172 *Management Control in CEE Subsidiaries*

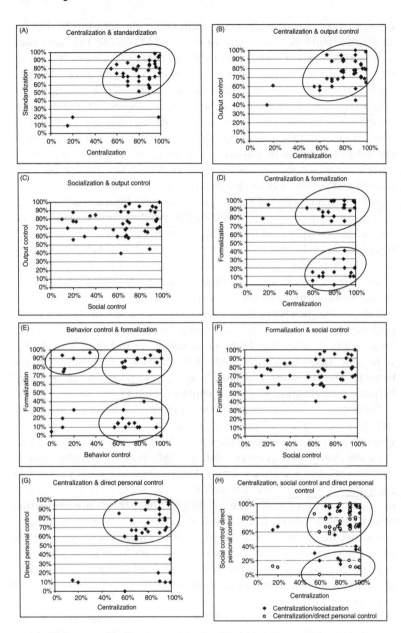

Figure 7.16 Combinations of control mechanisms.
Source: Data analysis.

a combination of those. Also, a rather high use of socialization seems to go somewhat hand in hand with a rather high centralization. Hence, socialization does not seem to be used as an alternative to centralized structures, but rather as a complementing instrument.

In short, our sample shows that MNCs operating in CEE rely on a mix of formal and informal control mechanisms to govern their subsidiaries. More specifically, our data clearly points to a high use of centralization, standardization, behavior control, output control and informal mechanisms. Rather than looking at various control mechanisms as alternatives, our findings show that they are used as complements which are only effective in combination. By granting access to embedded and soft information on subsidiaries informal control mechanisms serve as a pathfinder for formal mechanisms.

7.2.4.3 Control extent: operational versus strategic control

In order to determine the extent of control exercised by a parent, we resort to the distinction of operational and strategic control as defined by Doz (1981), Child (1984), Johnson (1987) and Groot (2000). As already described at length in the theory part, strategic control is the extent of influence an HQ has on a subsidiary concerning subsidiary strategy. Consequently, the interaction level between HQ and subsidiary is on the strategy level and the HQ does not interfere much on the operational level. Operational control, on the other hand, is control over the essential processes within an organization, in the sense of determining how employees of an organization perform their work (Child, 1984; Groot et al., 2000). Therefore, the interface between HQ and subsidiary is located on the operative management level and the extent and intensity of control and related activities is high. Furthermore, operational control is characterized by a high intensity of communication, detailed reporting, budgets and planning by the HQ, and personal and social coordinating mechanisms. Figure 7.17 depicts how operational control was reproduced in our interview data by linking several codes.

Most interviewees mentioned that a group-wide standardized integrated accounting system is a prerequisite for effective operational control. Operational control ensures transparency and is also positively correlated with the extent of centralized HQ decision making. Hence, a detailed evaluation and control system lays the ground for an operative holding.

65 percent of all CEE headquarters can be categorized as operative holdings exerting operational control over their subsidiaries and the remaining 35 percent as strategic or management holdings exerting

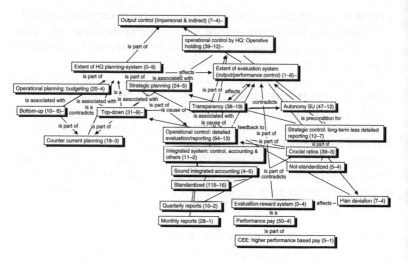

Figure 7.17 Extent/intensity of HQ control in CEE subsidiaries.
Source: Data analysis.

strategic control over their foreign ventures. Important strategic decisions regarding finance and investment are always made at the HQ.

7.3 Contingencies: the political and economic framework in CEE

Interviewees named a high political and economic risk, institutional upheaval in transition economies, obscure bureaucracy, corruption, risk of concealment and the lack of understanding of Western management concepts as primary challenges for governing FDI in CEE. Figure 7.18 shows the different codes established from the interview data.

At first sight, the market economy in CEE is fully established: convertible currencies, liberal prices and the majority of people working in private enterprises are a case in point. However, the soundness of structural reforms can be questioned and 'privatization' did not always work its magic since lacking macroeconomic coordination lead to dilapidation of enterprises. Kartte (1994) argues that transformation is bound to be rocky: '[...] every market economy starts with criminals – in the U.S. market economy was introduced with the colt and the Winchester. Rockefeller had a private army. I'd go so far and tell the Russian that in the U.S. criminal families appointed presidents from their ranks'.

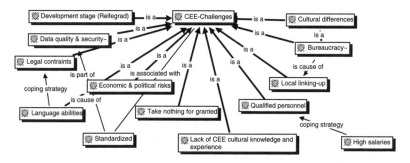

Figure 7.18 CEE challenges.
Source: Data analysis.

The collapse of the socialist system led to substantial regression in economic growth, GDP/capita, purchasing power, living standards, unemployment and inflation. The transition period is marked by a lose–lose pattern for many people in a lot of former communist countries. Many lost their jobs and had to face soaring market prices and new taxes, resulting in a substantially decreased discretionary income. At the same time, the cushion of social security was replaced by economic shock therapies. In a nutshell, people have to deal with new political systems and institutions, gradually renewed economic regulations, the collapse of traditional (Soviet/CIS) markets and the challenges of entering new (Western) markets, high inflation rates, new financial markets and the privatization of companies (Bakacsi et al., 2002).

In our study, interviewees perceive CEE markets as turbulent with quick and sometimes unpredictable environmental changes. FDI in CEE involves risk that is sometimes difficult to estimate (Marinov et al., 2003). MNCs face a changing external environment including economic, legal/political, social/cultural and technological forces (Hoskisson, Eden, Lau, & Wright, 2000; McCarthy & Puffer, 2003). Ongoing reforms and repeatedly changing legislation make it virtually impossible for HQ to be up-to-date with local laws and conditions. Therefore, effective governance is especially critical in emerging and transitioning economies (Dharwadkar, George, & Brandes, 2000). Arguing from an institutional theory view Peng (2003) states: 'the changing dynamics of institutional transitions have to make changes in strategic choices inevitable – both for domestic and foreign firms participating in these transitions and for economies embracing these transitions.' That context as described by executives:

> [t]he market in CEE is not very **regulated** [...] mechanisms are completely different than those we were used to in the Western markets. [...] Public tenders follow different rules. [...] there are strong political influences. (P18: 99)

> We encountered the **typical risks and dangers related to Eastern Europe**, such as theft and certain mentality related issues [...] but we got everything under control. (P24: 97)

> Payment behavior sucks in CEE [...] **in some countries we only sell for cash** and do not grant any time for payment. [...] Theft is also an issue [...] we had to put up fences in order to protect our assets. [...] The further eastward you go the worse it gets. (P24: 98)

> [m]acroeconomic parameters such as a low income, poor infrastructure, high unemployment and **political instability** [...] Political risk e.g. in the Ukraine and in Serbia is very high [...] also those factors must be taken into account. (P43: 32)

7.3.1 Political risk

7.3.1.1 Political instability

Things are different in transition economies and necessary conditions for a market economy in the Western sense are often not met. Ongoing reforms and frequent unprecedented changes in legislation make it virtually impossible for headquarters to be up-to-date with local laws and conditions. Therefore, effective governance is critical in emerging and transitioning economies (Dharwadkar et al., 2000). Some executives explain:

> There is an **increased political risk in CEE** [...] every time new elections take place our order intake comes to a still stand because the old administration does not dare to place new orders and the new administration is not yet established after the elections. [...] Since we also depend on other FDI the political situation has a direct effect on us. (P13: 33)

> **Political decisions are often far from market-economy rational** in Eastern Europe rather other mechanisms [...] are important. Often political decisions are rather bizarre since they are driven by how they might affect the outcome of the next elections. Therefore, necessary restructuring measures are often not undertaken [...] In

addition, there are **frequent changes in the legal framework** due to transition processes. (P18: 103)

> The **pace of reform** in many Eastern European countries is challenging for us, since changes in the local laws affect us. [...] Frequent amendments of the law make it difficult for us to keep ahead of things. (P32: 53)

However, political stability varies considerably within CEE. As a basic rule, the further East a nation is located the greater is the political instability as perceived by interviewees:

> All those countries are still **in their early stages of development towards a market economy**, it still is a very unsettled region, especially Russia and the Ukraine [...] Hungary, the Czech Republic and Poland are more stable economies, however, **they still do not match Western European standards.** [...] That's the reason why we have a centralized control and reporting system at the HQ. (P17: 70)

7.3.1.2 Bureaucracy

Moreover, economies in CEE are marked by a high level of intricate bureaucracy. Effectively dealing with local authorities requires local experts, and, therefore is often left to local subsidiary employees. Because of the high local involvement necessary to understand the number of rather unclear bureaucratic processes and changes in legislation, local managers act increasingly on their own without the understanding or supervision of the MNC's headquarter. This, then, increases information asymmetry between foreign subsidiaries and their HQ. Some 30 percent of respondents gave account of a high level of redtapism in CEE. As explained by another executive:

> We are constantly **struggling with bureaucracy and local authorities.** [...] Communication with authorities proved to be very tough. It takes ages to get things done. I suspect that there is **no logic but 'administrative discretion' behind those obscure authorities.** Closing our representative office and founding a new company took 10 months in Hungary; [...] there are a legion of little things [...] bureaucracy runs wild in those countries. (P17: 64)

> Polish bureaucracy [...] that's quite something! [...] **redtapism is aggravated even further by a general respect and fear of authorities.** (P29: 73)

7.3.1.3 Corruption

Corruption is a frequently reported phenomenon, and some 30 percent of interviewees talked rather openly about it. In the words of the executives:

> We try to **avoid cooperating with local godfathers** because that's extremely risky. You never know if you bet on the wrong horse. [...] Russia is the worst [...] We try to keep a clean record by all means but we have to deal with herds of people wanting something if we need a permit or whatever from a local authority. [...] Establishing goodwill is a challenge. (P24: 103)

> In **CEE connections are everything**, you need to have the right contact persons. It is quite common that people expect 'gifts'. In addition you have to be able to hold your drink, that's essential. (P38: 50)

> In CEE there is still the mentality that you have to bring **'gifts' to authority officials** if you need something. Those are not necessarily 'great presents' but gifts that adequately match the request. I don't talk about great amounts of money [...] But somebody needs a new TV, or a new video camera, or whatever. Those contacts have to be cultivated otherwise you can't do business successfully in CEE. (P17: 65)

> It can get quite dangerous the further you go East. Russia is definitely dangerous. **Protection money and stuff like that are no fairy tales.** You got to know your business there. (P38: 53)

Drawing on the literature, we find that the dominant logic for firms under communism included full employment, central planning outside the firm, and individual obedience (Newman, 2000). Firms developed resources and capabilities consistent with this dominant logic that allowed them to 'compete' effectively under central planning. Based on principles of Marxism, planned economies were characterized by exclusively state-owned property which resulted in inefficiencies at the firm and the macro-level (Filatotchev, Wright, Uhlenbruck, Tihanyi, & Hoskisson, 2003; Kornei, 1992). Low levels of competition among bureaucrats or among those being regulated increase the incentive for corrupt behavior. No or little competition enables companies to generate high rents, and regulators or bureaucrats who are the sole channel for regulated goods try to skim those high rents by demanding bribes. Under communist regimes competition was hardly existent and bureaucrats who had power over the allocation of resources had only limited control and oversight. Given the omnipresence of bottlenecks and shortages in communist economies, bribes and other forms of private payment kept the economy moving (Sandholtz & Taagepera, 2005). As our data indicates, imprints of such behavior are still found in CEE.

7.3.1.4 Legal constraints

Legal frameworks in CEE are often perceived as constraints by HQ as reported by 38 percent of the interviewees. Often, MNCs could not acquire 100 percent stakes when taking over firms and were forced to be content with minority stakes or JV agreements. Legal constraints were also reported to work at a more delicate level, for example by requiring a subsidiary CEO to fluently speak the local language. Moreover, different local legal requirements were found to be a barrier for more standardized accounting systems. In the words of an executive:

> We always bought companies which were previously owned by the state. That's why **we were forced to enter into JV agreements first although we wanted to acquire a 100% immediately.** [...] Local legal requirements forced us to enter into JVs. (P4: 33)
>
> You always have to consider the local requirements. Especially in **accounting people's way of thinking is shaped by local legal frameworks.** It takes some effort to communicate that, apart from acting according to local laws, we also want to be compatible with group standards and U.S. GAP. That takes a lot of time [...] (P17: 60)
>
> It was important to speak Polish fluently because there is a **law requiring that the CEO and at least one other member of the board speak the local language.** (P6: 76)

7.3.1.5 Summary political risk

Table 7.7 summarizes the above findings and gives an overview on how increased political risk in CEE influences HQ-subsidiary relations and management control. Additionally, the percentage of respondents per variable is given.

7.3.2 Economic and firm level risk

7.3.2.1 Risk of concealment of relevant information

Economic risk in CEE increases the likelihood of subsidiary failure or bad performance. Since subsidiary managers cannot diversify their employment, their jobs depend on the performance of the subsidiary. Therefore, local management is reported to frequently attempt to let

Table 7.7 Impacts of political risk on subsidiary control

Political risk	Impacts on management control due to	Exemplary quotes	%
Political instability	Frequently changing frameworks and institutional upheaval	Political decisions are often far from market-economy rational in Eastern Europe, rather other mechanisms [...] are important. Often political decisions are rather bizarre since they are driven by how they might affect the outcome of the next elections. Therefore, necessary restructuring measures are often not undertaken [...] In addition, there are frequent changes in the legal framework due to transition processes. (P18: 103) All those countries are still in their early stages of development towards a market economy; it still is a very unsettled region, especially Russia and the Ukraine [...] Hungary, the Czech Republic and Poland are more stable economies, however, they still do not match Western European standards. Just look at the development of the Forint for example [...] That's the reason why we have a centralized control and reporting system at the HQ. (P17: 70)	55
Excessive Bureaucracy	Complex and opaque governmental restrictions	We are constantly struggling with bureaucracy and local authorities. [...] Communication with authorities proved to be very tough. It takes ages to get things done. I suspect that there is no logic but 'administrative discretion' behind those obscure authorities. Closing our representative office and founding a new company took 10 months in Hungary. There are a legion of little things [...] bureaucracy runs wild in those countries. (P17: 64)	30

Corruption	Bribes and intransparent mob-like economic structures	In CEE connections are everything, you need to have the right contact persons. It is quite common that people expect 'gifts'. In addition you have to be able to hold your drink, that's essential. (P38: 50)
		In CEE there is still the mentality that you have to bring 'gifts' to authority officials if you need something. It does not necessarily have be 'great presents' but gifts that adequately match the request. I don't talk about great amounts of money [...]. But somebody needs a new TV, or a new video camera, or whatever. Those contacts have to be cultivated otherwise you can't do business successfully in CEE. (P17: 65)
	Goal conflict due to bribes	It can get quite dangerous the further you go East. Russia is definitely dangerous. Protection money and stuff like that are no fairy tales. You got to know your business there. (P38: 53)
Legal constraints	Prevent 100% owned subsidiaries	We always bought companies which were previously owned by the state. That's why we were forced to enter into JV agreements first although we wanted to acquire a 100% immediately. [...] Local legal requirements forced us to enter into JVs. (P4: 33)
	Being barriers to standardized accounting and MIS	You always have to consider the local requirements. Especially in accounting people's way of thinking is shaped by local legal frameworks. It takes some effort to communicate that, apart from acting according to local laws, we also want to be compatible with group standards and U.S. GAP. That takes a lot of time [...] (P17: 60)
	Influence board composition	It was important to speak polish fluently because there is a law requiring that the CEO and at least one other member of the board speak the local language. (P6: 76)

Source: Data analysis.

figures look better than they really are. Such practices can endanger the MNC as a whole since corrective action might come too late. This situation is aggravated since MNCs use to benchmark the performance of single CEE subsidiaries provoking competition among CEE locations for much-wanted foreign investments. Consequently, subsidiary managers whose subsidiaries do not perform very well may be tempted to conceal bad performance. Executives outline these occurrences as follows:

> Often **things were disguised in Central and Eastern Europe.** Until we [the parent] were able to discover what really happened it was already too late for corrective action and we had to deal with the consequences [...] this is aggravated by competition among the single subsidiaries. (P1: 70)

> We **try to have more centralized structures.** There is a very simple reason for that: We had a subsidiary executive who looked at his personal benefit only and did not share relevant information with the Headquarter. That's why we seek to handle things more centralized. (P29: 58)

7.3.2.2 Development stage (maturity) and poor data quality

A crucial challenge for managing CEE subsidiaries is the bad quality of organizational and financial data. In order to ensure plausible figures and reports, Western MNCs often implement Management Information Systems (MIS) and introduce accounting and bookkeeping from scratch. MNCs attempt to introduce standardized systems to ensure comparability and transparency of subsidiaries data. For example, one executive noted that:

> The **greatest challenge** in those countries is always to have **data which is reliable and secure**. We have to see to it that we have the greatest integration of systems possible for our subsidiaries in CEE to ensure that we have closed loops. Establishing integrated systems is the only way to establish at least some kind of data reliability. We put much effort into building integrated systems to get away from single reports which were not plausible. (P1: 45)

> The trouble was that they [subsidiary personnel] had **very different perceptions about management control**. Management control and reporting in the sense of a modern organization was alien to them. They run some wild calculations which could by no means be

retraced and which never matched with the results from accounting and bookkeeping. It was horrible [...] they were showing OK results throughout the year but at the end of the year came the big light-bulb moment of the truth which was a huge loss [...]. (P1: 117)

Clearly, less advanced management and information processing systems in CEE subsidiaries result in information asymmetry. This situation is aggravated by a rather poor education in accounting and management. In the words of an executive,

> [t]he trouble is that **we unite subsidiaries with varying degrees of maturity**. Our group as a whole and our Western European or U.S. subsidiaries have very advanced management and information systems and we grant our new Eastern subsidiaries **very little time to catch up to meet our standards**. We have to constantly watch that things which are taken for granted here are understood and interpreted correctly in CEE (P40: 50).

Only a constant coaching process by the HQ was found to prepare the ground for establishing integrated information and reporting systems. Thus, differing development stages of HQ and subsidiaries add to information asymmetry since much needed information systems must be implemented and understood before effective management is possible.

The degree of granted autonomy depends on the development stage of the subsidiary. The more mature a subsidiary is in terms of organizational structure, reporting and performance, the more leeway in decision making is granted.

> It depends. **I need to visit already established subsidiaries in more advanced countries less frequently** than new subsidiaries which we just set up. In the latter case I need to be there at least a week per month [...]. (P4: 68)

The question of how to manage subsidiaries in terms of structure, instruments and complexity depends on the development stage of the subsidiary. [...] The trouble is that we unite subsidiaries with varying degrees of maturity. Our group as a whole and our Western European or U.S. subsidiaries have very advanced management and information systems and **we grant our new Eastern subsidiaries very little time to catch up to meet our standards**. We have to constantly watch out that things which are taken for granted here are understood and interpreted correctly in CEE. (P7: 110)

7.3.2.3 Lack of understanding for Western management concepts and control

A general lack of understanding of Western management concepts and instruments was noted in CEE which causes a twofold information asymmetry between HQ and subsidiaries: In order to transfer knowledge from the parent to subsidiaries some organizational capabilities to understand the concept are required. However, absorptive capacity of CEE subsidiaries is limited due to their little prior exposure of Western management techniques and adapting to a market environment (Filatotchev et al., 2003; Newman, 2000). Absorptive capacity is the ability of firms to 'recognize the value of new information, assimilate it, and apply it to commercial ends' (Cohen & Levinthal, 1990). Knowledge to fulfill plans imposed by a central planning authority differs significantly from management and market knowledge necessary to succeed in a market economy. Information processing capacity, however, is critical for gathering, interpreting, preparing and synthesizing information for organizational decision making (Luo, 2005). According to information processing theory intra-MNC information processing is only effective when an organization's information processing requirements and its processing capacities are in line with each other (Thushman & Nadler, 1978). After 1989 the structural and moral institutions and the logic of central planning was abandoned resulting into a vacuum. 'New values and norms were slow to develop, as were the political, legal, and financial institutions that are legitimated by underlying values and norms' (Newman, 2000). New capabilities such as efficiency orientation, strategic thinking, entrepreneurial initiative and proneness to take risk were required, but those developed only slowly (Newman, 2000). Building on institutional theory, Kostova (1999) points out that 'if a practice is inconsistent with the cognitive institutions in the recipient environment [...] employees will have difficulties understanding, interpreting, and judging it correctly.' Thus, the parent cannot expect an Eastern subsidiary to speak the same corporate terminology but needs to create a common understanding first to reduce information asymmetry. The current study supports these findings. The following quotations illustrate a variety of problems associated with a noted lack of understanding of 'Western' management concepts:

> People had to **slowly learn to appreciate the necessity of information management** and management control. But that's clear they never worked with such concepts and instruments before. (P19: 73)

> Well **Western management techniques per se triggered a culture shock** to some extent. If you've always thought in terms of the organization or even society as a whole introducing profit centers was a culture shock. We had to slowly explain 'Western' management concepts. (P7: 117)

> We had to come up with a **glossary, which explains in detail all the terms, what they mean** and how they are applied. Then we set up a series of workshops where we went through it together. (P20: 60)

7.3.2.4 Qualified personnel

Last but not least, some 30 percent of interviewees indicated that it is difficult to find qualified personnel in the field of management control and accounting in CEE. However, at the same time, a number of interviewees were thrilled with top educated CEE personnel.

> The challenge lies in adhering to certain reporting standards [...] **very few people in CEE are used to report according to international accounting standards.** [...] We had to coach people and transfer know-how [...] it took some time to achieve a certain reporting standard. (P40: 50)

> Finding qualified personnel in CEE with a sound accounting background is difficult in CEE. [...] Most of our staff in management control still comes from Austria [...] we are constantly coaching and training local personnel in management control. (P39: 62)

7.3.2.5 Summary of economic and firm level risk

Table 7.8 summarizes the above findings and gives an overview on how the economic framework in CEE influences HQ-subsidiary relations and management control. Additionally, the percentage of respondents per variable is given.

Based on the data analysis we suggest the propositions.

P (31) The greater the perceived political and economic risk in the host country the more HQ control by expatriates is exerted

P (32) The greater the degree of maturity of a subsidiary the less stringent is HQ control

Table 7.8 The impact of economic risk on management control

Economic risk	Impact on management control due to	Exemplary quote	%
Transition economy	Different economic frameworks	Forget about certain basic prerequisites… I mean things which are taken for granted in Western Europe should not be taken for granted in Central and Eastern Europe. If you do so you'll be disastrously shipwrecked. It is not yet a real market economy […] the transition is going on…. But if you bear in mind the circumstances [transition economies] you'll tackle them. (P16: 115)	51
Data quality	No integrated management information systems Poorly qualified personnel	The greatest challenge in those countries is always to have data which is reliable and secure. We have to see to it that we have the greatest integration of systems possible for our subsidiaries in CEE to ensure that we have closed loops. Establishing integrated systems is the only way to establish at least some kind of data reliability. We put much effort into building integrated systems to get away from single reports which were not plausible. (P1: 45) The trouble was that they [subsidiary personnel] had very different perceptions about management control. Management control and reporting in the sense of a modern organization was alien to them. They run some wild calculations which could by no means be retraced and which never matched with the results from accounting and bookkeeping. It was horrible; they were showing OK results throughout the year but at the end of the year came the big light-bulb moment of the truth which was a huge loss […]. (P1: 117)	51
Maturity	Less advanced structures	The trouble is that we unite subsidiaries with varying degrees of maturity. Our group as a whole and our Western European or U.S. subsidiaries have very advanced management and information systems and we grant our new Eastern subsidiaries very little time to catch up to meet our standards. We have to constantly watch out that things which are taken for granted here are understood and interpreted correctly in CEE. (P7: 110)	51

Lack of exposure to Western Management concepts	Different perceptions of meaning	People had to slowly learn to appreciate the necessity of information management and management control. But that's clear they never worked with such concepts and instruments before. (P19: 73) Well Western management techniques per se triggered a culture shock to some extent. If you've always thought in terms of the organization or even society as a whole introducing profit centers was a culture shock. We had to slowly explain 'Western' management concepts. (P7: 117) We had to come up with a glossary, which explains in detail all the terms what they mean and how they are applied. Then we set up a series of workshops where we went through it together. (P20: 60)	40
Fierce competition & risk of failure	Concealment of relevant information	Often things were disguised in Central and Eastern Europe. Until we [the parent] were able to discover what really happened it was already too late for corrective action and we had to deal with the consequences [...] this is aggravated by competition among the single subsidiaries. (P1: 70) We try to have more centralized structures. There is a very simple reason for that: We had a subsidiary executive who looked at his personal benefit only and did not share relevant information with the Headquarter. That's why we seek to handle things more centralized. (P29: 58)	30
Poor education standards	Shortage of qualified personnel	The challenge lies in adhering to certain reporting standards [...] very few people in CEE are used to report according to international accounting standards. [...] We had to coach people and transfer know-how [...] it took some time to achieve a certain reporting standard. (P40: 50) Finding qualified personnel in CEE with a sound accounting background is difficult in CEE. [...] Most of our staff in management control still comes from Austria [...] we are constantly coaching and training local personnel in management control. (P39: 62)	45

Source: Data analysis.

7.4 Culture

In order to deepen our understanding of CEE culture we strive to triangulate existing findings on CEE culture with the insights drawn from our interviews and to explore how Western developed management and control theories apply in CEE. To capture potential cultural influences on the design and functioning of control and coordination systems and the mode of managing HQ–subsidiary relationships, the third set of questions of the present study focuses on perceptions of cultural differences and ways of dealing with it. While the Globe study produced measurable scales of cultural distance (Figure 7.19) between different cultural clusters we identified a number of perceptions on CEE culture from an Austrian, German and Swiss point of view by qualitative inquiry. Consequently, our findings do not allow for measuring cultural distance but provide a qualitative picture of cultural perceptions of CEE which are largely in line with the Globe findings.

The cultural perceptions identified in our data are basically stereotypes of implicitly perceived risk attributed to cultural differences by HQ managers in dealing with CEE subsidiaries. Those risk perceptions concerning CEE culture impact decisions on management control. One CEO got right to the point by stating that the trickiness involved with different mentalities and cultures lies in the perceived similarity of Austria and Eastern European countries. In his own words:

> Central and Eastern European culture is **misleading, because at first sight the mentality seems pretty similar.** If we would have

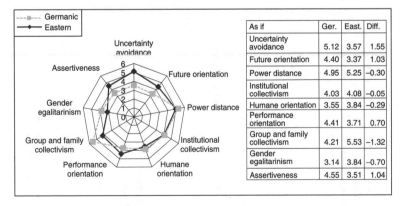

Figure 7.19 Differences in 'As if' scores: Germanic versus Eastern European cluster.
Source: Based on data from Bakacsi et al. (2002) and Szabo et al. (2002).

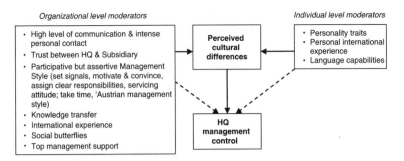

Figure 7.20 Perceived cultural differences and moderators.
Source: Author.

entered the Asian market we would have started to think about cultural differences immediately, because there are apparent differences. In the Czech Republic and in the Slovak republic we did not notice great differences at first sight, however, **at the second and third glance we noticed tremendous differences which need to be taken into account.** (P2: 39)

In general, the higher the perceived risk attributed to cultural differences is, the greater is the degree of HQ control in CEE subsidiaries. Following the culture standard method, perceptions on cultural differences identified in the interviews can be further validated to culture standards (see Fink et al., 2001; Fink et al., 2004a).

Our data not only shows perceptions of CEE culture but also effective ways of dealing with CEE culture as perceived by our interviewees. We identified seven moderators on perceived cultural differences on the organizational level and three moderators on the individual level (Figure 7.20).

In the following we first discuss the cultural perceptions as noted by our interviewees in some detail and compare those with the findings of the recent Globe study (House et al., 2002). Second, moderators on perceived cultural differences will be discussed. Lastly, we will develop propositions on perceived cultural differences and moderators.

7.4.1 Some CEE-wide parallels in cultural perceptions based on communism

In general, we found that CEE cultures differ among each other a great deal and cannot be lumped together. However, they do share a common history of communist regimes which caused interesting coping strategies which are widespread among different nations: Based on our data 18 categories of common characteristics of the CEE region are established. Figure 7.21 displays the percentage of interviewees who mention a certain characteristic at least one time during the course of the interview.

In the following the established categories are explained in some detail.

Passive resistance

Given the strong tradition of planning and centralization in a centrally planned economy (Krotz, 1998) one might expect that people are used to executing orders and act according to given rules and regulations. Obviously, however, people developed some creative coping strategies in order to avoid interference and orders from above. For example, Peng (2001) found a tradition of ignoring 'senseless' laws and mistrusting individuals which were not in the sphere of personal relations in socialist economies. Fink and Lehman (2006) explain that people in socialist regimes had developed a self-conscious form of individualism and subversive privacy in the workplace 'to get the best out of the system'. Paradoxically work itself allowed people to escape from rigid controls. Despite seemingly tight plans there was a lot of freedom at the workplace and plan targets were neither challenging nor usually met in time (Fink et al., 2006).

Based on our data, two strategies to avoid executing HQ orders were identified: *'Say yes but don't comply'* and *'Find 1000 ways around the rules or discuss orders to death'*. The first strategy implies seemingly taking the line of least resistance by agreeing to everything that is being said

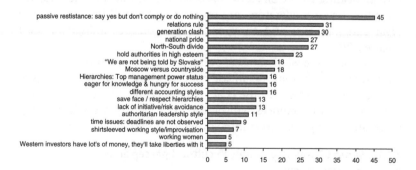

Figure 7.21 Common characteristics of CEE culture.
Source: Data analysis.

combined with taking no action to reach the agreed goals. This simple strategy obviously did the trick in communist times. Nearly half of our interviewees indicated that they experienced such situations and only slowly learned to cope with it. The following exemplary quotes of HQ executives who had been managing CEE subsidiaries before illustrate that point:

> [t]he Czechs obviously **learned under communist times to creatively find ways to resist orders.** If the communists – the Russians – demanded that they do something they found a legion of loopholes to avoid executing their orders. And they still use those strategies today. [...] There seems to be an attitude of 'we survived the communism we will also survive the MNCs' by resorting to prior field-tested strategies of avoidance. [...] there **were a lot of plans in communist times but the prescribed targets were rarely met** [...] that's why we need to be rather tough in those countries in order to get things done [...] otherwise they'll just trick us. (P2: 46)
>
> It's not easy to introduce guidelines and targets in CEE. We have had our fights [...] It seems that **people feel like back under communist times if somebody comes with guidelines and targets they fight them tooth and nail. We had to slowly learn how those patterns of resistance work** [...] **They just said 'yes' and put on a friendly face** [when we introduced guidelines and targets] **but then they did nothing at all.** First we thought, 'yea they got it, they'll do what they are told' [...] later we realized that they did not. That was a violent surprise. [...] If we pointed out difficulties they just looked at us and said OK, and went back to the agenda, it didn't matter to them. (P1: 87)
>
> My experience with meetings in our Czech subsidiary was that **everybody nods and is silent,** you think they accepted what you presented, but actually they didn't. If you don't know that, you think 'great that went well' but when you enter the control stage of the project you'll notice that **nothing happened.** Nobody did execute what we agreed on in the meeting! [...] After some time I became more sensitive [...] I ask them if there are any objections and most of all I assign responsibilities to single people and put everything down in writing. [...] Responsibilities need to be clearly assigned and consequences must be communicated if deadlines are not observed. [...] That's of utmost important. [...] Most [Western] newcomers make many mistakes. (P12: 40)

> We had a vast number of meetings where we discussed a many things and agreed on a lot of things which **were never executed** [laughs]. (P41: 45)

The most successful strategies of coping with such behavioral patterns reported are writing minutes on every single meeting and assigning clear responsibilities combined with regular checkups, controls and drastic action. Although *'passive resistance'* patterns are reported to be found in the whole CEE region, it seems to be exceptionally common in the Czech Republic and in Hungary. These findings are in line with Novy (2003) who found that Czechs avoid direct conflicts and dislike explicit communication about it. In contrast to Germanic cultures, Czechs are skeptical about structures and much rather value flexibility and improvisation. Being able to improvise and not rely on structures and timetables is regarded as a sign of excellence and capability (Fink et al., 2000).

A second strategy to avoid executing orders is labeled as 'finding 1,000 reasons why a something cannot be implemented'. An executive gets to the point:

> I noticed that people try to avoid implementing new things by seeking for problems and barriers. I would say the **Czechs are World Champions in finding a vast number of details why something does not work** [...] as a newcomer I thought 'whew they are right, that is an important issue which I did not consider' [...] but actually whatever they come up with is not important. [...] **They just try to baffle us 'foreigners' with lots of country specifics until we say yea, that really can't work here.** [...] **You need to watch out for that!** (P2: 43)

> The **'not invented here' syndrome** is found all over CEE – something does not work here because things do not work like that in Poland or Hungary, or wherever. Surely, we have to act according to the local law, but that's another thing. (P15: 81)

In order to avoid falling for the 'passive resistance' traps, executives reported that it is important to set clear signals by praising followers and eliminating persons who repeatedly block headquarters decisions and orders. An illuminating example of a prior subsidiary CEO:

> You need to be pretty assertive each change management process is met by people trying to obstruct changes. Those people need to be

identified and fired. **You need to set signals – both positive and negative ones. Positive ones by praising followers and negative ones by dismissing blockers.** [...] That is very important because otherwise they won't take you serious [...] they would just think they survive their new owners just as they survived under communism. (P2: 90)

Another way of dealing with such strategies is to involve people in the decision making process and assign clear responsibilities:

Clash of generations
A number of authors point to the dramatic turmoil provoked by fundamental political and economic changes in CEE. Roth & Kostova (Roth et al., 2003) suggest that the fall of communism entailed not only an institutional upheaval but also a radical change in fundamental values, beliefs and assumptions. Newman states that not only political systems, laws, regulations, and financial markets but also 'the underlying assumptions about the purpose of economic activity were destroyed or significantly changed within a short time' (Newman, 2000). Our data supports those findings: A key theme noted by the interviewees is a tremendous rift in the behavior and motivations of CEE employees based on age. While the 'older' generation which grew up in communism is not yet acquainted with market economic thinking, the younger generation is jumping at chances and is extremely performance and success oriented. Younger people are also more prone to take risk, for example by welcoming performance-based pay.

These opposing behaviors impact the choice and appropriateness of control mechanisms of MNCs. While the 'older generation' cannot be motivated by performance-related pay schemes, the younger generation welcomes such incentives. Consequently, MNCs need to use a combination of output and behavior control. In the words of an interviewee:

Young people in CEE welcome performance-based pay. [...] There is a lot of drive [...]. Therefore, we primarily try to recruit young people who are very performance oriented. [...] There is a tremendous rift between the older and the younger generation. (P11: 78)

Market economic thinking patterns have not penetrated all people in CEE [...] the young generation is already very market oriented. (P13: 62)

There are **huge differences based on age.** [...] People who grew up under socialism sometimes do not push enough [...] they don't show much initiative. (P20: 73)

Eagerness to learn to hungry for success
In general, CEE employees are marked by a thirst for knowledge and hunger for success resulting in a work attitude that can hardly be matched by Western European employees. Especially in the big thriving cities people work long hours including weekends and accept up to 100 percent performance-based pay. Young people in particular are determined to succeed and catch up. Some 15 percent of the interviewees gave account of this phenomenon:

> They were **starving to learn from us** [...] (P12: 81)

> The **eagerness, drive and ambition to catch up and learn is unmatched in CEE** [...] People are ready to perform and determined to succeed in business [...] (P15: 86)

> **People are hot and ready to go** [...] People **accept 100% performance-based pay schemes** [...] I think people in Moscow are already more American than the Americans. Business goes round the clock there. We cannot even do maintenance work on our server on the weekend because there are at least 30 people permanently working in the office over the weekends. [...] employees call me at 6 AM in the morning as well as at 2 AM at night. (P16: 84)

> Our CEE employees are substantially **more dedicated than our Austrian employees.** [...] They are ambitious and avid [...] you can literally feel the drive in the cities bursting with energy. [...] They all work like maniacs [...] that atmosphere of departure runs through all the countries. (P43: 79)

Moscow vs. countryside
'He who knows Moscow does not know Russia' (Bayer, 1996). Already under communist time regionally and nationally different levels of development triggered different moral concepts and behavioral norms (Bayer, 1996). Hence, a universal model of management know-how transfer is doomed to fail given the vast contextual and situational differences found in CEE. Our present findings underscore the tremendous differences between big cities and congested areas on the one hand and a rather poorly developed countryside on the other. The following quotations illustrate differences perceived by executives:

> People are partly **incredibly aggressive and greedy.** [...] But essentially they are well-educated and good to work with. [...] That's how it is in the cities, such as Warschau or Krakov [...] in the countryside things are different [...] it is still very traditional. (P16: 51)

In Moscow **people work day and night** [...] the city is booming it's incredible [...] it's like New York [...] You got to see it to believe it. [...] Outside Moscow, however, it's different, very different; the market potential is not yet developed there. (P17: 30)

Hierarchies: top-management power status
Our data clearly shows that top management in CEE has an absolute power status and should be treated with respect. Power and status of top-managers are displayed openly and decisions are usually made on the top, thus, participative decision making is not practiced. An executive remarks:

[t]**op management plays an important role** [...] in Moscow, e.g. they have offices were money doesn't count. Top managers express their status through their office [...] we developed colors, designs, and materials especially for such markets. [...] It's all about demonstrating power. (P16: 77)

Some interviewees noted a relation between development stages of a nation and hierarchical structures. In the words of an executive:

[t]he Slovak republic and Slovenia, e.g., are more progressive but in other countries it is still common that there is **one general director who dominates the decision making** [...] there is hardly anybody else with decision making power apart from the general director. What the top-manager decides is the law. [...] it takes some time to get used to that. (P18: 110)

Our findings are once more in line with prior research, which noted a strong power–distance culture in CEE (5.25), reflected by hierarchical structures and a prominent role of top management (House et al., 2004). People who grow up in such societies usually avoid taking on responsibility and rather depend on their superiors (Bakacsi et al., 2002). Even more so, they expect superiors to take care of them. In communist times large consultative bodies practiced a paternalistic and only officially 'participative' management style Bakacsi (2002). At the same time, there is a widespread feeling of learned helplessness (Pearce et al., 1994).

Save face/respect hierarchies
Given the high status of top management in CEE it does not come as a surprise that the concept of 'saving face' is important. Top management

in CEE has to be treated with utmost respect. Consequently, critique however modest should never be raised in front of employees but always be dealt with in confidence. Hierarchies are respected and should always be adhered to. Also, the Globe findings on power distance with a score of 5.25 in CEE, points to the importance of treating top-managers with respect. The following quotations address the critical role of status and power in CEE:

> A **boss is respected in CEE and has a certain standing** [...] you need to pay careful attention to never criticize a local subsidiary manager in front of his employees. [...] Even if we just discuss things in a larger round with other subsidiary managers **I need to carefully watch my words** [...] I've been learning by doing believe me [laughs] [...] In CEE you need to be alert and always **see to it that nobody loses his face**. (P8: 102)
>
> I'll give you a current example: An employee in our Slovak subsidiary made a huge mistake and we lost a considerable amount of money. Her immediate boss took a disciplinary measure [...] later that employee called directly at the HQ without telling her immediate boss who would have been the local subsidiary CEO. [...] by doing so the local **manager lost his face and we had to cancel everything and let him deal with her.** [...] Losing face in front of their own people is the worst. [...] that's a question of mentality. (P5: 103)

Pride
Along the lines of hierarchy and respect, national pride is mentioned as a shared characteristic among CEE countries. CEE employees are reported to be rather proud and it is important to show appreciation for their achievements.

> People in CEE are **very proud**, especially people in management positions. It is **crucial that our CEO speaks personally with the subsidiary CEO**. (P6: 83)
>
> [p]eople in CEE are **very proud** of what they achieved during the last 10 years and we need to show appreciation for their achievements. [...] At the same time, we need to be outspoken when they make a mistake. The carrot and the stick are important tools, especially when dealing with Hungarians. The Hungarians are the proudest of all and need to be directed back to earth from time to time. (P27: 82)

Relations rule
The importance of personal relations for doing successful business in CEE is underlined by some 30 percent of interviewees. These findings can be backed up by prior studies on Eastern European culture which found that CEE cultures are much more diffuse than Western ones (Hall, 1959; Trompenaars & Hampden-Turner, 2000). Diffuse cultures do not strictly divide private and professional spheres rather the underlying relationship rules (Hall, 1959; Hall et al., 2000). Also, compared with other clusters in the Globe study this cluster stands out with high scores on group-orientation (House et al., 2004). With a score of 5.53 on group and family collectivism the Eastern European cluster outreaches the Germanic cluster by 1.32 points. In Eastern Europe there is a tendency for citizens to distrust individuals, groups, and organizations that fall outside their sphere of personal relationships (McCarthy et al., 2003). Throughout communism people's attempt to accomplish goals through official channels often lead to frustration and failure. As a consequence, people resorted to personal networks to obtain goods and services, jobs, financing and so on (McCarthy et al., 2003; Peng, 2001). People developed survival strategies based on a network of trust among individuals at the workplace. Under a seemingly untroubled surface, insiders established close personal ties and shared tacit knowledge which enabled them to achieve a great degree of freedom at the workplace (Fink et al., 2006). Peng and Luo (2000), for example, found that firm performance in transition economies is positively related to a firm's personal connections to authority officials. Securing rights through 'private payments' to public officials and politicians is common in transition economies (Hellmann, Jones, & Kaufmann, 2000). Consequently, establishing intra-organizational personal networks within the MNCs may help to align HQ and subsidiary interests and prepare the ground for effective governance. A CEO explains:

> Basically, the whole **reporting system** which I have described at length before **has a limited explanatory power** [...] because our Polish CEO and our main owner know each other very well, and are on excellent terms with each other, and jointly decide what will happen and what won't. (P34: 39)

Once a sound personal relation is established between HQ and subsidiary personnel, the HQ can exert much more pressure on the subsidiary because people feel personally responsible and will not let their 'buddies' down. One CFO explicates the importance of personal relations as follows:

> Establishing sound personal relations in CEE is beneficial and crucial. [...] I have had my fair share of troubles with our subsidiary managers [...] the trick is to make them feel that you are doing them a favor then they'll return that favor. [...] That's also important for transferring knowledge. You always have to give him [the CEE manager] the feeling that he is more important than you and that he knows more than you. That will do the trick in the beginning. [...] After you got to know each other, you switch to the informal and personal 'you' and then things change. Once you have established a good personal relation you can exert much more pressure [...] There is no clear separation between private and professional spheres. (P43: 74)

Caution needs to be exercised when criticizing as critique is often taken personally in diffuse cultures. Therefore, as an HQ CEO had to experience himself, some cultural sensibility is needed to be successful in CEE:

> [s]ometimes I write a rather harsh e-mail to our local managers to trigger some action [...] but I made the experience that people in **CEE take critique personal** [...] e.g. our Bosnian manager thought I assaulted him personally. [...] Those people **are very proud** [...] now I'm a lot more careful. (P5: 100)

Since personal relations are a door opener in CEE it is essential to have good contacts not only within the corporation but also to other stakeholders such as potential clients and the government:

> **Relations are of utmost importance in CEE.** [...] Relations rule in every aspect, politics, clients, etc. (P18: 111)

North-south divide
Some culture-specific behavior was noted to change along a North-South divide: Employees from Southern CEE subsidiaries were perceived as being more emotional, more prone to negotiate, and more enthusiastic in their forecasts as compared to their Northern counterparts. Those differences do not only impact business conduct but also seemingly 'hard facts' such as the way business forecasts are made. The network view below summarizes the evidence gathered on the North-South divide.

In the following the individual aspects are discussed in more detail.

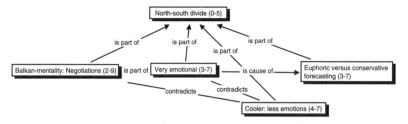

Figure 7.22 North-south divide.
Source: Data analysis.

Emotional vs. less emotional. A North-South divide in terms of emotions is noted among our interviewees. In general, the more Southern the more openly emotions are displayed, thus emotionally charged business encounters are common practice. Northern CEE nations, including Poland, Russia, and Czech Republic, are 'cooler' and emotions are not openly shown. Those findings are supported by the literature on cultural standards on CEE cultures (Fink & Meierewert, 1999).

> That's different in **Northern countries**. [...] Polish people are **less emotional**, the same is true for people from the Baltic States and from Russia, their mentality is cooler, they are less prone on negotiating. (P4: 113)

Southern Europeans were reported to act much more emotional and direct in business encounters. Consequently, some interviewees perceived their Southern European employees as being rather aggressive and direct:

> Somebody from the Balkans expresses **spontaneously what he thinks and feels**. [...] Russians or Czechs, on the other hand, are more reserved and do not show emotions openly. There are huge differences [...] (P43: 63)

> Our Rumanian manager is **very emotional and speaks up** even in a meeting with the MNC board [...] he dares to speak up although he should keep his mouth shut given his performance. [...] He still speaks up. [...] I like him but he needs to pace himself sometimes. (P4: 118)

> **Southern mentality is less diplomatic** [...] If they are not content with something they address it directly [...] often an aggressive wording is chosen [...] in general they have a very direct approach. (P39: 57)

Euphoric vs. conservative forecasting. Emotions are reported to impact the way forecasts are made. Southern cultures seem to be more euphoric in their forecasts while Northern cultures were reported to be more conservative. Those different styles need to be taken into account by the HQ managers. A top executive shares his experience:

> Some subsidiaries are very conservative in their forecasts and plan very conservatively. [...] Other subsidiaries – mostly **our Southern subsidiaries – are very enthusiastic in their forecasts**. [...] It's a subjective logic [...] In order to have realistic forecasts we need to think how the culture of the country is reflected in their estimation [...] **is it a very euphoric culture or a rather pessimistic one**. [...] We need to sort of reassess their forecasts with a human element. (P10: 46)

Southern/Balkan Mentality
A number of interviewees talked of a 'Balkan mentality' which is marked by a great liking for lengthy budget negotiations. An executive astutely described his experiences regarding budget negotiations with Southern European colleagues:

> [t]he **more Southern** we get the more we notice a Balkan mentality, [...] **the more they want to negotiate**. [...] Lengthy budget negotiations are a case in point. [...] They come up with 1001 reasons why they need more budget [...] they just love negotiating. [...] That's totally different in our Northern subsidiaries. (P4: 112)

'We are not being told by the Slovaks'
The transfer of employees between single subsidiaries in the East is found to be challenging since people of differing CEE nationalities do sometimes prefer not to cooperate. Some 13 percent of respondents point to the issue that managers of different Eastern European nationalities than the one of the host country are not easily accepted. While PCNs or Western third-country nationals are readily accepted in management positions this is not true for Eastern European third-country nationals. Mostly, historical reasons are thought to render explanations for that phenomenon. An executive vividly warns against underestimating the dynamics between single nationalities:

> I made an interesting experience by trying to use Slovak consultants in Hungary. [...] We had very successfully worked with Slovak consultants before when implementing our control system in the Slovak Republic. [...] Since those consultants also spoke Hungarian perfectly I thought I would be a good idea to have them facilitating the

implementation process of same system in Hungary. [...] After half a year, however, I had no choice but to exchange them with a Hungarian enterprise. [...] I was at a loss in trying to understand why the project failed [...] Months later a Hungarian explained that there are discrepancies between Slovaks and Hungarians based on historic reasons [...] **Hungarians won't be told what to do by Slovaks. Never.** [...] The Slovak consultants never had even the slightest chance [...] Nationality cannot be underestimated even if we think well we are all Central Europeans. [...] Nationalities and cultures need to be dealt with more care, that was our experience. (P1: 92)

Mentalities are important also in terms of appointing managers. What I'm saying here is not very 'quotable' but anyway, **if you appoint a Hungarian as a CEO in Rumania you are bound to encounter much more difficulties** [...] than e.g. appointing an Austrian. The same is true for Slovaks and Czechs [...] or having a Croatian working Serbia, etc. That's reality. (P15: 83)

Mentalities matter! [...] **Don't even think of sending a Moslem sales representative to a Serbian-orthodox client.** Or any other combination [...] Eastern Hungarians do not want to deal with people from Budapest. [...] It's crazy! (P27: 63)

Sending a Russian employee to Poland for training purposes or to work there is a delicate issue. [...] Polish and Russians simply do not go together. [...] Well Russians in general do not enjoy the best reputation in CEE [...] (P39: 83)

Such attitudes have a major impact on the intra-organizational transfer of knowledge and best practices. Nevertheless, a large percentage of MNCs are successful in establishing CEE-wide networks by sending trainees not only to the HQ but also in other subsidiaries for learning purposes.

Short-sleeved working style
Eastern European managers are reported to make decisions rather fast compared to PCNs who usually decide only after careful consideration. The rather low scores on future orientation of 3.37 among the Eastern European cluster might render an explanation for this lack of long-term planning in CEE. In comparison with the Germanic cluster there is a difference of 1.03 points in terms of future orientation. Those two management styles can also be perceived as mutually complementary:

> There is a rather **short-sleeved working style in CEE**, decisions are often made quick and dirty [...] we [HQ] tend to decide only after careful consideration. [...] At the moment we are striving for a happy medium from which both sides benefit. (P16: 48)

However, the downside of a rather improvised management style is less discipline in terms of timeliness and attention to detail:

> **It's a question of managerial discipline,** there are still some major deficiencies compared to Austrian standards. But we are slowly getting there. Still, managerial discipline needs to be improved. (P19: 48)

Time issues: deadlines are flexible
Respondents repeatedly complain that deadlines are often not observed and Eastern European subsidiary personnel have a relaxed view on time issues. Again, our findings are in line with prior research on time in Eastern Europe: As culture determines the conception of time, time is rather an idea than an object (Trompenaars et al., 2000). Different attitudes towards time can be explained by high scores in a synchronic or polychronic understanding of time of CEE nations. While Western nations including Austria and Germany have a monochronic or sequential understanding of time, many Eastern European nations have a polychronic or synchronic understanding of time (Fink & Meierewert, 2004b; Hall, 1959; Hall et al., 2000; Trompenaars et al., 2000). A monochronic time approach entails 'that time is conceived as a line of sequential events passing at regular intervals' (Trompenaars et al., 2000). Moving from A to B as straightforwardly as possible with minimal effort and maximum effect is defined as efficiency and impacts the business norms in Western Europe and the United States However, this concept is flawed as adhering to 'straight lines' might not always be the best way. The synchronic or polychronic approach, however, entails that people track and execute various tasks at a time or as Hall describes it, as the number of activities run in parallel (Hall, 1959). While sequential people tend to schedule everything very tightly, synchronic cultures are less insistent upon punctuality. Rather, a final goal can be reached by numerous and possibly interchangeable ways. Both, synchronic and polychronic styles are the source of many misunderstandings in international business (Fink et al., 2004b). Our data clearly supports those findings:

> **Time ticks differently in CEE.** To pursue a straight line to a certain target as seems logic for an Austrian brain is not common in Croatia, or Slovenia, or Hungary. Additionally, those nations even differ

among each other in their perception of time. [...] **There is a general attitude of 'relax, we'll do it somehow' [...] deadlines are not observed.** (P22: 78)

Not observing deadlines is common. [...] We need to permanently communicate our reporting deadlines [...] however, that a deadline is a deadline is still not understood everywhere. (P24: 88)

Lack of entrepreneurial spirit & risk avoidance
Customer orientation and competition were not an issue in the former monopoly situation (Bayer, 1996). Some 10 percent of interviewees indicate that they still perceive a lack of entrepreneurial spirit and initiative of Eastern European employees compared with their Western counterparts. The Globe scores for performance orientation differ by 0.70 between CEE and the Germanic cluster, pointing to a less pronounced performance orientation in CEE. However, these perception stands in sharp contrast to the enthusiasm and drive of the younger generation in CEE and the mentality perceived in the metropolitan areas.

Work mentality is different in CEE. [...] It takes time to get things done. [...] If people don't know how to progress **they rather stop working than taking initiative.** [...] that behavior is grounded in their past. [...] A Western European employee would not let things unfinished and wait till somebody addresses him [...] **Our Eastern European employees need to be reminded of their responsibilities and deadlines.** (P17: 62)

[w]e can only be profitable if **we spread our entrepreneurial spirit** to the last white-collar employee. [...] Therefore, people need some training to understand a P&L and to see his or her own personal benefit in it. [...] We need to spread that understanding and spirit in our CEE subsidiaries. [...] **Many people come from a culture where performance didn't matter** [...] we need to introduce performance oriented thinking and efficiency principles. [...] (P19: 76)

A general uncertainty and a tendency to hedge one's bet by asking for orders from the top was noted among CEE employees. Such behavior goes hand in hand with the authoritative management style and high status of top management discussed before. Furthermore, a certain lack of initiative and entrepreneurial spirit is mentioned repeatedly by the interviewees. Some managers feel that employees do not push enough and rather remain passive instead of taking initiative to improve things. As described by an executive:

> [t]hey need **close interaction and contact to their superiors**, and orders [...] I noted lots of uncertainty [among CEE employees] [...] they are **not very self-confident**. [...] Additionally, they usually try to hedge their bet by talking to superiors. That behavior is rooted in their past [...] if something has been discussed with a superior it's OK. Even our board members do that – except for the young ones. (P6: 87)

> [p]eople tend **to be extremely cautious when it comes to making autonomous decisions and deciding on their own** [...] **they are very insecure and procrastinating in discerning their responsibilities**. They asked me for advice twice rather than come to a decision on their own. [...] I got pretty impatient and told them to just go ahead. (P5: 99)

Again, the communist heritage renders possible explanations for example Pearce et al. (1994) noted a feeling of 'learned helplessness' in former communist countries. A paternalistic and authoritative management style was practiced in socialism, which did not foster entrepreneurial initiative (Bakacsi et al., 2002). A successful coping strategy for that sort of behavior is to give orders and carefully monitor how these orders are executed. That approach works best when being personally on the spot.

> **They appreciate direct contact and orders from superiors** because they are not very confident in decision making [...] They are not really fit in mastering all managerial skills yet. (P6: 86)

> **I just say what I want from them and give pretty detailed orders** [...] **later I control** if and how my orders were implemented [...] that works pretty well. (P29: 66)

Authoritarian leadership style
In some countries a very authoritarian leadership style is reported to be commonplace. If an expatriate or third-country national takes over, he needs to be aware of certain expectations regarding leadership styles. Employees do not expect too many degrees of freedom in their daily work and are used to being carefully monitored. Fink and Lehmann (2006) explain that people in socialism tried to never stick out and showed their official loyalty to superiors by executing their orders

carefully. Only under a seemingly untouched surface they undermined that system by close networking and sharing their important tacit knowledge only within their networks and never with their superiors. We found that expatriates who pursue a more participative management style can be perceived as not being serious about their orders if they fail to monitor the execution of them. A former subsidiary CEO describes his experiences:

> Let's compare an Austrian executive with a Czech executive: [...] Czech executives pursue an authoritarian leadership style and keep a check on everything. Austrian managers are perceived as somebody who assigns tasks and responsibilities but who fails to supervise and control their employees closely. That's weird for a Czech employee [...] he does not understand such a behavior. [...] Consequently, he does not execute given orders because he is not controlled and therefore lacks direct feedback. [...] All the more alien it seems to him that he is criticized from behind later on. [...] In fact there is huge underlying cultural misunderstanding. [...] The Austrian executive perceives his Czech employee as unreliable while the Czech employee perceives the Austrian executive as lacking leadership qualities. [...] Only looking at both sides enables us to get to the bottom of the misunderstanding. Both sides are caught in certain culturally based thinking patterns. (P2: 125)

> **Command structures are prevailing in CEE** [...] at least in some countries. Bulgarians and Serbians like straight orders. [...] Russians too, that's the order that's what we will do. Period. (P6: 97)

> My **experience is that Eastern European males** who come out of the post-communist era **are still coming from the old school** [...] their **behavior is anything but cooperative** [...] they are heavy-handed lacking any sort of tactfulness and are extremely authoritarian. (P43: 48)

However, as we will see later, a number of interviewees indicate that a mix of authoritarian and participative leadership elements work best for introducing HQ controls.

'Not in writing'
Scholars of corruption point out that both structural and cultural factors lead to higher levels of corruption (Klitgaard, 1987; Rose-Ackerman, 1978). Empirical research in this field mainly focuses on structural factors (Sandholtz et al., 2005). Few scholars (Lipset & Lenz, 1999;

Sandholtz & Gray, 2003; Treismann, 2000) empirically studied the effects of culture on corruption. 'Communism created structural incentives for engaging in corrupt behaviors, which became such a widespread fact of life that they became rooted in the culture of these societies – that is the social norms and practices prevailing in communist societies' (Sandholtz et al., 2005). The transition towards democracy and market economies could not leave those traditions behind but rather opened up new opportunities for corruption. Sandholtz and Taagepera (2005) found empirical evidence that reforming communist and post-communist countries experience higher levels of corruption than otherwise similar countries. Using Inglehart's (1997) value dimensions, Sandholtz and Taagepera (2005) show that a strong 'survival' orientation and a strong 'traditional' orientation are positively related with high levels of corruption. Post-communism and communism increased those levels even further both directly and by adding a higher emphasis on 'survival' values (Sandholtz et al., 2005). As culture does change only slowly, the authors suggest that post communist countries will have to deal with high levels of corruption for decades (Sandholtz et al., 2005). We refrain from labeling corruption as a cultural characteristic of CEE; nevertheless, our data suggests that it is at least grounded in the norms and behavior of people. Alternatively, the strong emphasis on personal relations in CEE might also render an explanation for 'corrupt' behavior, which might very well be a means of cultivating and fostering a strong personal network. In the words of an executive:

> People **are prone to arrange things among themselves preferably without written evidence.** [...] Personal contact and **cultivating relations is all-important** [...] I try to talk to all my managers on the phone at least once a week and see them in person at least once a month. (P6: 88)
>
> Having the **right connections and contact persons in CEE is core** [...] it is common practice that people expect 'gifts' [...] and you need to be able to hold your drink (P6: 88)

Hold authorities in high esteem and bureaucracy
A general phenomenon of CEE countries reported by our informants is that employees have a deep respect for local authorities. Russian accountants for example tend to be more loyal to the local tax authorities than to the corporation they work for. Apparently, the communist regime left its imprints on people's minds since they still closely obey

bureaucratic regulations. However creative people might be in findings ways of evading orders, our data clearly shows that some authorities – especially tax authorities – are not only held in high esteem but also impact the design of entire accounting systems. Respondents explained that accounting systems in private corporations are still primarily designed to satisfy authority regulations rather than providing essential business information for the firm. An executive explains:

> You cannot compare Russian accounting to our accounting or even international accounting standards. An accountant in **Russia are more loyal to local tax authorities** than to the corporation they work for, because if he does not act a 100% according to the Russian laws he sails close to the wind. According to the law a Russian accountant has almost the same responsibility as a CEO. If something goes wrong not only the CEO but also the accountant goes to jail. [...] Try to teach such an accountant who has lived up to those standards for 20 years to use group-reporting standards. (P3: 69)

> When I started here in 1998 I was stunned [...] **terms like 'depreciation' or 'provision' were alien to them**. All they had were tax statements. Everything they did was targeted towards the tax authorities [...] corporate reporting was not an issue. (P20: 62)

Additionally, locals are reported to somehow fear authorities and adhere closely to official governmental regulations. Although those findings might appear to conflict the nifty attempts of avoiding orders from above as discussed before, they might very well just round off the picture: By an unquestioning and scrupulous adherence to official requirements and orders – which can be influenced by the organization anyway – attention might be drawn away from other undertakings. In the following, some executives share their experiences on that point:

> Poles are complicated in a lot of ways and **extremely anxious about everything which has to do with tax rules or authorities in general**. They are virtually scared when it comes to dealing with authorities. (P20: 76)

> [t]hat **exaggerated communistic respect towards authorities is still there**. [...] Nobody questions authorities [...] they don't dare to voice protest or even the slightest harmless critique on authorities. [...] Nobody in Western Europe would deal with authorities like that. (P29: 71)

Western companies have lots of money – they'll take liberties with it
Our interviewees note that Western MNCs are often perceived as financially sound and are therefore regarded as taking liberties in terms of finances. In the words of a former subsidiary CEO who is now working for the HQ:

> If a Western MNC enters the market we noted a general attitude à la **Well those guys have plenty of money – they'll take liberties with it**. [...] It's crucial to establish a stringent regime from the very beginning to counteract such attitudes. (P1: 110)

Working woman – more gender egalitarianism
Our data shows, that women are more easily accepted in the workplace and in top-management positions in CEE than in Western nations. In communist times women were treated very egalitarian and that acceptance seems to prevail. Our findings are in line with the literature: With a score 3.84 out of 7, the Globe study (House et al., 2004) found rather egalitarian ratings for the Eastern European cluster. Two female executives describe their experiences:

> When I took the job as the CEO of our Slovak subsidiary **I was fully accepted as the boss from the very beginning**. [...] In Austria I had to put up a fight all the time to be accepted. In CEE a female boss was considered to be normal. (P23: 10)

> There are **clearly less troubles in being accepted in a top-management position [as a woman] in CEE as compared to Western nations**. [...] Women in top positions were taken for granted [...] Our Slovenian subsidiary, e.g., is run by a woman. (P9: 56)

Interestingly, some MNCs even prefer to employ women in top positions since they found their female CEE managers to be more successful and diplomatic in business interactions. In the words of a male HQ executive:

> I made the experience that **males in CEE act rather authoritarian** [...] they lack tactfulness and cooperativeness. [...] We had a Russian CEO in our subsidiary who failed badly. [...] After we exchanged him with a woman sales soared within no time. [...] Interacting with Eastern European males I noticed that they are personally offended if they fail to put their ideas through [...] women are much more diplomatic [...] that's why more than half of our CEE subsidiaries are

run by women [...] **we consciously prefer to employ woman because they achieve better results.** (P43: 47)

7.4.2 Moderators

Factors having a moderating effect on the perceived risk of cultural differences were identified on both the organizational level and on the individual level (Figure 7.23). In the following all moderators are discussed in some detail.

7.4.2.1 Moderators on the organizational level

The following moderators are identified as having a moderating effect on the perceived risk of cultural differences: Intense Communication and direct personal contact, knowledge transfer, a participative but assertive management style, the assignment of clear responsibilities, a servicing attitude of the HQ, support from subsidiary top management, trust-building efforts, the use of a clear control jargon, the establishment of local linkages, some degree of adaptation, and taking time. Figure 7.23 indicates the percentage of interviewees who mentioned single moderators. Clearly, intense communication and personal contact are most important in CEE subsidiary management, mentioned by an overwhelming 93 percent of respondents.

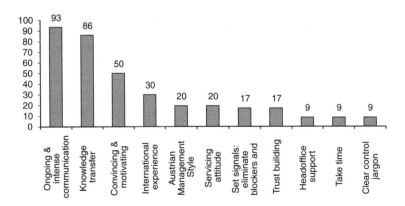

Figure 7.23 Moderators on the perceived risk attributed to cultural differences on the organizational level.

Source: Data analysis.

Intense personal contact and communication. Ongoing and intense communication between the parent and the subsidiary is crucial for effectively dealing with CEE subsidiaries. 43 out of 46 interviewees underline that being personally on the spot at regular intervals is of utmost importance. The higher the frequency of communication and the extent of personal contact between HQ and subsidiary personnel the better are the parent–subsidiary relations. Good relations between the HQ and the subsidiary in turn provide the ground for effective managerial control by the HQ. The following quotations of our interviewees illustrate the salience placed on intense personal interaction:

> Personal contact is immensely important in CEE. [...] If you rely exclusively on output control you will fail badly. [...] Face-to-face interaction is crucial [...] vital information can only be gathered in time via personal interactions. [...] I need to see every subsidiary at least once a month. Statistically spoken I spend most of my time in the plane [...] but that effort pays off. (P14: 70)
>
> **Personal contact** is the most important thing. [...] Given that we all have different mother tongues and are rooted in different cultures misunderstandings are pre-assigned. [...] **The probability for misunderstandings is enhanced given that often two persons communicate in their second language.** [...] Such interactions require lots of patience on both sides and regular checkups if we are both still talking about the same thing. (P16: 114)
>
> **Without personal interaction nothing goes.** There is not a single controller out there who I do not see at least once a month. (P31: 52)
>
> Personal contact rules [...] You cannot manage effectively by simply giving order [laughs] there is much more to effective management [...] and **face-to-face interaction is crucial in CEE.** (P15: 78)

A high intensity of communication and personal interactions lays the foundation for trust building.

Trust building

> Interpersonal and inter-organizational trust have been widely cited as important components of economics exchanges. However, rarely have these concepts been measured and their implications examined.
>
> J. B. Barney on Zaheer (1998)

Given the importance placed on personal relations in CEE and the blurred borders of personal and professional spheres in diffuse cultures, building trust is essential. Trust building requires an intense communication between the HQ and the subsidiary and a great deal of personal interaction between HQ and subsidiary personnel. The following quotations underscore the role of trust in management control:

> We control our subsidiaries centrally from our HQ in Vienna [...] in order to make sure that the subsidiaries act according to our intentions we have person designated and responsible for each country here at the HQ. Those persons are confidants for the subsidiaries. [...] They **need to establish a high degree of mutual trust between themselves and the subsidiaries. That's of utmost importance.** (P4: 63)

> We take **our time and strive to look after our subsidiaries personally. That's vital for trust building.** If **I have persons here at the HQ who permanently interact with the subsidiaries** I can build trust and I have immediate access to all the information. The communication and information flow between us [HQ] and our subsidiaries is excellent. (P4: 81)

> **Soft and tacit information can only be accessed based on mutual trust.** Trust needs to be built up carefully and must never be abused. It's like fostering and cultivating a plant [...] someday it's big and that's very important to us. (P24: 67)

Figure 7.24 below shows a network view on how trust is established and which factors influence the creation of trust. It displays how trust adds to group-wide transparency and relates to personnel policy and personal control mechanisms.

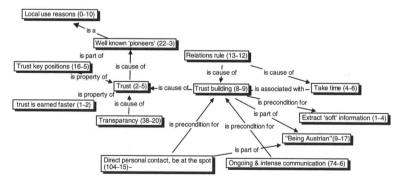

Figure 7.24 Network view on trust building.
Source: Data analysis.

Trust building takes time. However, the time invested is well spent, since trust provides a basis for a sound long-term headquarter–subsidiary relationship. In the words of an executive:

> In the beginning, Czechs are very suspicious towards foreigners. [...] If you succeed to win their trust, however, you can rely on them a 100% and they become some sort of friends. Frankly spoken I had my most loyal employees in the Czech Republic. It only takes longer to win their trust. (P2: 114)

Once a trust based relationship is developed the quality and intensity of information flows between the HQ and the subsidiary is greatly improved, since also 'soft' information is passed on. Thus, trust prepares the ground for transparency and effective knowledge exchange. As one executive explicates:

> You can only learn that much from figures [...] sometimes the crucial information cannot be displayed and is of more 'subtle' nature. [...] You can only extract that information in a personal encounter. [...] Such information can only be accessed based on mutual trust. (P4: 65)

> **Going out with the subsidiary managers and creating mutual trust is important.** You need to spread the message that we are all in the same boat, we are friends [...] informal personal encounters lay the ground for trust building. (P38: 72)

Moreover, since key positions are mostly awarded to people who have been proven reliable and trustworthy, trust is a major a criterion for selecting managers. As PCNs are usually better known by the HQ they are often awarded key offshore positions. However, if local managers are appointed for key positions, our data clearly shows that they are usually well-known and had been working for the MNCs for a while. Thus, they have proven to be reliable and loyal and enjoy the HQ confidence. A CEO explains:

> Basically we appoint key positions to whom we trust the most. (P11: 49)

> We always have host-country nationals in charge of our profit centers. **As a general rule the first employee we recruited in a country eight or ten years ago is now in charge of the profit center.** [...] Most of our local CEOs or board members have been with us from the very beginning. (P5: 55)

Knowledge transfer
There is a growing recognition of the importance of knowledge generation and transfer knowledge as a source of competitive advantage in MNCs (e.g., Dixon, 2000; Gupta et al., 1991; Takeuchi & Nonaka, 2004). With 58 quotations underscoring the crucial role of knowledge transfer for effective subsidiary management our data clearly supports those findings. Figure 7.25 gives an overview on relations established on knowledge transfer based on the data.

Knowledge transfer basically means that HQ knowledge is transferred to CEE subsidiaries. Not only specific knowledge about the HQ and its way of doing business is transferred, but also best practices are spread. Some 18 percent of MNCs strive to spread best practices group-wide:

> **Being a large internationally operating group we try to create synergies by spreading 'best-practices' identified in one country to other countries.** At the same time we have to take into account that very few markets are comparable. (P10: 106)

According to our data, knowledge transfer is caused by both a general lack of understanding of management control in CEE, and the need to transfer prior international experience within the MNC. More than

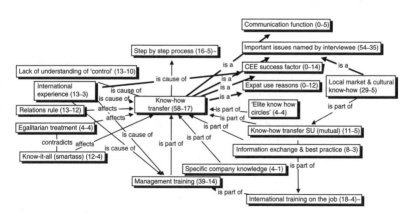

Figure 7.25 Network view on knowledge transfer.
Source: Data analysis.

30 percent of the interviewees vividly state that international experience must be passed on:

> Every acquisition adds to our learning experience [...] and we try to document what went well and in which areas we need to improve [...] which processes should be used for future acquisitions and which processes need to be changed [...] we are about to put together a standardized procedure [...] In addition, we also pass on personal impressions of the acquisition but this is done rather informally, e.g. at the coffee break. (P31: 79)

Another executive explains how a general lack of understanding of Western management control concepts triggers knowledge exchange:

> A major challenge was to establish understanding for the difference between accounting and management control because people thought accounting alone does the trick. (P1: 79)

Although most companies attempt to share knowledge on all levels of hierarchy, Japanese MNCs tend to exchange crucial knowledge via elite know-how circles.

> We have different layers of communication channels: Japanese channels and 'non-Japanese' channels [...] The key persons are communicating in Japanese and others are communicating in English [...] **the Japanese channels have access to more information than others.** (P17: 80)

Additionally, an increasing number of companies stress that rather than focusing exclusively on top-down transfer of HQ knowledge to subsidiaries, they foster a mutual knowledge transfer by accessing subsidiary knowledge and transferring it to the HQ.

> Mutual knowledge exchange is fostered. Sometimes exchanging different points of view helps adding value. (P17: 81)

> People from different cultural environments **gave our organizational culture new impulses.** (P37: 65)

> Locals [people from CEE] are experts on their culture and how to do business there. We appreciate that expertise. [...] At the same time they can learn from us [...] If both sides appreciate and values the knowledge of the other side learning takes place and we are both better off. (P16: 113)

Management training and the use of inpatriates are also used as knowledge transfer channels. Given the great importance placed on personal contacts and relations in CEE, expatriates and training are very effective means of knowledge transfer mentioned by 75 percent of interviewees. As already discussed at length, know-how transfer is an important function of communication and a major driver for using expatriates in CEE subsidiaries. Moreover, know-how transfer is perceived as a success factor in CEE and is ranked as a very important issue by the interviewees.

> Employing expatriates enables us to keep knowledge within the MNC. **We actively seek to transfer knowledge within the whole region.** (P26: 45)

Egalitarian treatment of CEE subsidiaries facilitates knowledge transfer. Along those lines, a know-it-all approach is found to be a major barrier for knowledge transfer indicated by 30 percent of interviewees. The pitfalls of a know-it-all approach as explicated by executives:

> If you go to a country [...] with a know-it-all approach you are doomed to fail. With such an attitude you better stay at home. (P1: 161)
>
> **What I can't stand is people going abroad thinking 'I'm the Western smartass, I come from Vienna, I know-it-all and you guys know** nothing' [...] that does not work at all. (P5: 97)
>
> A major pitfall is to appear as a know-it-all [...] Rather, you need to give your counterpart the impression that his knowledge is valuable and that he is important. (P43: 67)

Knowledge transfer takes time. Therefore, management knowledge on control systems should be carefully introduced step by step rather than at a single blow. Often organizational learning for the whole group is enticed by transferring control systems into CEE subsidiaries. In the words of a CEO:

> **You cannot dictate managerial control.** [...] Of course we could have stepped into our new subsidiary four years ago and try to dictate structures no matter if they fit or not. [...] **Today, however, we know that the control system we are using at the HQ here in Vienna is not ideal in every aspect.** Additionally, dictating terms de-motivates peoples [...] Looking back we have learned a great deal watching them designing the MCS within the degrees of freedom we granted. [...] Now, after five years of dealing with new subsidiaries and learning from them we are ready to design a common standard for new entities. [...] **We underwent an incredible learning experience.** (P12: 95)

Some 17 percent of interviewees outlined that it is important to transfer insights from prior international experiences and pitfalls of intercultural interactions within the MNC. Although most MNCs do not have institutionalized cross-cultural training programs, knowledge is transferred informally between employees. Often, information exchange is initiated by expatriates. The following quotations outline the salience of knowledge transfer:

> Intercultural experiences are passed on rather informally and unstructured. [...] **Passing it on to new colleagues is important.** (P1: 96)
>
> The exchange of experience was initiated by former expatriates. We institutionalized a regulars' table and met once a month to mutually exchange our experiences. **Talking about pitfalls and different ways of handling things helps.** (P2: 21)
>
> I've accumulated quite some experience in CEE and **I'm trying to pass it on to our youngsters.** [...] If people see that some strategies in dealing with people were successful they need not much convincing [...]. (P25: 77)

International experience
Prior international experience of parents is reported to greatly improve the effectiveness of transferring management practices and management control to CEE subsidiaries. Although most companies do transfer their accumulated experience rather informally and not in a systematic way, interviewees mention quite often that prior international experience has a moderating effect on managing and controlling CEE subsidiaries. As one executive explicates:

> Expanding Eastward is a lot easier now that we can build on our prior experience. (P6: 105)
>
> We have subsidiaries in every CEE country now [...] **naturally we learned from the sum of experiences.** By now we can look back on a decade of experiences how to do business in CEE. [...] Having people with a lot of **'Eastern' expertise and drawing on a huge pool of knowledge is beneficial.** At the same time, however, every new country is a new challenge. (P16: 107)
>
> We learned a great deal in CEE. Actually we still do. It's a process. (P38: 28)
>
> I would say we already agglomerated some expertise in CEE, however, every acquisition presents new challenges to us. [...] **Undoubtedly we developed some sensitivity for appropriate**

behavior and a general susceptibility to cultural issues. [...] we learned how to deal effectively with local authorities and how to lobby [...] Regarding 'soft facts' we have a great deal of experience. (P40: 64)

Participative management style
A participative but assertive management style comprises the following sub-codes: Convincing, motivating and involving people, setting signals, assigning clear responsibilities, a servicing attitude, and taking time. This participative management style has a moderating effect on perceived cultural differences by the interviewees. Furthermore, some interviewees identify a certain 'Austrian' management style which comprises all elements of the participative management style and some additional aspects such as egalitarian treatment, diplomatic communication, a proneness to compromise and fostering personal relationships. Also, a general cultural proximity to the East was perceived to be beneficial for Austrian managers in CEE. In the following the single elements of a participative management style are discussed in some detail:

Convincing, motivating & involving people. 'If you want your people to build a ship, teach them the longing for the sea', an executive borrowed Saint-Exupery's famous words in the course of an interview. Some 50 percent of respondents underpinned the importance to convince and motivate people in CEE subsidiaries. Only highly motivated and devoted employees will achieve optimal results. Given the history of taking and receiving centrally planned orders during communism interviewees agree that it is all the more crucial to create perspectives and to foster goal commitment on a personal level. Executives report that once people experience that they benefit personally by achieving organizational goals the whole work ethic changes. Some selected insights from executives:

> If I can motivate my employees they will implement orders no matter if it is a large or a small subsidiary. **It's decisive to convince people to do something [...] once they are convinced they'll do it [...]** that involves providing perspectives for people. [...] it's important that people can identify with what they do. (P2: 61)

> People – no matter which nationality they belong to – **are much more motivated to do something if they understand the rationale behind a measure.** [...] I tell me people to not go out in the

subsidiaries 'as the HQ'. That's wrong. You cannot compel obedience just because you are coming from the HQ! I tell my people that they need to be consultants not enforcers. (P13: 81)

You simply need to produce followers [...] if people are convinced of something they'll follow you automatically [...] that's why we need to explain, motivate and convince our employees and CEE managers. (P15: 89)

In line with convincing and motivating it is important to involve people in a change process. Executives repeatedly outline that if people are given the chance to have a say and contribute their ideas to HQ concepts, more or less the same concepts as originally intended by the HQ are produced by a joint decision making process. By doing so, an understanding for the necessity of certain measures is created and people can identify themselves with the concepts and are committed to the objectives. An executive describes how it works:

You need to **involve people in the decision making process rather than showing up with readymade concepts**. [...] We invited the key players to Austria to show them how we work and then jointly discussed how we could improve things in the Czech subsidiary. [...] **If people have a chance to bring in and discuss their own ideas** [...] **you will see that you'll finally get to the same solution as you originally intended**. [...] But people can identify themselves with it. (P2: 86)

Trying to force ideas to people is a mistake [...] convincing people by jointly working on concepts works much better. (P3: 70)

Set signals: Eliminate blockers and praise followers!. An absolute necessity for operating successfully in CEE is to set signals both positive and negative ones. Given that people sometimes resort to strategies which were proven very effective in communist times such as finding thousands of reasons why something does not work in a specific context or simply agreeing to orders but not executing them, HQ need to be very assertive in proving that such behavioral patterns do not work. Two former subsidiary CEOs explain:

You need to be pretty consequent each change management process is met by **people trying to obstruct changes. Those people need to be identified and fired.** You need to set signals – both positive and negative ones; positive ones by praising followers and negative ones by dismissing blockers. [...] That is very important because **otherwise they won't take you serious** [...] they would just think they survive their new owners just as they survived under communism. (P2: 90)

[w]e need to be outspoken when they make a mistake. The carrot and the stick are important tools [...] they need to be directed back to earth from time to time. (P27: 82)

Assignment of clear responsibilities and competencies. Assigning clear responsibilities and competencies proved to be a successful coping strategy in dealing with CEE employees. Especially when confronted with nifty ways of avoiding orders as outlined above, such as presenting a legion of causes why something does not work, assigning clear responsibilities combined with some degree of assertiveness is found to be very helpful. Basically, this approach is similar to the cadre building in Soviet times (Fink et al., 2006). As explained by an executive:

We need to keep minutes for almost everything. [...] Responsibilities need to be clearly assigned and sometimes even consequences for failing of keeping deadlines need to be communicated repeatedly in advance. [...] a little information on what happens if things are not done in a certain way and at a certain time works miracles sometimes. (P2: 42)

Servicing attitude. For an effective and smooth management control in CEE subsidiaries HQ control units should ideally be perceived as a service provider for subsidiaries. If the subsidiary management and personnel perceive parent controllers as 'helpers' and not as dictators, barriers and negative attitudes towards HQ control can be overcome. Consequently, HQ executives caution their people of playing the HQ card:

I tell my people to not go into the subsidiaries with the mentality of 'being the HQ'. That's doomed to fail. You cannot compel obedience just because you are coming from the HQ! I tell my people that they need to be consultants not enforcers. [...] People **in the subsidiaries should perceive us as service providers** who contribute to their success. (P13: 82)

The image of a 'controller' changed over the years [...] rather than being grey boring eminences we understand ourselves as service providers. And service means helping. **Once our CEE subsidiaries perceive us as helpers it works.** (P3: 75)

> Our success in Eastern Europe is based on our **partnership principle** [...] We try to bring them new skills and help them exploring new management and reporting instruments. [...] **We want people to perceive us as somebody who makes them acquainted with new stuff from which they will benefit it in the long run.** (P25: 63)

Take time. Although the implementation of control often takes place rapidly, some time should be taken to give people a chance to get used to the novel tools and provide optimal support for learning. An MNC's head of corporate control explains:

> We need to **make sure to grant enough time for people to get acquainted with new management control instruments and ratios** in order to use them correctly. It is our responsibility that people understand the relevancy of certain ratios correctly otherwise we set the wrong signals. (P7: 108)

> We are extremely cautious and slow in implementing new systems. (P17: 46)

'Austrian' Management Style. A recurring theme during the interviews arose on the issue of what makes Austrians successful in CEE. Given that Austria is used as a hub for CEE by many MNCs, and given our data, this question seems worthwhile to explore. An executive put it in a nutshell:

> Given our German international HQ I noted that we [Austrians] do have some advantages in dealing with Eastern Europeans vis-à-vis our German colleagues, based on our attitude and emotionality. [...] Germans are often perceived as smartasses who like playing the know-it-all card [...] we [Austrians] did not encounter such difficulties as much [...] Maybe it is due to our shared history [...] Maybe it is because we are more prone to compromise and involve them [CEE people] in the decision making. I don't know [...] it might be in our genes. (P1: 99)

> Our strength in dealing with our CEE subsidiaries as compared to our German parent is that **we take our time and take care of the people personally** which is very important in CEE. That's how we build long-term relations and trust. (P4: 82)

Apart from the successful participative management style as identified above, interviewees found that there is something about Austrian mentality and leadership style which makes Austrians more successful in CEE than other nationalities. Although we did not specifically ask

Empirical Results 221

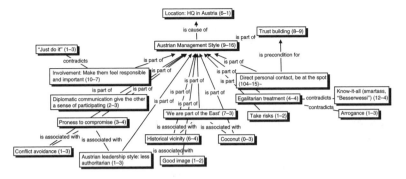

Figure 7.26 Austrian management style.
Source: Data analysis.

for it, we can identify the following specifics of an Austrian management style in CEE subsidiaries based on our data.

In a nutshell, an 'Austrian management/leadership style' can be described as a participative but nevertheless assertive leadership style (see Figure 7.26). It comprises the following elements: egalitarian treatment, diplomatic communication, a proneness to compromise, involvement of subordinates, a proneness to take risks and fostering personal relationships. Furthermore, a general cultural proximity to the East was noted based on a common history. In the following, the single elements of an 'Austrian' leadership style are discussed in some detail.

Egalitarian treatment. Going into CEE with a 'know-it-all' attitude is considered as a major cultural pitfall by many interviewees. Some respondents note that it is vital to treat people in CEE as equals and never appear as the 'Western smartass' who knows everything better. In the words of an executive:

> Our export manager is a Viennese of the old school. [...] He is charming and polite to everybody [...] and people from [**CEE appreciate it that there is a person who treats them as equals.**] (P28: 91)

We found that it seems crucial to hold existing knowledge of Eastern Managers in high esteem and not impart that their knowledge is not valuable. These findings are in line with prior research for example Turner (1994). As an executive explains:

> A major pitfall is to appear as a know-it-all [...] Rather, you need to give your counterpart the impression that his knowledge is valuable and that he is important. (P43: 67)

We never use a 'we know everything better and you know nothing' approach. **We treat our CEE colleagues as equals and try to jointly come up with solutions.** That does not imply that we have no rules and regulations. Some things are standardized and have to be adhered to, but we communicate why. (P33: 93)

A quarter of the interviewees mention that their German colleges met more resistance in their approach of trying to strictly implement plans one-to-one. As a consequence, many Germans are perceived as arrogant in CEE. As a matter of fact a number of German HQ moved their regional CEE HQ to Austria. As some executives explain:

Germans are often perceived as arrogant in CEE, I think that's why we [Austrians] are more successful in CEE than our German colleagues. (P28: 94)

Germans and Austrians differ in terms of cosmopolitanism. [...] **Many Germans – I have observed that myself pretty often – just show that they are Germans and act like 'masters' [...] which is not appreciated in CEE.** (P28: 90)

Diplomatic communication. Our study shows that Austrians make use of an indirect and diplomatic communication style. Prior research for example Brück (1999; 2002) also found that Austrians are clearly more indirect communicators and a more diffuse culture as compared to Germans or Swiss. As one executive put it:

Maybe we [Austrians] are more diplomatic communicators. [...] We do not run straight to one point, rather we sometimes take twists and turns. [...] Maybe we just give our counterparts the feeling that they can also have a say. That doesn't mean that by doing so we lose sight of our goal. [...] That might be more time-consuming than simply setting targets but it seems far more effective to achieve our goals. (P1: 105)

Diplomacy and lots and lots of communication are important. (P3: 74)

Proneness to compromise and learn. Along the lines of a more indirect communication style, the Austrian management style is characterized by willingness to compromise instead of forcing it by any means necessary. That way the parent not only reaches its goals and gains acceptance for it, but also learns and improves its own practices. As explained by an executive:

> We might turn and twist in the face of obstacles, and pursue a more indirect path, but during our detours we learn important things for the group as a whole. Germans, e.g., would not deviate from their path, and thereby miss out on learning opportunities. We on the other hand learn something, and next time we already know about it. [...] I think our way is the better one. (P10: 94)

> **We are simply more prone to compromise and to involve others in decision making.** In addition, we are open for different ways to achieve a goal. (P1: 99)

Involvement: Make people feel responsible and important. Apart from indirect communication and proneness to compromise, the Austrian management style involves people in decision making and gives them a feeling of importance. Executives reported that if people are given the chance to have a say and contribute their ideas to HQ concepts more or less the same concepts as originally intended came out of the joint decision making process. By doing so, however, understanding for the necessity of certain measures is created and people can identify themselves with the concepts and are more easily committed to the objectives. As one CEO explains:

> You need to involve people in the decision making process rather than showing up with readymade concepts. [...] We invited the key players to Austria to show them how we work and then jointly discussed how we could improve things in the Czech subsidiary. [...] **If people have a chance to bring in and discuss their own ideas [...] you will see that you'll finally get to the same solution as you originally intended.** [...] But people can identify themselves with it. (P2: 86)

> It is difficult to appreciate the national specifics of each country individually and to try not to force our ideas on our subsidiaries but **to realize ideas jointly by convincing, involving and motivating people**. (P3: 69)

> Every change process is difficult. [...] but it is even more difficult if people do not understand the rationale behind the change. People constantly questioned the necessity of the change. [...] Every change causes stress and friction [...] but we got better every time [...] after

the third time everything went smoothly and we had created a new standard process. (P35: 61)

Involving people and delegating responsibilities must not be confused with laissez-faire, as it still comprises some guidance and leadership by the parent. An American 'just do it' approach is reported to fail badly in CEE:

> I worked jointly with American colleagues in CEE [...] Americans come with a 'just-do-it' approach and do not go in a lot of detail. [...] that approach often triggered conflicts between Americans and Czechs because basically they were just the opposite. Austrians are somewhere in between those two extremes. (P2: 113)

Take risks. Instead of overanalyzing, Austrian managers take some risk to try out new ideas, which fits in well with a more short-sleeved working style in CEE. An executive explains:

> We **just start working while our German HQ ponders for ages if that is the right approach or not.** That way ideas slowly peter out. [...] We take more risks; that's why we were heaps faster and more successful in CEE. Naturally sometimes we failed but overall it worked out. (P4: 109)

Foster personal relations. In contrast to other nations, Austrian based CEE HQ emphasizes ongoing direct personal interaction with their subsidiaries. Measures involve PCNs being personally at the subsidiaries on a regular basis and subsidiary personnel being brought to the HQ for training purposes. Valuing personal relations fosters trust building and knowledge transfer.

> My people need to be directly on the spot [at the subsidiaries] at least once a month. **Our people need to go out with them and establish close personal ties.** That way they can extract vital information and get the whole picture [...] alternatively, we also bring in people from the subsidiaries to us. (P4: 66)
>
> **We take our time and strive to look after our subsidiaries personally.** That's vital for trust building. If I have persons here at the HQ who always in touch with the subsidiaries I can build up trust and I have immediate access to all the information. The

communication and information flow between us [HQ] and our subsidiaries is excellent. (P4: 81)

Cultural proximity: 'We are part of the East'. Maybe one explanation why Austrians are successful in CEE lies pure and simple in the relative cultural proximity of Austrians and their CEE neighbors as compared to their other Western European counterparts. Therefore, cultural effectiveness might be a function of cultural distance. The Austrian somewhat laid back and unhurried mentality accommodates Eastern cultures pretty well. Interestingly, executives are aware of the 'closeness' of the Austrian culture to Eastern Europe:

> I rather not say historical roots because I rather let the emperor Franz Joseph rest [laughs]. I think it's just the fact that Prague is located more Western than Vienna. **The main reason why we deal with Eastern Europeans pretty well is that we are part of the East, even if we disavow that sometimes.** (P6: 82)
>
> It's a question of mentality. **Our engineering people are in tune with the Czechs [...] on the Christmas party they all dance Polka, Germans would be way too stiff for that. [...] There is some sort of connection between Austria and the East. Austrians are simply closer to the East than other nations.** (P24: 86)
>
> I'm sure that other nations, such as England, who never had a tradition in CEE, cannot operate there successfully. They are simply lacking to understand those cultures. [...] **I'm sure Austrians do have an advantage because we share a common history which is still somehow present there. [...] It's not hard for an Austrian to be accepted there and the cultures somehow match with the Austrian touch.** That's my experience. (P25: 59)

Cultural proximity of Austrians and Eastern Europeans can also be documented by prior research: Austrians and Eastern Europeans both seem to belong to the G-type or diffuse (Lewin, 1936; Trompenaars et al., 2000) cultures which are marked by a large private and a rather small public space. As outlined by an executive:

> We perceive Americans as superficial while Americans perceive us as coconuts and themselves as peaches. Peaches because one gets pretty far for some time and then nothing goes once you hit the stone. Coconuts, on the other hand, are very hard to penetrate due to their hard paring, but once you are through you can get to the stone pretty

easily. **It's the same with the Czechs, only that their paring is even harder than ours. But once you are through everything is fine.** (P2: 117)

Less cultural distance between Austrians and Eastern Europeans in comparison to other Western European nations in terms of mentality was noted among executives. Some even traced the ability to deal effectively with CEE cultures back to a common history of Austrians and CEE. A common history, however ancient, seems to have a positive impact on cultural distance and creates some basis for understanding. In the words of an executive:

We are a large MNC and there are plenty of attractive regions, such as Singapore, the U.S. and South Africa, where key managers are dying to go to. [...] **We [Austrians] have always been keen to go to Eastern Europe, maybe due to historical reasons, and we were the only ones who liked going there. Sure, we have a lot of experience with our Eastern neighbors and we also have a lot of prejudices, which we like to cultivate.** [...] But you need to go there to see if those stereotypes and prejudice are true or not. (P10: 73)

Furthermore, Austrians are reported to have a good image in most CEE regions:

In sum I can say we work together very well despite of all the differences. E.g. in Southern Poland people are very Austrian minded based on the history [...] interestingly we still have a very good image there [...] Additionally, I think we have an advantage in terms of mentality compared to Germans or Swiss, despite all differences. (P16: 52)

In a nutshell, egalitarian treatment of fellow CEE employees, a diplomatic communication style, a certain proneness to compromise and making sure that CEE managers are involved in the decision making and an emphasis on personal relations evidently work well in CEE. Therefore we conclude, that a sound understanding about cultural differences and the historic background of management styles and behavior is essential for effectively managing and transferring control and management know-how into CEE (Bayer, 1996). Also, the effectiveness and selection of expatriate managers may be based on how strongly their leadership styles overlap with predominant leadership styles in the target country (Brodbeck et al., 2000; Szabo & Reber, 2001). The cultural proximity of Austrians and their CEE neighbors might make them more effective as expatriate managers than for example their German counterparts.

Support from the top. Backup and commitment from the top management is essential for implementing management control and keeping a control system running. Essentially, control prepares the ground for top-management decision making and it can only function if enforced by the top management. Given the power status of top management in CEE, support from the top is essential for smooth control structures. Two executives explicate:

> The most important thing is **that we are supported by the board, not just the CFO, but the whole board**. Therefore, we as controllers need to be well-connected and on good speaking terms with all board members. (P9: 19)
>
> Support from our CFO and the whole board actually is crucial – because these people are the ones working with our data [...] controlling per se is no end in itself. If nobody works with our drudgingly collected data we could as well have no management control at all. (P12: 67)

Social butterflies. As already described at length before, expatriates acting as 'social butterflies' can reduce the friction caused by cultural distance and are therefore classified as moderators.

Establish a clear control jargon. Control and Management terms are not necessarily understood correctly in CEE and should therefore be handled with care. Not only language itself is a barrier but also the lack of understanding for underlying management theories. Therefore, an increasing number of companies establish glossaries of managerial terminology to leave no room for misunderstandings and varied interpretations. Doing so prepares the ground for standardization. In the words of a CFO:

> When I started here in 1998 I was stunned [...] **terms like 'depreciation' or 'provision' were alien to them**. All they had were tax statements. Everything they did was targeted towards the tax authorities [...] corporate reporting was not an issue. [...] we needed to introduce new concepts [...] We started to create an English

accounting manual, it's actually a glossary where all terms are listed and explained in detail [...] including how to book them. Any changes in and amendments to our manual are presented in meetings and jointly discussed. [...] We make sure that everybody understands them. (P20: 60)

It is important to be clear on the meaning of certain terms. An interaction between marketing and controlling persons in Austria is already challenging [...] communicating in different languages adds to complexity. At some point we need to start translating our controlling jargon into Czech and Russian. (P23: 55)

7.4.2.2 Moderators on the individual level

On the individual level, language abilities, personality traits, cultural sensitivity, and prior international experience of the interacting person are found to have a moderating effect on cultural differences. Personal international experience is mentioned by 22 percent of the interviewees, language capabilities are mentioned by 26 percent of the interviewees and personality traits are mentioned by 43 percent of the interviewees.

Personality traits. Some 43 percent of the interviewees indicated that the effectiveness of dealing with foreign cultures depends on the personality and attitude of the interacting person. The more open, and tolerant, and socially competent that person is, the more effective he or she is in dealing with other cultures. In the words of interviewed managers:

People who are sent abroad need a certain attitude of openness and tolerance to accept that there are differences and that he or she needs to adapt to those differences. (P1: 98)

It always depends on the person. Some people who have been abroad for 10 years still don't know how it works and others learn it within a year. [...] It all comes down to personality [...] an openness and willingness to accept different mentalities and to learn. (P2: 45)

[i]t all depends on how people interact with others and how their behavior and personality is perceived by others. I think an effective controller in CEE needs to accept different mentalities and needs to be ready to intensively spar with people and develop long term personal relation with them. (P36: 7)

It depends on the personality of the people. Some get on very well with our Eastern employees and some just don't. (P31: 45)

Cultural sensitivity. Some cultural sensitivity is needed to identify and become aware of differences and to develop strategies of effectively coping with those. Without a certain susceptibility to differences, foreign subsidiaries cannot be integrated successfully since management practices cannot necessarily be implemented one-to-one. Evidently, the ability to deal effectively with cultural differences can be learned during a foreign assignment. However, whether or not a learning process takes place depends largely on the personality and attitude of the expatriate. Learning might be accelerated in case of prior international exposure. In the words of the executives:

> It is **necessary to deal with different nationalities sensitively.** It is naïve to think that one can just go there and do stuff. Effectively pressing ahead things takes time, lots of time. [...] **Different nationalities and cultures need not be underestimated, even if some people say, well we are all Central Europeans. From my experience, culture has a greater impact than one might expect.** [...] Some of our expatriates did not understand that and failed badly. Others learned very fast [...] It is a learning experience. (P1: 93)

> **It is not possible to implement things one to one without considering cultural differences.** [...] Although mentality might look similar at first sight there are notable differences which need to be adhered to. (P2: 33)

> **Granted it is very tricky to deal with each nationality individually** [...] Some never learn. (P3: 71)

> I do expect some cultural sensitivity from my employees. I expect them to approach people [in CEE] in a sensitive manner and to listen to them [...] rather than appearing as Western smartasses who deal with ex-communists. [...] **We are looking for cultural competence and openness when hiring people.** (P5: 96)

The importance of such soft skills is acknowledged by the top management; if PCNs lack cultural skills the parent often has no alternative but to recall them:

> Unfortunately, **cultural sensitivity seems to be a personality trait.** Some people are very effective from early on [...] with

other people we have no alternative but to recall and replace them. (P9: 14)

Personal international experience. The amount of personal international experience is paramount for operating successfully in CEE. All respondents who had been abroad for an extended period of time point out that they made many mistakes during their first foreign assignment and that the learning process they underwent during that time is invaluable. Having been exposed to the complexity of dealing with foreign cultures before made them much more effective in dealing with foreign employees later on, no matter what cultural background they had. Therefore, prior international experience has a moderating effect on cultural distance.

> During my first year abroad I made many mistakes, I simply lacked understanding for the Czech market. [...] It is a learning process. (P2: 36)

> If I would not have been abroad before I would not be able to handle my current position. Currently I'm confronted with five different mentalities at a time. That's a challenge. It is even more difficult than my prior job as subsidiary manager in the Czech Republic. **Back then I learned a lot. And now I'm still learning on a daily basis.** (P29: 52)

Intercultural training and specific preparation for foreign assignments is perceived as valuable but cannot offset the actual experience:

> It is nice to listen to other peoples experiences in dealing with cultures or even participate in a specific training, but **at the end of the day it is your own experience that counts.** The value of your own experience cannot be matched by anything. (P1: 97)

Language proficiency. The capability to speak the native language is essential for establishing good relations with foreign managers and employees. Since relations rule in CEE, language capabilities should not be underestimated. Interestingly, opinions on the importance and necessity to speak the native tongue of the host country were divided: Those interviewees who spoke the language underlined that speaking the language makes all the difference, since it facilitates trust and relationship building. Furthermore, they outlined that the ability to speak the native tongue is a sign of respect and appreciation for the national characteristics which is greatly appreciated by locals. Moreover, information flows are greatly improved. Those interviewees who did not master the native tongue did not consider that capability as important. Some examples given by executives on the importance of language:

> Speaking the local tongue is essential in a lot of ways. [...] e.g. when it comes to reading contracts [...] being able to communicate in the local language enabled me **to build up relationships much faster**. [...] You can be the best educated business man but without being able to communicate well with locals you are at a loss. [...] People appreciate it when their boss speaks their language. (P43: 66)

> I personally think that people open up much faster and at a much deeper level when you are able to communicate with them in their local **tongue. [...] Speaking their language is a sign of respect and is therefore deeply appreciated by the people.** [...] **Additionally I have access to much more information because not only do people open up much more** but also because I can address those who cannot speak English very well. (P2: 97)

> Four out of seven board members speak an Eastern European language. [...] that shows the importance we attach to mastering the local tongue. (P6: 74)

> **If I would not be able to master Hungarian I would encounter major difficulties.** [...] Even if the people in the subsidiaries can communicate in English or German **a great deal of information would just pass by** me. (P41: 29)

Those who did not speak a native language, however, insisted that language ability as a door opener is pure myth and speculation.

> **Mastering the local language is negligible,** I mean it wouldn't be a disadvantage to master it but in business English prevails anyway. (P19: 60)

Speaking native languages is no doubt challenging in CEE due to the large variety of different languages, or as one CEO puts it:

> Sure it would be nice to speak a Slavic language but that does not help me in Hungary, and I am not able to learn every tongue, I can never master Polish, Czech, Slovak and Hungarian at the same time. (P29: 83)

7.4.3 Propositions and managerial implications

Based on our analysis of culture and moderators the following propositions regarding MNC management control can be made:

Propositions regarding CEE culture and MNC control in general:

P (33) The greater the perceived risk attributed to cultural differences the greater is the extent of HQ control.
P (34) Given the importance placed on personal relations in CEE personal control is an effective means of MNC control in CEE.
P (35) Given that managers from other CEE countries are not easily accepted in CEE subsidiaries, HQ rather send out parent-country or third-country nationals as expatriates.
P (36) The generation clash in CEE impacts the choice of control mechanisms: Older people refrain from performance-based pay schemes, while younger people welcome such incentives.
P (37) Southern CEE subsidiaries are more euphoric in their forecasts than Northern ones

Propositions regarding CEE culture and organizational level moderators and MNC control:

P (38) Given the importance of personal relations and the high scores on group-collectivism in CEE, HQ control in CEE subsidiaries is facilitated by relation and trust building based on intense personal contact and communication between HQ and subsidiaries.
P (39) Expatriates in the function of social butterflies have a moderating effect on the perceived risk attributed to cultural differences of CEE.
P (40) A participative but assertive HQ management style is effective in dealing with culture-based behavior of CEE employees such as 'passive resistance', non-observing of deadlines, national pride and a short-sleeved working style.
P (41) The importance of hierarchies in CEE requires that management control in subsidiaries has top-management support and that subsidiary top management is treated with respect.
P (42) Prior international experience of the HQ decreases the perceived risk of cultural differences.
P (43) Intra-group knowledge transfer has a positive impact on the perceived risk of cultural differences.

Table 7.9 Perceived cultural differences and the managerial implications

	Perceived cultural differences and the managerial implications
Passive resistance	Two strategies of CEE employees rooted in the communist past were found to impact HQ management control by aiming at avoiding executing HQ orders. First, people seemingly take the line of least resistance by agreeing on everything that is being said by the HQ but take no action at all to reach agreed-on goals. Second, people are very creative in finding thousands of reasons why something cannot be implemented or does not work in the subsidiary. ⇨ HQ executives need to be aware of such strategies and need to set clear signals and exert a rather assertive management style in order to not fall for 'passive resistance traps'.
Relations rule	Personal relations are of utmost importance in CEE. These findings can be backed up by prior studies on Eastern European culture which found that CEE cultures are much more diffuse than Western ones (Hall, 1959; Trompenaars et al., 2000). Diffuse cultures do not strictly divide private and professional spheres rather the underlying relationship rules (Hall, 1959; Hall et al., 2000). Also, compared with other clusters in the Globe study this cluster stands out with high scores on group-orientation. ⇨ HQ needs to maintain a high level of communication and intense personal contact with subsidiary employees and engage in trust-building activities.
Hierarchies	Top management in CEE has an absolute power status and need to be treated with respect in order to avoid that top-managers lose face. Our findings are once more in line with prior research, which noted a strong power-distance culture in CEE (House et al., 2004), reflected by hierarchical structures and a prominent role of top management. ⇨ Implementation of management control systems should be supported by top management. HQ executives must respect local hierarchies.
National pride	National pride is a common characteristic of CEE employees. ⇨ Showing appreciation for the local expertise of CEE employees is important. HQ executives need to avoid appearing as 'know-it-alls' by all means.

Continued

Table 7.9 Continued

	Perceived cultural differences and the managerial implications
'We are not told by the Slovaks'	The transfer of employees between single subsidiaries in the East was found to be challenging since people of differing CEE nationalities did sometimes prefer not to cooperate. While PCNs or Western third-country nationals were readily accepted in management positions this was often not true for Eastern European third-country nationals. ⇨ Caution needs to be exercised regarding international human resources transfers.
Time issues: Deadlines are not observed	Respondents repeatedly complained that deadlines are often not observed and Eastern European subsidiary personnel have a relaxed view on time issues. Eastern European nationals have a polychronic (Hall, 1959) understanding of time which entails that people track and execute various tasks at a time and regard deadlines as flexible. ⇨ A participative but assertive management style is effective in dealing with time issues.
Hold authorities on high esteem	CEE employees have a deep respect for local authorities. Apparently, the communist regime left its imprints on people's minds since they still closely obey bureaucratic regulations. Respondents explained that accounting systems in private corporations are still primarily designed to satisfy authority regulations rather than providing essential business information for the firm. ⇨ HQ executives need to transfer management knowledge on managerial control and need to create an understanding for the need and purpose of organizational control.
Clash in generations	A key theme noted by the interviewees is a tremendous rift in the behavior and motivations of CEE employees based on age. While the 'older' generation who grew up in communism is not yet acquainted with market economic thinking, the younger generation is jumping at chances and is extremely performance and success oriented. A number of authors point to the dramatic turmoil provoked by fundamental political and economic changes in CEE explaining that the fall of communism entailed not only an institutional upheaval but also a radical change in fundamental values, beliefs and assumptions. We found that younger people are also more prone to take risk for example by welcoming performance-based pay. ⇨ A combination of explicit and implicit control is needed in CEE. Younger employees can be motivated by output control (e.g., performance-based pay).
Lack of entrepreneurial spirit & risk avoidance	Some 10% of interviewees indicated that they perceive a lack of entrepreneurial spirit and initiative of Eastern European employees compared with their Western counterparts. Customer orientation and competition were not an issue in the former monopoly situation. However, these perception stands in sharp contrast to the enthusiasm and drive of the younger generation in CEE and the mentality perceived in the metropolitan areas. ⇨ HQ executives need to transfer knowledge on management practices and assign clear responsibilities.

Moderators on cultural distance on the individual level:

P (44) Personality traits of HQ personnel such as a high level of tolerance and cultural sensibility have a positive impact on perceived cultural differences.

P (45) Prior personal international experience of HQ personnel has a positive impact on the risk perceived attributed to cultural differences.

P (46) Proficiency in the local language of HQ personnel has a positive impact on the perceived risk attributed to cultural differences.

Table 7.9 gives a short overview on the most important cultural differences and its managerial implications as perceived by HQ executives.

8
Major Findings

8.1 Conclusion: cultural differences, contingencies, moderators and management control in MNCs

The above analysis of control mechanisms, the contingencies, and the cultural specifics that affect the choice and effectiveness of management control in Central and Eastern Europe (CEE) allows us to answer our research questions:

Which Management Control Systems (MCS) do MNCs use to control their CEE subsidiaries?

- How does culture influence the design and management of HQ control systems in foreign subsidiaries?
  - What are the major cultural differences in CEE as perceived by MNC HQ personnel?
  - What are successful strategies adopted by MNC HQ to cope with cultural differences?
- How do context factors, such as the environment and organizational characteristics, influence the design and functioning of coordination and MCS in the CEE subsidiaries?

Grounded on findings from rich semi-structured interviews we propose a model which sheds light onto how the context and perceptions of CEE culture influences the applicability and choice of control mechanisms of MNC HQ in their CEE subsidiaries. Figure 8.1 below depicts the relationships established based on the analysis of our data.

Our findings show that the perceived risk attributed to cultural differences affects the applicability of MNC management control in CEE. Eighteen cultural characteristics of CEE based on the perception of our

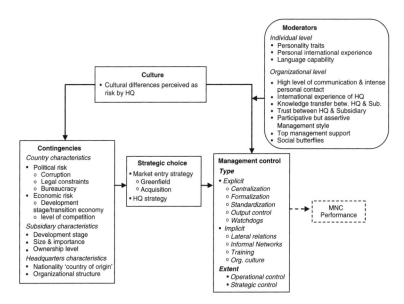

Figure 8.1 MNC management control in CEE.
Source: Author.

interviewees are found to be important in a management control context. Those perceptions are based on Austrian, German and Swiss respondents, thus their explanatory power is limited. In general, the higher the perceived risk attributed to cultural differences by HQ executives the greater is the degree of centralized HQ control. Culture also affects contingencies, since HQ, subsidiary, and country characteristics are influenced by the 'country of origin effect', which implies that a nation's institutional structures and practices are heavily shaped by its culture. Given that most of the nations in CEE experience great changes due to economic transition, a general upheaval in values was noted in our data which also impacts the effectiveness of MCSs. For example, while the 'older generation' in CEE is not motivated by performance-related pay schemes the younger generation welcomes such incentives.

In line with the findings of the literature review, a number of contingencies are found to impact the type and choice of MCS: We find that a high environmental uncertainty on the country level, such as political risk, a frequently changing legislation, an opaque bureaucracy, and some degree of corruption have a bearing on both the type and extent of control exerted by HQ. Economic risk caused by the transition process, the development stage of a nation, and the intensity of regional competition also impacts management control. On the subsidiary level, the size and importance of a subsidiary as perceived by the HQ and the degree of maturity influence MCS design. Majority ownership is beneficial for operational HQ control. Lastly, we note that the nationality of the HQ might have an impact on MCS preferences; however, given our limited sample and the exploratory nature of our research design our latter findings should be taken with care and are therefore only displayed in Figure 8.1.

HQ strategy and market entry strategy also impact the type and extent of management control exerted in CEE subsidiaries. For example, a standardized group-wide MCS is found to be more easily put up in Greenfield operations.

A number of moderators on the organizational and individual level which have a moderating effect on the perceived cultural differences are identified: A high level of communication including intense personal contact, knowledge transfer between HQ and subsidiaries, a high level of trust between the HQ and the subsidiary, some past HQ international experience, a participative but assertive management style, top-management support, and expatriates as social butterflies are found to have a positive impact on the perceived risk attributed to cultural differences on the organizational level. Additionally, some personality traits which bring forward cultural sensitivity, a personal experience of working abroad and language capabilities are found to offset potential negative effects triggered by perceived cultural differences on an individual level.

Our empirical findings show that both contingencies and perceptions on CEE culture determine the applicability and choice of MCSs in CEE subsidiaries. Together with the presence or absence of moderators they impact an HQ design in terms of type and extent of management control: The great majority of MNCs rely on personal centralized control and output control and use a combination of explicit and implicit management control types in order to effectively govern their CEE ventures. Therefore, we propose that MNCs need to use a combination of both explicit and implicit control mechanisms to effectively manage their CEE subsidiaries. Ultimately, the level of fit between the chosen extent and type of control and a given scenario of culture and context, impacts effective subsidiary control and at last, an MNC's performance. We hope that this study provides a first step towards more empirical research on the role of context and culture on MCSs in International Business (IB).

We conclude that neither research based on cultural theory nor research based on contingency theory alone can explain the phenomenon of cross-border diffusion of managerial control adequately.

Research conducted under the contingency paradigm (e.g., Burns and Stalker, 1961; Lawrence and Lorsch, 1967) assumes that patterns of perception and preferences of organizational members are dictated by the environment and are therefore universal across borders. The culture based perspective, however, sees culture as a determinant for human action and, hence, explaining international variations in management controls. Although the world-wide diffusion of knowledge, technologies, information and the increasing harmonization between national policies – commonly known as the globalization effect – would be expected to decrease the importance of national differences (e.g., Hunt, 2000; Mueller, 1994; Ohmae, 1990, p. 94; Parker, 1998), both our literature review and our empirical findings show that this is not the case. However, the role of culture might not be evident at first glance, or as Triandis (1983) put it:

> Its [culture's] influence for organizational behavior is that it operates at such a deep level that people are not aware of its influences. It results in unexamined patterns of thought that seem so natural that most theorists of social behavior fail to take them into account. As a result, many aspects of organizational theories produced in one culture may be inadequate in other cultures.

Existing cultural research on management control is mainly based on Hofstede's taxonomy of cultural dimensions which seems to have a limited explanatory power for the cross-border applicability of management control. Both paradigms provide valuable insights and should not be looked at in isolation, since our findings show that external and internal factors, institutional consequences, and the risk perceptions attributed to culture influence the process that produces control systems.

8.2 Directions for future research

Our propositions regarding MCS for CEE subsidiaries need to be empirically tested. Future research could test the level of 'fit' between the MNC strategy, the control system, and the host-country environment in terms of both culture and context. The assessment of the appropriate congruence among these components might yield new insights into managerial behavior, headquarter–subsidiary relations, and subsidiary performance.

Future research can attempt to shed more light onto the interaction of contingencies and culture in the diffusion of MCS. Furthermore, the crucial role of trust in establishing MCS across borders is at most scarcely present in current empirical IB research although there is ample evidence that this factor does have significant explanatory power in international control contexts.

Lastly, we join a number of scholars (Capelli & Sherer, 1991; Kostova, 1999; Modway & Sutton, 1993; O'Reilly, Chatman, & Caldwell, 1991) calling for a multilevel and multimethod approach for studying complex issues such as the cross-cultural transfer of organizational practices in order to allow for 'a more thorough and innovative examination of the process of transfer and the determinants of transfer success' (Kostova, 1999). Given the complex nature of cross-cultural issues employing more qualitative research methods could be a way of gaining a better understanding of the cross-border diffusion of management practices.

8.3 Discussion

Our study does have some limitations which will be discussed in some detail below. At the same time, we strive to give some recommendations for further research:

First, with the exception of ten MNCs, our results are based on the opinions of a single respondent in each organization. We tried to validate given answers by cross-questioning and triangulating them with additional sources such as company statements wherever possible. Future researchers might try to question more than one person per firm in order to further increase data objectiveness.

Second, our sample contained only executives from HQ; consequently, we have to be aware of the biased view on management control issues. Only some interviewees had worked in subsidiaries before returning to the HQ. Adding the subsidiary view to our analysis would undoubtedly yield a different picture based on perception gaps between HQ and subsidiaries. (For an overview on this topic, see Chini (2005). By triangulating both the HQ and the subsidiary view, a better window on reality might be generated.

Third, the qualitative nature of inquiry allowed us to gain insights into causal relationships, such as why a certain control type was chosen. Thus, we were able to suggest causal relationships derived from the open question format, which are presented in the form of propositions. For instance, the role of international transfers in establishing control over foreign ventures did not remain a black box but yielded insights into the different layers of direct and indirect expatriate control of MNCs. At the same time, the open format of the questions may impact the comparability of data since not all interviewees explored each topic in the same depth.

Fourth, the interview setting creates a shared context where meaning, ideas and experiences are exchanged, and is therefore subject to bias. Given that the same researcher conducted all interviews a bias caused by more than one interviewer could be avoided. Nevertheless, we are fully aware that our study is subject to different levels of bias, discussed in depth in the method section of our paper. By choosing the method of the semi-structured interview, we made sure that we collect comparable data since the interview guide ensured that the same line of inquiry was pursued with all respondents. However, the answers to our questions might contain an element of perception.

Fifth, the generalizability of our findings is limited given the qualitative research approach. Qualitative content analysis and the comparability of data due to the interview guide approach enabled us to quantify our findings to some extent. Careful attention was paid to putting qualitative data into a 'quantitative' perspective. We always indicated the number of quotations forming an identified data category and the number or percentage of interviewees represented per category. We could, for example, clearly distinguish different MCS in the various MNCs, and were able to categorize those, and account for their frequency of use. Given that the underlying population of regional and international HQ for CEE in Austria is approximately 200, a sample of 40 HQ represents some 20 percent of the investigated population.

Sixth, our study includes MNCs with direct investments in the form of subsidiaries and/or International Joint Ventures (IJVs) in CEE. Only two out of 40 MNCs also operate via Joint Ventures(JVs), and all the others rely exclusively on subsidiaries. One of the two MNCs operating via IJVs was forced into a JV agreement by local laws and would rather have entered the market by wholly owned subsidiaries. Consequently, the level and composition of control mechanisms used might very well be different for JVs or other forms of minority participations. Some executives mention that the higher the level of ownership the 'easier' it is to implement HQ control. On the other hand, given the local legal requirements of joint ownership, our sample might have been distorted by excluding IJVs.

Seventh, our study looks at how regional or international HQ for CEE based in Austria manage and control their CEE ventures. The number of countries they operate in range from two to all of the countries in CEE. When asked for perceptions of culture in dealing with subsidiaries many interviewees describe in depth their experiences in managing and controlling their subsidiaries in a specific cultural context. Although some characteristics described in different cultural settings show some parallels this does not mean that there is a CEE-wide culture. Rather, there are some common characteristics which are mentioned throughout the region and are mainly derived from a common experience of decades of communism. However, some countries might be overrepresented and some might only be represented in the sample once or twice. Contingencies on the country level such as the degree of perceived political and economic risk differed quite a bit, ranging from very little political risk to very risky environments depending on the stage of maturity in the various countries.

8.4 Managerial implications

Many MNCs continue to grow by expanding further eastward into new countries. At the same time, the dramatic shift in the political structure in CEE in recent years implies that all MNCs face a new set of host governments with emerging economies and shifting sets of government restrictions and an upheaval of norms and values among CEE people caused by the transition context. MNCs must find means to effectively manage and control their Eastern subsidiaries given this increased level of complexity and the diminished discretion of the parent's ability to assess the subsidiary and its management. Increasing levels of Foreign Direct Investment (FDI) in CEE make the primary area of inquiry of this study both important and urgent. The model proposed in this paper is an important step in understanding how MNCs can control their subsidiaries effectively in increasingly complex and uncertain foreign environments. In the following, some determinants of effective subsidiary management and business success in CEE which were perceived to be of high importance to our interviewees are briefly recounted.

8.4.1 Determinants of effective management control and business success in CEE

Table 8.1 gives an overview over various determinants of successful management control in CEE identified as highly important by the interviewees. Interviewees mention centralized control, ongoing direct personal contact, finding the right mix of expatriates and locals, and a mutual know-how transfer between HQ and subsidiary as most important in successfully managing CEE subsidiaries.

Table 8.1 Determinants of effective management control and business success in CEE

Success factors	Impacts on management control	Exemplary quote	Quotations
Centralized control	The majority of interviewees outline in some 118 quotations the importance of centralized control as a prerequisite for successful management in CEE. Only centralized structures seem to generate much wanted synergies in MNCs. Centralized control prepares the ground for group-wide network structures with various competence centers being spread out over the whole group. Hence, in the future we might see new network style organization structures. Moreover, in a recent discussion with some 30 HQ executives, who were not in the current sample underlying our findings, this trend could be acknowledged. The greater the perceived risk attributed to cultural differences and the political and economic situation, the greater is the extent and centralization of HQ control in subsidiaries.	We have an **extremely well structured and centralized reporting** in all our CEE subsidiaries. We have a group-wide standardized software and account system. [...] our group-wide SAP enables that we manage our subsidiaries optimally [...] **Vienna is our central CEE hub** [...] I can see everything from here [...] that's essential for an optimal management and control [...]. (P24: 35)	118
Combining explicit and implicit control	35 out of 40 HQ rely on personal centralized control while 32 HQ rely on output control. Given the high group-collectivism and the importance placed on personal relations in CEE, personal control and control by socialization and networks is an effective means of control in CEE. Mostly, a combination of explicit and implicit control mechanisms is used to effectively govern CEE subsidiaries.	**Personal contact is immensely important in CEE.** [...] **If you rely exclusively on output control you will fail badly.** [...] Face-to-face interaction is crucial [...] **vital information can only be gathered in time via personal interactions.** [...]. (P14: 70)	25

Continued

Table 8.1 Continued

Success factors	Impacts on management control	Exemplary quote	Quotations
Ongoing direct personal contact	Ongoing and intense communication between the parent and the subsidiary is crucial for effectively dealing with CEE subsidiaries. 43 out of 46 interviewees underlined that being personally on the spot at regular intervals is of utmost importance. The higher the frequency of communication and the extent of personal contact between HQ and subsidiary personnel the better are the parent-subsidiary relations. Good relations between the HQ and the subsidiary in turn provide the ground for effective managerial control by the HQ.	**Without personal interaction nothing goes.** There is not a single controller out there who I do not see at least once a month. (P31: 52) Personal contact rules [...] You cannot manage effectively by simply giving order [laughs] there is much more to effective management [...] and **face-to-face interaction is crucial in CEE**. (P15: 78)	104
The right mix of locals and expatriates	MNCs need a right mix of expatriates and local employees to be successful in CEE: a) Locals: Having good relations to stakeholders such as local authorities is considered to be vital in CEE. In order to establish necessary connections outside the firm 33% of MNCs rely on locals. Only locals have the necessary cultural and language background to nurse existing and foster new business relations on the spot. This knowledge is paramount when it comes to handling local authorities. b) Expatriates: In order to successfully manage and control CEE subsidiaries, HQ rely on expatriates to control subsidiaries explicitly and implicitly.	[...] in order to be successful in CEE you need **connections and networks** [...] only local have access to those networks. (P44: 20) the key to success is to employ the 'right' locals [...] **well connected people whom you can trust** (11:79) you do need a watchdog for certain things. If you let things slide in the subsidiaries you are bound to experience some nasty surprises. (P6: 92) extract 'soft information' expats need to [...] socialize. Only by doing so they are able to get access to the really important information and get a complete picture. The key to get access to soft information is to establish trust. (P4: 65)	40 46

Know-how transfer	Mutual know-how transfer between HQ and subsidiaries is crucial. Detailed knowledge about local markets is essential for market success in CEE. A combination of local know-how and HQ global strategic know-how builds the ground for a unique competitive advantage and success in CEE markets	We transfer our know-how within the group [...] the local business is run by locals who **know their region, business environments, markets, business conduct and cultural specific best.** Only somebody with expertise in local markets and cultures can run be successful. [...] we call that 'glocal' [...] **A local CEO who is rooted and well connected in the region can never be matched by an expatriate.** (P42: 38)	58
Keep it simple	The more simple output oriented management control is, the easier control mechanisms can be applied in CEE subsidiaries. A balance is needed between the levels of complexity of MCSs on the one hand, and the development stage of a CEE subsidiary on the other. As a general rule, Chief Financial Officers (CFOs) call for the design of intelligible systems, which are able to depict complex relations, and at the same time, are easy to comprehend and simple.	The question of how complex MCSs need to be is important. [...] sometimes they get so complex that the wood can't be seen for the trees. [...] complexity of control systems needs to be **aligned with the degree of maturity of subsidiaries.** [...] we do not grant our subsidiaries much time to catch up. (P7: 106)	14

Source: Author.

8.4.2 Managerial implications of perceived cultural differences

Table 7.9 gives a brief overview on the most important perceptions of CEE culture of HQ executives and its managerial implications:

8.4.3 Strategic success factors for implementing management control

In order to achieve group-wide standardization of reporting and control systems, MNCs are required to implement and/or adjust control and Management Information Systems (MIS) into CEE subsidiaries. The present study identified a number of challenges which impact the implementation process. At the same time, executives named a number of factors which proved to be very helpful for implementing management control in foreign subsidiaries. Figure 8.2 visualizes the challenges and moderators identified on different levels of analysis.

8.4.3.1 Implementation challenges

Transfers of organizational practices within MNCs are not always smooth and successful (Kostova, 1999). Barriers to transfer are either related to characteristics of the organizational practices which should be transferred or to cultural and organizational characteristics (Kostova, 1999; Szulanski, 1996; Zander & Kogut, 1995). Table 8.2 summarizes the challenges and barriers to implementing and transferring HQ management control into subsidiaries mentioned by the interviewees including the number of quotations found in the data and the percentage of interviewees.

Non-acceptance of transparency

Implementing control and reporting systems enhances group-wide transparency. Whether a greater degree of transparency is welcomed or not depends on the performance of a subsidiary. The better the performance of a subsidiary, the more welcome is management control. In the words of a Chief Executive Officer (CEO):

> **It is human nature that transparency is only welcomed if one looks good.** This conflict can never be solved. [...] Naturally we strive for a high level of transparency within the group [...] we need to benchmark investments in order to make good economic decisions [...] **thus some subsidiaries benefit from transparency and some come under pressure.** (P2: 106)

> Basically **implementing our control system was well received** because our subsidiaries had noted that they needed more transparent

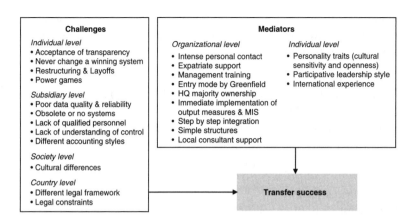

Figure 8.2 Challenges for implementation and mediators at different levels of analysis.
Source: Author.

Table 8.2 Implementation: challenges & facilitators of implementing HQ control

Challenges	No of quotations	% of interviewees
Qualified personnel	30	24
Differing accounting styles & legal constraints	24	22
Data quality & security	20	17
Acceptance of transparency	17	16
Lack of understanding of 'control'	13	13
Restructuring: lay off people	9	7
Never change a winning system	5	5
Obsolete or no systems	3	3
Political games/power	2	2

Source: Data analysis.

information tools [...] they had nothing hide [...] that was a way of **showing local success within the group** and the business units. As long as they [subsidiaries] couldn't show their success, they couldn't benefit from it. [...] Transparency builds trust and the HQ invests more. (P3: 41)

Some interviewees trace the reluctance to accept greater levels of transparency in subsidiaries to the communist past where central authorities were not welcome:

> Well you need not to forget their history, 60 years central **planning cannot be deleted in just a few years**. [...] Transparency is clearly **not welcomed** in CEE. (P6: 55)

> There is some **fear of disinvestment** in our subsidiaries. [...] standardized reporting allows us to **benchmark** all subsidiaries [...] that exerts quite some pressure. (P26: 86)

Power/political games
Implementation of management control and group-wide standards curb the power of subsidiary managers, and is therefore not always welcomed. Some interviewees mention that political power games hinder successful implementation of management control. As explicated by an executive:

> The more guidelines, **standardized processes and rules** we have the more competences are pooled [...] and decisions are made centrally at the HQ [...] That in turn **reduces the influence and power of the local subsidiary managers**. [...] it's all about power [...] they don't like being deprived of their power base. (P34: 53)

> The technical part of the implementation of SAP went well [...] the **political games** involved were more troublesome [...] who has full access rights to the system? Where will be server be located and the like. (P12: 32)

> Some people are never satisfied [...] **they fight against everything** although their arguments do not make any sense from a groups point of view [...] people and power ... (P24: 35).

Never change a winning system
Interviewees indicate that the introduction of new control systems is rarely welcomed since people tend to dislike changing established 'winning' systems. The intricacies involved with change as described by executives:

> We encountered fierce resistance when we tried to implement our controlling system. **'Why don't we leave things as they are?'** That's the typical question. [...] We needed to make them understand that we need ONE standard and not thousands of modifications (P43: 56).

> Of course **we ran against resistance** by trying to implement our systems. **Who welcomes a change anyway?** [...] we had no alternative but to exchange the existing obsolete management information system [...] it does make sense to introduce one group-wide standard (P33: 57).
>
> **Standardization is not welcomed** [laughs] but we solved all conflicts amicably. If somebody says no, I'm not doing it, he needs **to name a very good reason** [...] and nobody could voice a good reason. [...] Now we have endless data to run the most sophisticated analyses [...] I can see everything, every process in every subsidiary [...] I can ask why somebody takes three times longer for a certain process than others. [...] clearly the underlying process must be less than ideal. Then he has to proof to me that everything is in order. (P20: 54)

Restructuring/Laying people off
Every change has its consequences. MNCs restructure acquired firms in CEE which tend to be overstaffed and not competitive. Restructuring and streamlining of management and control systems often result in substantial layoffs and other unpopular measures.

> If I take over an enterprise [...] with 1,500 employees of which 1,200 are working in production and 300 doing administrative work. [...] the **firms have monopoly-like** structures [...] nowadays we face competition and the market changes to an oligopoly structure with marketing and sales becoming more important. [...] For production we usually **cut some 50–60% of the jobs** within an agreed-on period of time of some 3 to 5 years. That's necessary in order to be competitive in the long run. (P4: 73)
>
> The administration of the **acquired enterprise had more than 50 people in the accounting department** – not a single controller was among them by the way – and we have no clue what they did. [...] a **comparable enterprise** of that size and complexity is doing OK with some **15 accountants**. [...] We **have no choice but to resize** the accounting department and specifically train and coach some 10 accountants and bring in some 5 new people which we build up as controllers. (P4: 74)

Rigorous measures like replacing the old management and introducing new people and structures at the same time result in a crash in terms of organizational and national cultures. Such measures are never welcomed by local personnel. A middle manager describes the course of a recent restructuring project as follows:

> We **introduced SAP** in our last large acquisition in Poland **within four months** from scratch, just like that. [...] actually we are still trying to digest it [...] we need to do **major restructuring** [...] The old management resigned because they didn't want to cooperate. Thus, **we changed the management, the electronic data processing** [...] and kept only some employees. [...] That was a **major crash**. Personally, I would not have dared to move that fast, but our manager just said, we'll go through with it at one go [...] surely, that was a **major culture crash** which is not optimal. [...] Basically that's our strategy that's the only way we can achieve synergies. **When we will take over the next plant, we'll do the same** we abstain from taking over the existing administration and sales department and only keep the best people. [...] If you are convinced of your strategy you gotta stick to it. (P24: 55)

Poor data quality and reliability
The poor quality of data is a major challenge for implementing integrated control, accounting and reporting schemes. Some 50 percent of the interviewees stress that the poor reliability of data in CEE subsidiaries make implementing integrated systems a priority. Given a rather poor standard to start with, implementing new systems is challenging:

> The **greatest challenge** in those countries is always to have **data which is reliable and secure**. We have to see to it that **we have the greatest degree of integration of systems possible** for our subsidiaries in CEE to ensure that we have closed loops. **Establishing integrated systems is the only way to establish at least some kind of data reliability**. We put much effort into building integrated systems to get away from single reports which were not plausible. (P1: 45)

Obsolete or non-existent systems
Often management control or reporting systems in acquired CEE subsidiaries were either not existent at all or were obsolete. Implementing control systems and establishing a group-wide standard and comparability of data is challenging. In the words of an executive:

> For our calculations **we need exact figures** regarding provisions, precisely accrued and deferred interests and so on per account. **Most**

of the existing systems in CEE were not equipped for that. [...] At the moment we are working on achieving that standard group-wide [...] next year we'll have some 95% group-wide standardization. (P12: 24)

Different accounting styles & legal constraints
Comparability of accounting data is often flawed due to different accounting styles which are partly caused by differing legal frameworks but also by cultural differences. However, MNCs spare no pains to achieve as much standardization as possible. A CFO broods over the long way to standardization:

> Achieving **standardization is a long and rocky path** [...] it takes time to **discover how people in the single subsidiaries do accounting in practice** [...] that's not something you can learn from a textbook. It's not as much a legal challenge than a practical challenge. Don't laugh but **there are cultural differences in how people do the bookkeeping**. It doesn't have anything to do with an Austrian or U.S. GAAP but how people are socialized during their education impacts how they do accounting. I think we'll never be finished with our standardization process. [...] but I try to constantly restrain their room for maneuver. (P14: 42)

For example, letting the books open till March rather than closing them by the end of December by accruals and deferrals is reported to be common practice in CEE. Getting people to change long-practiced habits proved to be challenging.

> [o]ur CEE **subsidiaries don't close the books till March**!! If a new invoice of € 10 comes in March they still book it in December. We would book that in March or whenever. [...] We can't get them to change that [laughs]. (P20: 79)
>
> We try to make accounting more transparent in CEE [...] But there are still practices like **'cash-based accounting' in Russia**, that means not what's indicated on the invoice counts but what is actually spent. Delete that, I'm afraid that's not very quotable, but it's true! [laughs] [...] **there is no double-entry accounting like we are used to** [...] only when an invoice is settled an entry is made. (P38: 62)

Respondents underpinned that people need to learn to not only think in terms of their local accounting rules and regulations but also in terms of international accounting standards. This learning process takes time and support by the HQ.

> Accountants always think in terms of the local rules and guidelines. [...] **We need to make them understand that they need to stretch in both directions** [...] According to the locals regulations but also according to the U.S. GAAP. [...] It's damn hard to get them to do that (P17: 60).

Lack of understanding for Western management concepts and control
There is a lack of understanding for Western management concepts and instruments in Central and Eastern Europe. In order to transfer knowledge from the parent to subsidiaries some organizational capabilities in order to understand the concept are required. Absorptive capacity of CEE subsidiaries is limited due to their little prior exposure of Western management techniques and adapting to a market environment (Filatotchev et al., 2003; Newman, 2000). This lack of understanding of Western management hinders the transfer of MCSs. Management control per se was not known in CEE. In the words of an executive:

> People had **to slowly learn to appreciate the necessity of information management and management control**. But that's clear they never worked with such concepts and instruments before (P19: 73).

> We are about to implement a tool in our countries which lists different costs and earnings [....] **I'm noticing that the understanding of accounting and costing terms within CEE differs considerably**. Some countries are more progressive than others (P8: 23).

In order to bridge the gap in relevant control and management knowledge MNCs created glossaries and accounting manuals to overcome knowledge, language and perception barriers and curb misunderstandings:

> We had to come up with a glossary, which explains in detail all the terms, what they mean and how they are applied. Then we set up a series of workshops where we went through it together (P20: 60).

Lack of qualified personnel & understanding of control
The poor data quality and the little-advanced information processing systems in CEE subsidiaries are reported to be further aggravated by a rather poor education in management control and accounting.

They have more than 50 accountants [...] those 50 accountants deliver a considerably worse data quality than my comparable 15 'good' accountants in our Hungarian subsidiary which is of a comparable size. It's amazing [...] management control does not exist (P4: 75).

The lack of understanding of Western management control concepts in CEE makes implementation and standardization even more difficult. Employees from Eastern subsidiaries often do not speak the same management terminology, thus HQ have to establish a common ground of understanding first.

People had no clue that management control is not just accounting. People thought a few simple figures from accounting are enough to effectively govern a firm (P13: 79).

8.4.3.2 Implementation mediators

Interviewees outline not only challenges and obstacles to implementing management control but also describe in detail strategies to overcome barriers to transfer. Often, implementation requests for new practices by the parent add to the frustration of foreign subsidiary managers. The more alien the underlying parent motives are to foreign subsidiary managers the more likely such requests are not welcome. The key to create good-will for implementing new practices lies in creating a shared meaning of why it is important to do so. Table 8.3 summarizes findings on factors which facilitate the implementation of MCSs in CEE subsidiaries.

Table 8.3 Implementation mediators

Facilitators	No of quotations
Direct personal contact, be at the spot	104
Expatriate, personal control	46
Immediate implementation of output control & MIS	23
Greenfield	38
Management training	39
Participative leadership style: less authoritarian & set signals	31
Personality rules	22
Step by step integration process	16
Ownership	14
Personal international experience	10
Support by local consultants	4

Source: Data analysis.

Direct personal contact. Intense personal contact between the parent and the subsidiary is not only crucial for effectively managing and controlling CEE subsidiaries but also for implementing control and MIS. 43 out of 46 interviewees underline that being personally and frequently on the spot are essential for a successful transfer of management systems. A CFO underscores that it is important that he is personally on the spot to implement the Balanced Scorecard in all the CEE subsidiaries. In his own words:

> Face-to-face contact and interaction is crucial [...] Important projects such as introducing the BSC in all our subsidiaries can only be a success if it is done based on personal interaction. [...] I was personally present in all countries in all subsidiaries in order to talk to the people in person [...] that's the only way to gain acceptance, and approval, and commitment for HQ projects [...] the effort paid off. (P28: 60)

Only personal interaction is reported to prepare the ground for a common understanding and acceptance of the necessity of management information and control systems.

> Personal contact rules [...] the HQ can decide on things but whether things are implemented or not depends on the collaboration of the subsidiaries. Good cooperation is based on personal contacts and joint efforts [...] on mutual understanding and goodwill. If that is not the case things are bound to get difficult. The joint effort, the common ground and the shared understanding is the basis for everything. (P18: 97)

Personal interaction reduces the great potential for misunderstandings due to differences in language and culture and managerial thinking. It cannot be taken for granted that the HQ and the subsidiary personnel define a financial ratio in the same way, thus, personal discussions are essential for transferring MIS:

> I was personally present after acquiring our Hungarian and second Czech subsidiary. [...] Both times we came into the firm and analyzed everything [...] that was some sort of due-diligence. [...] After we had analyzed everything we started talking to the local controllers and laid out in detail what we expect of a monthly reporting system. [...] We discussed in detail how every ratio is composed. [...] That can only be done face-to-face [...] otherwise you end up in chaos. (P31: 46)

Personal contact implies that managers and controllers from the HQ are sent abroad for longer period of times:

> I spent a year in Hungary after we merged with an enterprise [...] it took that long till we reorganized and restructured everything [...] It took a considerable effort to restructure [...] and to implement our management control and information systems (P1: 94).
> To integrate cross-border acquisitions we need to be on the spot in person. [...] It doesn't work if we don't go there (P12: 98).

Even after a successful implementation frequent personal contact is reported to be necessary to keep the system running smoothly:

> We meet at least every month and I'm on the phone with every larger subsidiary at least five times a day the same is true for e-mail. Rather than trying to control our subsidiaries I try to advance things in the subsidiaries. Therefore, communication is intense and rather informal. [...] All controllers here at the HQ are in permanent contact with the subsidiaries. (P20: 56)

At the same time, local managers and controllers are brought to the HQ to discuss and decide on implementation issues. By doing so, a great level of commitment by the subsidiary personnel is created:

> We always invite the key players [from the subsidiary] to Austria to show them our way of doing things and to jointly discuss how we can improve things in the subsidiary (P2: 88).

Expatriate support. Some HQ transfer their controlling systems by sending expatriates into CEE subsidiaries to make sure the HQ managerial control practices are adhered to. If expatriates stay at the subsidiaries for an extended period of time, implementation of MCSs is usually pretty smooth. Having expatriates in place on a permanent basis facilitates transferring managerial practices to an even greater extent than intense personal contact which is often limited to the implementation phase. In the words of two executives:

> Basically we established management control by sending people into the subsidiaries on a permanent basis. That works well for us (P22: 43).
> [w]e originally intended to also put expatriates in charge at the second management level as well [...] especially in the field of control, finance and risk management. [...] In any case, the CFO and the head of corporate control are always expatriates.

Management training. Management training is essential for transferring management control. Our data clearly shows that training has several dimensions: Ad hoc training is offered whenever needed, for example in case of acquiring new subsidiaries. At the same time, MNCs increasingly commit to a long-term personnel policy by bringing trainees into the HQ and establishing international best breed cadres, which are ready to be sent to newly acquired firms or to help building up Greenfields.

> Trainees from CEE subsidiaries are here [at the HQ] all the time [...] they are here for six months before being sent back to their subsidiaries. [...] For future leaders and top managers we have an international assessment center and an international management program where those people undergo training at the HQ and various subsidiaries. (P6: 100)

Training also comprises permanent workshops. In order to sustain successfully integrated MCSs, controllers from subsidiaries and the HQ meet on a regular basis to keep up with new developments.

> At least two times a year we have group-wide workshops for all our local controllers [...] we all met here and discuss relevant management control issues (P7: 83).

Immediate implementation of output control & MIS. Many interviewees explained that implementing output control systems and MIS immediately is crucial. They illustrate their point as follows:

> Our last acquisitions were rather **radical**. [...] We were moving speedily ahead [...] Marketing and sales was integrated as fast as possible [...] production was either shut down or maintained [...] Restructuring plans were immediately drafted [...] electronic data processing and accounting was immediately replaced with our systems. [...] **Within two days after the acquisition we had our data processing system up and running.** That was a shock for the people. (P24: 53)

> We **introduced our systems immediately** after the acquisition. We are very best-practice oriented, SAP is our basis [...] sometimes we analyzed existing management information systems, but mostly **we restructured everything within no time and introduced our systems.** (P24: 53)

Our data suggests, that reorganizing and integrating foreign ventures demands a certain rigor to be successful. In the words of an executive:

> Our most successful man in CEE often had sayings such as: 'if you restructure you need to look at it as if there a ravens sitting on a field. They sit there quietly, then you come clap your hands, and they all fly up and then they sit down again fast.' [...] He was right. (P10: 77)
> **Implementing transparency is met with resistance if you don't do it from the very beginning.** [...] Well, we mostly operate with Greenfields which makes it easy to set a certain standard right from the start. [...] Everybody has to adhere to that standard [...] no discussions, no debates, no resistance. (P1: 79)

At the same time, informants stated that the extreme pace of implementing systems and processes causes a shock for newly acquired ventures. Even if systems and structures are introduced with an enormous pace, the actual integration of subsidiaries and people takes times. Executives guess that until integration is processed in the heads of the people it takes at least some four to five years or even longer. Nevertheless, a fast integration and transfer of reporting and control structures is perceived as essential:

> Well, [laughs] **integrating reporting and MCS is the first thing we do, there is no alternative to that.** After we acquire a firm we need to know the results immediately. That's the first thing which NEEDS to be in place! [...] **On the other hand, we are well aware that every firm we acquired has its own history, self-image, organizational culture and way of seeing things [...] that cannot be eradicated within no time.** [...] **Many of the firms we acquired some 4 to 5 years ago have mentally processed the integration only recently. An entire mental integration might never take place** [...] but at least to a substantial degree. (P32: 78)

Step by step integration process. 16 executives describe implementing control systems and integrating new ventures as a step-by-step process. First, an appropriate data processing base is established as a basis for a future integrated MIS system. Again, an immediate introduction is considered to be of vital importance. Second, a sound accounting framework is created and, finally, management control instruments can be introduced. All steps require training and some time, otherwise the risk of failure or misleading interpretations is high. Although these findings might appear to contradict the above discussed immediate implementation of output control and MIS at first sight, they are rather in line with each other as both perspectives consider it as vital to start with the first step immediately.

> It always starts with data processing. Before I can introduce MCSs I need the right data processing. [...] First I need to **create orderly and integrated systems, and second, I need to set up a precise and comprehensive accounting.** [...] only after everything runs smoothly accounting wise I can start introducing management control instruments. (P1: 121)

> We give our new subsidiaries some time – mostly 3 years – until we are actually able to introduce SAP. [...] It simply takes some time to set the stage for SAP [...] we need to build up organizational processes and structures and a sound accounting. [...] However, **we start IMMEDIATELY preparing the ground** for the introduction of our MCS. (P4: 57)

> We are following a **step-by-step procedure** [...] we need time to train and educate people [...] they start with transferring simple financial statement into Excel files [...] **knowledge is transferred step-by-step** (P17: 49).

Entry mode: Greenfield. Market entry by Greenfield operations facilitates group-wide standardization of MCS, as systems can be introduced from scratch. In case of takeovers, existing systems need to be replaced or adapted which requires a change process. Therefore, start-up operations are reported to provide a more beneficial setting for implementing management control than acquisitions.

> Since we only have Greenfield operations we were able to introduce one group-wide standard in all subsidiaries from the very beginning (P7: 68).

> It depends whether we entered the market via Greenfield operations or not. In Greenfield operations we build up our standardized system from scratch. If we took over firms we were confronted with an existing organizational culture, and process, and structure and had to adjust that to our standards. (P8: 19)

High ownership degree. Similarly, a high degree of ownership of subsidiaries facilitates implementing standardized control and reporting systems. In the words of an executive:

> Majority ownership made it easier to push our systems through than in case of JVs. That's why we avoid entering in JV agreements (P8: 12).

> We always strive for having fully owned subsidiaries. [...] That way we can best implement our systems (P15: 28).

Keep it simple. The more simple output-oriented management control is the easier control mechanisms can be applied in CEE subsidiaries. A balance is needed between the levels of complexity of MCSs on the one hand, and the development stage of a CEE subsidiary on the other. Caution should be exercised to make sure that systems are understood correctly. As a general rule, CFOs call for the design of intelligible systems, which are able to depict complex relations, and at the same time, are easy to comprehend and simple. In the words of the executives:

> The question of how complex MCSs need to be is important. [...] **sometimes they get so complex that the wood can't be seen for the trees.** [...] complexity of control systems needs to be aligned with the degree of maturity of subsidiaries. [...] we do not grant our subsidiaries much time to catch up. (P7: 106)

> Control systems need to **be easily understood and comprehensive.** [...] It doesn't help to have the most sophisticated system which produces outputs that can only be interpreted by an expert. [...] Rather, we need intelligible systems which produce comprehensible and clear results which can be interpreted by everybody. [...] The underlying complexity of such systems can be sophisticated but the outputs must be simple and traceable. [...] that we make sure that we talk about the same thing. (P35: 64)

> **Only simple things work.** [...] Simple structures do not rule out detailed and sophisticated reports. [...] It is essential that the underlying basic structure is simple though (P3: 115).

> It is **essential to focus on some key ratios and at the same time ensure data quality.** [...] There is no need for a very complex system when the data quality sucks (P14: 79).

Support from local consultants. Executives outlined that using local consultants facilitated the implementation process. One executive explicates the importance of local consultants as follows:

> We have been cooperating with the firm XY for a year now, that's one of the largest software providers worldwide and we outsourced our management control IT to them. [...] They are operating in every CEE country with locals [...] that works very well for us (P19: 66).
>
> We work with SAP consultants [...] they are based in every CEE country and follow us on our expansion. [...] Once everything is customized it gets easier to implement it in the single countries (P33: 55).

Personality traits. The success of transferring management concepts and implementing control structures always depends on the personality and goodwill of the parties involved. However trivial that might appear 20 percent of interviewees find it worth mentioning. As one executive explains:

> **Implementation success also depends on the type of persons involved** [...] Are they rather stubborn and **headstrong and condemn everything which comes from the HQ** [...] or do they have a liking for structures. [...] I think it's not a question of mentality but a question of personality (P24: 35).
>
> [i]n addition the success depends on the persons involved (P9: 59).
>
> I personally think it depends on the maturity of the subsidiaries and **on the personality of the people how well a management control system is received** (P8: 27).

Personal prior international experience. Furthermore, prior personal international experience greatly improves the effectiveness of people implementing control systems. In the words of an executive:

> **I did nothing but taking an idea further which I have already been applying in Turkey.** I've been implementing MCS in some 60 subsidiaries now [...] It gets better every time (P3: 35).
>
> **implementing our MCS abroad for the first time was a huge challenge** [...] **now it's everyday work** [...] the more experience you get the better it works (P2: 36).

Participative but assertive management style. Involvement and participation of employees is of utmost importance for successfully transferring management control concepts. A good start and a participative management style are crucial as an executive explains:

> It all depends on how you go into a newly acquired subsidiary. [...] if you try to create a common ground and understanding or rather resort to giving out orders (P31: 45).

Involving people in the implementation process and being able to accept some compromises does not mean that the mechanisms and concepts are not put through. An absolute necessity for operating successfully in CEE is to set clear signals and be very assertive:

> **You need to be pretty consequent each change management process** is met by people trying to obstruct changes. Those people need to be identified and fired. You need to set signals – both positive and negative ones. Positive ones by praising followers and negative ones by dismissing blockers. [...] That is very important because otherwise they won't take you serious [...] they would just think they survive their new owners just as they survived under communism. (P2: 90)

9
Summary

9.1 Key findings on a glimpse

Table 9.1 Key findings

The Study	
Main contribution	Our study contributes to the understanding of international management control by MNCs • theoretically, by providing a comprehensive framework of factors determining the cross-border diffusion of management control based on a literature review of 95 articles in International Business (IB)journals, and • empirically, by analyzing the type and extent of management control exerted by Western MNCs in their subsidiaries in Central and Eastern Europe (CEE), and by proposing a model of fit between the type and extent of management control, contingencies, perceptions of culture and moderators.
Method and Sample	Based on the findings of an extensive literature review, an interview guide was developed and **46 semi-structured interviews** were conducted with executives from **40 Austrian-based MNC headquarters.** The companies were selected following a non-probabilistic sampling method from an identified population of approximately 200. The **sample represents some 20% of the population.** In order to control for extraneous variation across industry sectors, firms were selected from various industries. Findings were analyzed with **qualitative content analysis** using Atlas.ti software.

Continued

Table 9.1 Continued

Key empirical findings	
Culture	We found **18 cultural characteristics of CEE** based on the perception of our interviewees which are important in a management control context. Some of the most important perceptions of CEE culture impacting management control include passive resistance, the importance attached to personal relations, strong hierarchies and the power status of top management, national pride, a different perception of time resulting in a relaxed view on HQ deadlines, a high esteem for local authorities, and a lack of acceptance for Eastern European third-country nationals in management positions. In general, **the higher the perceived risk attributed to cultural differences by HQ executives the greater is the degree of centralized HQ control.** Culture also affects contingencies, since HQ-, subsidiary-, and country-characteristics are influenced by the **'country of origin effect'**, which implies that a nation's institutional structures and practices are heavily shaped by a nation's culture. Given that most of the nations in CEE experience great changes due to economic transition, a general **upheaval in values** was noted in our data which also impacts the effectiveness of Management Control Systems (MCSs).
Moderators on the perceived cultural differences	A number of moderators on the organizational and individual level which have a moderating effect on the perceived cultural differences were identified: A **high level of communication including intense personal contact, knowledge transfer between HQ and subsidiaries, a high level of trust between the HQ and the subsidiary, some past HQ international experience, a participative but assertive management style, top-management support, and expatriates as social butterflies** were found to have a positive impact on cultural distance on the **organizational level**. Additionally, some **personality traits** which bring forward cultural sensitivity, a personal experience of working abroad and language abilities were found to offset potential negative effects triggered by cultural distance on the **individual level**.
Contingencies	In line with the findings of the literature review, a number of contingencies were found to impact the type and choice of MCS: We found that a high environmental uncertainty on the country level, such as **political risk**, a

Continued

Table 9.1 Continued

Key empirical findings	
	frequently changing legislation, an **opaque bureaucracy**, and **some degree of corruption** have a bearing on both the type and extent of control exerted by HQ. Economic risk caused by the **transition process**, the **development stage of a nation**, and the **intensity of regional competition** was also found to impact management control. On the **subsidiary level**, the **size and importance of a subsidiary** as perceived by the HQ and the **degree of maturity** influence MCS design. **Majority ownership** was found to be beneficial for operational HQ control. Lastly, we noted that the **nationality of the HQ** might have an impact on MCS preferences, however, given our limited sample and the exploratory nature of our research design our latter findings should be taken with care. Moreover, **strategic choice** was found to impact the type and extent of management control exerted in CEE subsidiaries.
Conclusion	Our empirical findings show that **both contingencies and perceptions on CEE culture determine the applicability and choice of management control** in CEE subsidiaries. Together with the presence or absence of **moderators** they impact an HQ design in terms of type and extent of management control. We found that the **great majority** of MNCs rely on **personal centralized control and output control and use a combination of explicit and implicit control mechanisms** in order to effectively govern their CEE ventures. Rather than looking at single control mechanisms as alternatives, MNCs rely on a combination of mechanisms in order to effectively control their foreign subsidiaries. Most interestingly, implicit control is found to be a vital precursor for formal control mechanisms, such as integration and centralization. Ultimately, the **level of fit between the chosen control type and the given scenario of culture and context impacts effective subsidiary management** and an MNC's performance. Therefore, we propose that MNCs need to use a combination of both explicit and implicit control mechanisms to effectively manage their CEE subsidiaries. We hope that this study provides a first step towards more empirical research on the role of context and culture on MCSs in IB.

9.2 Summary

Controlling and coordinating a network of geographically and culturally dispersed subsidiaries is probably one of the longest standing challenges in international management. Given the pressures for local responsiveness and global integration a firm's global network needs to be coordinated effectively in order to explore new local resources or to exploit resources within the international network of subsidiaries (Bartlett & Ghoshal, 1989). The great diversity of MNC operations increases the complexity of its system interdependence which, in turn, demands more coordination (Lawrence & Lorsch, 1967) and affects information processing and control systems (Egelhoff, 1993; Vachani, 1999). Consequently, the question of how to coordinate an MNC's dispersed-value-creation activities has become prominent and widely discussed in the literature (Bartlett s., 1989; Pugh, Hickson, Hinings, & Turner, 1968). However, despite this ongoing and widely held discussion on coordination and control in MNCs surprisingly few generalizable insights have endured time and empirical results are mixed (e.g., Egelhoff, 1991; Gencturk & Aulakh, 1995; O'Donnel, 2000).

Given the rapid increase in levels of foreign direct investment in CEE over the last decade (OECD, 2005), we explored how Western developed management and control theories and techniques apply in CEE. Investing in CEE bears some risk since most markets are in a state of transition which is marked by a fundamental change in the norms, values, and assumptions underlying economic activity (Roth et al., 2003). Communism was abandoned speedily but is only slowly replaced with new norms, values, and assumptions that are more consistent with democracy and a market-based economy (Napier et al., 2004; Newman, 2000). New capabilities such as efficiency orientation, strategic thinking, entrepreneurial initiative and proneness to take risk are required, but those develop only slowly (Newman, 2000). Austria can be seen as a gateway to the East, since not only Austrian firms invested heavily in CEE but also MNCs use Austria as a hub for their regional CEE headquarters (Breinbauer et al., 2003). The growing dynamic and complexity of markets in CEE transition economies call for control mechanisms which maintain flexibility and transparency at the same time (Gigouline et al., 2001). Management control plays a crucial role for effectively managing foreign direct investments since it forms the basis for decision making in MNCs (Reichmann, 1995; Vogel, 1998). Building on those observations we undertook a study aimed at advancing the state of our theoretical and empirical understanding of how MNCs govern their CEE subsidiaries. It represents a first attempt to identify contingencies and perceived cultural characteristics that determine the applicability of management control in CEE. Understanding the factors that influence the adoption of HQ management control practices in CEE enhances the success with which such practices are disseminated and in turn affects a firm's economic performance (O'Connor et al., 2004).

Our study contributes to the understanding of international management control by MNCs

- theoretically, by providing a comprehensive framework of factors determining the cross-border diffusion of management control based on a literature review of 95 articles in IB journals, and
- empirically, by analyzing the type and extent of management control exerted by Western MNCs in their subsidiaries in CEE, and by proposing a model of fit between type and extent of management control, contingencies, perceptions of culture and moderators.

First, a literature review on existing studies on management control in MNCs in major IB journals was conducted. The journals were selected based on their relevance and impact in the field of management control in international ventures. There are basically two approaches found in the literature on cross-cultural studies of the transfer of management control mechanisms: research based on contingency theory, which considers contextual variables as major determinants of MCS and the culture based perspective, which sees culture as explaining international variations in management control. The following contingencies were identified as major influences on management control: subsidiary size, the level of interdependence between HQ and subsidiary, uncertain and complex environments, economic and technological imperatives, and resources and ownership structure. The presence, degree of intensity, and combination of those factors determine their magnitude on the diffusion process and the level of appropriateness and 'fit' of different control mechanisms. Culture also impacts management control as cultural distance plays a pivotal role on the transfer success of management practices. The cultural proximity or distance between organizational units of an MNC affects the applicability of management control and presents a major challenge to the diffusion of MCS. The effect of culture is twofold: on the one hand it directly affects management thinking, styles and preferences through values, on the other hand it shapes an HQ nature, structures and modes of control through the 'country of origin effect' arising through distinctive features in national institutional structures. Most analyzed studies focused on Anglo-American vs. Asian societies and none of the analyzed studies dealt with managerial control in a Central and Eastern European setting. Expatriate presence, international experience, and trust were identified as having a moderating effect on the friction caused by cultural distance on the applicability of management control in offshore units. Ultimately, a comprehensive framework was developed unifying findings from both paradigms.

Second, the type and extent of MNC control, and the salience of context and cultural factors impacting MNC management control identified in the literature review were tested by an empirical study in the context of CEE. So far, empirical studies on international management control have predominantly used quantitative methods to obtain data, which might have yielded to a lower level of understanding of the underlying phenomena than required. Given the novelty of analyzing HQ control in the context of CEE, we used the qualitative method of the semi-structured interview. This allowed us to follow up why and how questions while the comparability of data was assured by the use of the interview guide. Interview data was analyzed with computer-aided qualitative content analysis (Mayring, 2002b). The use of Atlas.ti software was highly helpful for 'quantifying' our qualitative analysis, for example by allowing us to account for the frequency of quotations and the number of respondents represented by quotation.

Semi-structured interviews were conducted with 46 interviewees on a sample of 40 MNCs having their international or regional HQ for CEE located in Austria. The companies were selected following a non-probabilistic method from an identified population of approximately 200. Hence, the sample represents some 20 percent of the population. In order to control for extraneous variation across industry sectors, firms were selected from various industries likely to differ on factors affecting the motivation to adopt more formal and transparent MCS. In all companies the ownership percentage of the CEE-subsidiaries was at least 50 percent, and in most companies this percentage was 100 percent. All HQ had at least two subsidiaries and/or joint ventures in CEE ranging from two to forty subsidiaries. The investigated international or regional HQ were of Austrian (47 percent), German (40 percent), Japanese (5 percent), American (2.5 percent), Swiss (2.5 percent) and Danish (2.5 percent) ownership. All HQ were located in Austria and relied mostly on Austrian and German personnel. In addition, these firms have had to be in place for a minimum time of five years in order to have a history of operating data.

9.3 Culture, contingencies and MNC management control in CEE

Grounded on our data analysis, we proposed the following model of management control in CEE (Figure 8.1) which sheds light onto how the context and cultural specifics of CEE as perceived by HQ executives, influences the design and extent of HQ control exerted in CEE ventures.

We find that both, perceived cultural characteristics which are to some degree rooted in a communist past and the current political and economic risk, have a bearing on the extent and type of control exerted by Western HQ in their CEE subsidiaries.

9.4 Culture

Our findings show that the perceived risk attributed to cultural differences affects the applicability of MNC management control in CEE. We found eighteen cultural characteristics of CEE based on the perception of our interviewees which are important in a management control context. Some of the most important perceptions of CEE culture impacting management control include passive resistance, the importance attached to personal relations, strong hierarchies and the power status of top management, national pride, a polychronic perception of time resulting in a relaxed view on HQ deadlines, a high esteem for local authorities, and a lack of acceptance for Eastern European third-country nationals in management positions. Those perceptions are based on Austrian, German and Swiss respondents, thus their explanatory power is limited. In general, the higher the perceived risk attributed to cultural differences by HQ executives the greater is the degree of centralized HQ control. Culture also affects contingencies, since HQ-, subsidiary-, and country-characteristics are influenced by the 'country of origin effect', which implies that a nation's institutional structures and practices are heavily shaped by a nation's culture. Given that most of the nations in CEE experience great changes due to economic transition, a general upheaval in values was noted in our data which also impacts the effectiveness of MCSs. For example, while the 'older generation' in CEE is not motivated by performance-related pay schemes the younger generation welcomes such incentives.

9.5 Contingencies

In line with the findings of the literature review, a number of contingencies were found to impact the type and choice of MCS: We found that a high environmental uncertainty on the country level, such as political risk, a frequently changing legislation, an opaque bureaucracy, and some degree of corruption have a bearing on both the type and extent of control exerted by HQ. Economic risk caused by the transition process, the development stage of a nation, and the intensity of regional competition was also found to impact management control. On the subsidiary level, the size and importance of a subsidiary as perceived by the HQ and the degree of maturity influence MCS design. Majority ownership was found to be beneficial for operational HQ control. Lastly, we noted that the nationality of the HQ might have an impact on MCS preferences, however, given our limited sample and the exploratory nature of our research design our latter findings should be taken with care. Moreover, strategic choice was found to impact the type and extent of management control exerted in CEE subsidiaries.

9.6 Moderators

A number of moderators on the organizational and individual level which have a moderating effect on the perceived cultural differences were identified: A high level of communication including intense personal contact, knowledge transfer between HQ and subsidiaries, a high level of trust between the HQ and the subsidiary, some past international experience of the HQ, a participative but assertive management style, top-management support, and expatriates as social butterflies were found to have a positive impact the perceived risk attributed to cultural differences on the organizational level. Additionally, some personality traits which bring forward cultural sensitivity, a personal experience of working abroad and language capabilities were found to offset potential negative effects triggered by perceived cultural differences on an individual level.

9.7 Conclusion

Our empirical findings show that both contingencies and perceptions on CEE culture determine the applicability and choice of MCSs in CEE subsidiaries. Together with the presence or absence of moderators they impact an HQ design in terms of type and extent of management control.

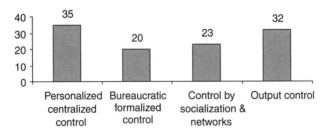

Figure 9.1 Distribution of control types.

The majority of MNCs rely on personal centralized control and output control, and use a combination of explicit and implicit management control types in order to effectively govern their CEE ventures. The layout of our interview guide allowed us to account for the frequency of control types as distinguished by Harzing (1999): 35 of the investigated HQ conduct personal centralized control, 20 pursue bureaucratic formalized control, another 23 score high on control by socialization and networks and 32 score high on output control. In terms of control extent, 65 percent of all CEE headquarters can be categorized as operative holdings exerting operational control over their subsidiaries and the remaining 35 percent as strategic or management holdings exerting strategic control over their foreign ventures. Important strategic decisions regarding finance and investment are always made at the HQ.

Ultimately, the level of fit between the chosen extent and type of control and a given scenario of culture and context, impacts effective management control in CEE subsidiaries and at last, an MNC's performance. Therefore, we propose that MNCs need to use a combination of both explicit and implicit control mechanisms to effectively manage their CEE subsidiaries. We hope that this study provides a first step towards more empirical research on the role of context and culture on MCS in IB.

9.8 The management challenge

Many MNCs continue to grow by expanding further eastward into new countries. At the same time, the dramatic shifts in the political structure in CEE in recent years implies that all MNCs face a new set of host governments with emerging economies, a shifting sets of government restrictions and an upheaval in norms and values of CEE societies. MNCs must find means to effectively manage and control their Eastern subsidiaries given this increased level of complexity and the diminished discretion of the parent's ability to assess the subsidiary and its management. Increasing levels of FDI in CEE make the primary area of inquiry of this study both important and urgent. The model proposed in this paper, is an important step in understanding how MNCs can control their subsidiaries effectively in increasingly complex and uncertain foreign environments. Determinants of effective management control in CEE subsidiaries which were perceived to be of high importance by our interviewees include centralized control, a combination of explicit and implicit control types, an ongoing and intense contact with CEE subsidiaries, a 'right' mix of expatriates and locals, and a mutual know-how transfer between HQ and subsidiaries.

Appendix

Cultural dimensions: Hofstede (1980) and House et al. (2004) and Trompenaars (1997) on a glimpse

Hofstede's (1980) cultural dimensions

Using a survey of some 116,000 individuals from 72 countries, Hofstede (1980) identified four important dimensions of work-related national culture and suggested (1983, 1984, 1991) that specific relationships exist between these cultural dimensions and individual's preferences and actions in an employment setting. Hofstede's four cultural dimensions are as follows:

Individualism vs. collectivism

Individualism is a measure of the relative importance of the individual's self-interest and immediate family compared to the wider group interest (with which the individual associates), his/her extended family. In organizations, goals and independence are stressed in high individualistic societies while more dependence on the organizations is favored in a low individualistic (collectivistic) society (Hofstede, 1980: 79).

Large vs. small power distance

A measure of the extent to which a society accepts the fact that power in institutions and organizations is distributed unequally. The level of power distance is related to the degree of centralization of authority and the degree to which cultures prefer a more autocratic leadership (Hofstede, 1980: 97)

High vs. low uncertainty avoidance

Uncertainty Avoidance indicates the extent to which a society feels threatened by uncertain and ambiguous situations and tries to avoid these situations by providing greater career stability, establishing more formal rules, not tolerating deviant ideas and behaviors, and believing in absolute truths and attainment of expertise (Hofstede, 1980: 155).

Masculinity vs. femininity

Masculinity is a measure of the extent to which the dominant values in society are masculine – that is, assertiveness, the acquisition of money and things, compared to the importance of work relations, cooperation and security (Hofstede, 1983: 83).

Confucian dynamism (based on Hofstede and Bond (1988))

Confucian Dynamism is a measure of the relative positioning of the values in a society between long-term and short-term orientation poles based on the teachings of Confucius. The long-term orientation pole comprises the values of persistence, status, thrift and having a sense of shame. On the opposite pole, 'short-term orientation', the values of personal steadiness and stability, protecting one's face, respect for tradition and reciprocation of greetings, favors, and gifts are emphasized (Hofstede, 1991) (Hofstede, 1991: 165–166)

Globe dimensions

'The meta-goal of Globe is to develop an empirically-based theory to describe, understand, and predict the impact of specific cultural variables on leadership and organizational processes and the effectiveness of these processes' (House, Javidan, Hanges, & Dorfmann, 2002).

- **Uncertainty avoidance** is defined as the extent to which members of an organization or society strive to avoid uncertainty by reliance on social norms, rituals, and bureaucratic practices to alleviate the unpredictability of future events.
- **Power distance** is defined as the degree to which members of an organization or society expect and agree that power should be unequally shared.
- **Collectivism I**: Societal collectivism reflects the degree to which organizational and societal institutional practices encourage and reward collective distribution of resources and collective action.
- **Collectivism II**: In-group collectivism reflects the degree to which individuals express pride, loyalty and cohesiveness in their organizations or families.
- **Gender egalitarianism** is the extent to which an organization or a society minimizes gender role differences and gender discrimination.
- **Assertiveness** is the degree to which individuals in organizations or societies are assertive, confrontational, and aggressive in social relationships.
- **Future orientation** is the degree to which individuals in organizations or societies engage in future-oriented behaviors such as planning, investing in the future, and delaying gratification.
- **Performance orientation** refers to the extent to which an organization or society encourages and rewards group members for performance improvement and excellence. This dimension includes the future-oriented component of the dimension called Confucian Dynamism by Hofstede and Bond (1988).
- Finally, **Humane orientation** is the degree to which individuals in organizations or societies encourage and reward individuals for being fair, altruistic, friendly, generous, caring, and kind to others. This dimension is similar to the dimension labeled Kind Heartedness by Hofstede and Bond (1988).

Source: House et al. (2002)

Trompenaars Dimensions (1997)

Universalism vs. particularism

People in **universalistic** cultures share the belief that general rules, codes, values and standards take precedence over particular needs and claims of friends and relations. In a universalistic society, the rules apply equally to the whole 'universe' of members. Any exception weakens the rule.

Particularistic cultures see the ideal culture in terms of human friendship, extraordinary achievement and situations; and in intimate relationships. The 'spirit of the law' is deemed more important than the 'letter of the law'. Obviously there are rules and laws in particularistic cultures; but these merely codify here how people relate to each other. Rules are needed – if only to be able to make exceptions to them for particular cases – but we need to be able to count on our friends.

Individualism vs. communitarianism

Each one of us is born alone. In a predominantly **individualistic** culture people place the individual before the community. Individual happiness, fulfillment, and welfare set the pace. People are expected to decide matters largely on their own and to take care primarily of themselves and their immediate family. In a particularistic culture, the quality of life for all members of society is seen as directly dependent on opportunities for individual freedom and development. The community is judged by the extent to which it serves the interest of individual members.

Each one of us is born into a family, a neighborhood, a community, which existed before we did, and will continue after we die. In a predominantly **communitarian** culture people place the community before the individual. It is the responsibility of the individual to act in ways which serve society. By doing so, individual needs will be taken care of naturally. The quality of life for the individual is seen as directly dependent on the degree to which he takes care of his fellow man, even at the cost of individual freedom. The individual is judged by the extent to which he serves the interest of the community.

Specific vs. diffuse

People from **specific** cultures start with the elements, the specifics. First they analyze them separately, and then they put them back together again. In specific cultures, the whole is the sum of its parts. Each person's life is divided into many components: you can only enter one at a time. Interactions between people are highly purposeful and well-defined. The public sphere of specific individuals is much larger than their private sphere. People are easily accepted into the public sphere, but it is very difficult to get into the private sphere, since each area in which two people encounter each other is considered separate from the other, a specific case. Specific individuals concentrate on hard facts; standards; contracts.

People from **diffusely oriented cultures** start with the whole and see each element in perspective of the total. All elements are related to each other. These relationships are more important than each separate element; so the whole is more than just the sum of its elements. Diffuse individuals have a large private sphere and a small public one. Newcomers are not easily accepted into either. But once they have been accepted, they are admitted into all layers of the individual's life. A friend is a friend in all respects: tennis, cooking, work, etc. The various roles someone might play in your life are not separated. Qualities cherished by diffuse cultures include style, demeanor, ambiance, trust, understanding, etc.

Affective vs. neutral

In an **affective** culture people do not object to a display of emotions. It isn't considered necessary to hide feelings and to keep them inside. Affective cultures may interpret the less explicit signals of a neutral culture as less important. They may be ignored or even go unnoticed.

In a **neutral** culture people are taught that it is incorrect to show one's feelings overtly. This doesn't mean they do not have feelings, it just means that the degree to which feeling may become manifest is limited. They accept and are aware of feelings, but are in control of them. Neutral cultures may think the louder signals of an affective culture too excited, and over-emotional. In neutral cultures, showing too much emotion may erode your power to interest people.

Achievement vs. ascription

Achieved status refers to what an individual does and has accomplished. In achievement-oriented cultures, individuals derive their status from what they have accomplished. A person with achieved status has to prove what he is worth over and over again: status is accorded on the basis of his actions.

Ascribed status refers to what a person is and how others relate to his or her position in the community, in society or in an organization. In an ascriptive society, individuals derive their status from birth, age, gender or wealth. A person with ascribed status does not have to achieve to retain his status: it is accorded to him on the basis of his being.

Time: sequential vs. synchronic cultures

Every culture has developed its own response to time. The time orientation dimension has two aspects: the relative importance cultures give to the past, present, and future, and their approach to structuring time. Time can be structured in two ways.

In one approach time moves forward, second by second, minute by minute, hour by hour in a straight line. This is called **sequentialism**. In another approach time moves round in cycles: of minutes, hours, days, years. We call this synchronism. People structuring time sequentially tend to do one thing at a time. They view time as a narrow line of distinct, consecutive segments. Sequential people view time as tangible and divisible. They strongly prefer planning and keeping to plans once they have been made. Time commitments are taken seriously. Staying on schedule is a must.

People structuring time **synchronically** usually do several things at a time. To them, time is a wide ribbon, allowing many things to take place simultaneously. Time is flexible and intangible. Time commitments are desirable rather than absolute. Plans are easily changed. Synchronic people especially value the satisfactory completion of interactions with others. Promptness depends on the type of relationship

Relations with nature: internal vs. external

Every culture has developed an attitude towards the natural environment. Survival has meant acting with or against nature. The way we relate to our environment is linked to the way we seek to have control over our own lives and over our destiny or fate.

Internalistic people have a mechanistic view of nature. They see nature as a complex machine and machines can be controlled if you have the right expertise. Internalistic people do not believe in luck or predestination. They are 'inner-directed' – one's personal resolution is the starting point for every action. You can live the life you want to live if you take advantage of the opportunities. Man can dominate nature – if he makes the effort.

Externalistic people have a more organic view of nature. Mankind is one of nature's forces, so should operate in harmony with the environment. Man should subjugate to nature and go along with its forces. Externalistic people do not believe that they can shape their own destiny. 'Nature moves in mysterious ways', and therefore you never know what will happen to you. The actions of externalistic people are 'outer-directed' – adapted to external circumstances.

Source: Trompenaars (1997)

http://www.7d-culture.nl/Content/cont042.htm

Bibliography

Adler, N. 1984. Understanding the ways of understanding: cross-cultural management methodology reviewed. *Advances in International Comparative Management*, 1: 31–67.

Adler, N. J. 2002. *International Dimensions of Organizational Behavior* (4 ed.). Canada: South-Western/Thomson Learning.

Ahrens, T. 1996. Styles of accountability. *Accounting, Organizations and Society*, 21: 139–173.

Ahrens, T. 1997. Talking accounting: An ethnography of management knowledge in British and German Brewers. *Accounting, Organizations and Society*, 22: 617–637.

Alvesson, M. 1993. Organization as rhetoric: knowledge intensive firms and the struggle with ambiguity. *Journal of Management Studies*, 30(6): 997–1015.

Alvesson, M., & Deetz, S. 2000. *Doing Critical Management Research*. London: Sage.

Ambos, B., & Reitsperger, W. D. 2004. Offshore centers of excellence: social control and success. *Management International Review*, 44(2 special issue): 51–65.

Amburgey, T. L., & Dacin, T. 1994. As the left foot follows the right? The dynamics of strategic and structural change. *Academy of Management Journal*, 37(6): 1427–1452.

Andersen, P. H., & Skaates, M. A. 2004. Ensuring validity in qualitative international business research. In R. Marschan-Piekkari, & C. Welch (Eds), *Handbook of Qualitative Research Methods for International Business*: 464–485. Cheltenham UK: Edward Elgar.

Anthony, R. N. 1965. *Planning and Control Systems: Framework for Analysis*. Boston: Graduate School of Business Administration, Harvard University.

Anthony, R. N., Dearden, J., & Bedford, N. M. 1989. *Management Control Systems* (6 ed.). Irwin: Homewood.

Anthony, R. N., & Govindarajan, V. 2000. *Management Control Systems*. McGraw-Hill, Irwin.

Arnold, D. F., Bernardi, R. A., & Neidermeyer, P. E. 2001. The association between European materiality estimates and client integrity, national culture, and litigation. *The International Journal of Accounting*, 36: 459–483.

Arrow, K. J. 1974. *The Limits of Organization*. New York: W. W. Norton.

Atteslander, P. (Ed.). 2000. *Methoden der empirischen Sozialforschung* (9 ed.). Berlin: Walter de Gruyter.

Awasthi, V. N., Chow, C. W., & Wu, A. 2001. Cross-cultural differences in the behavioral consequences of imposing performance evaluation and reward systems: An experimental investigation. *The International Journal of Accounting*, 36: 291–309.

Bakacsi, G. 1999. The pendulum effect: culture, transition, learning. In C. Makó, & C. Warhurst (Eds), *The Management and Organisation of Firm in the Global Context*: 111–118. Budapest: The Institute of Management Education, University of Gödöll and the Department of Management and Organisation, Budapest University of Economic Sciences.

Bakacsi, G., Takacs, S., Karacsonyi, A., & Imrek, V. 2002. Eastern european cluster: tradition and transition. *Journal of World Business*, 37(1): 69–80.

Baliga, B. R., & Jaeger, A. 1984. Multinational corporations: Control systems and delegation issues. *Journal of International Business Studies*, 15(Fall): 25–40.

Barden, J., Steensma, H. K., & Lyles, M. A. 2005. The influence of parent control structure on parent conflict in Vietnamese international joint ventures: an organizational justice-based contingency approach. *Journal of International Business Studies*, 36(2): 156–175.

Barnard, C. I. 1968. *The Functions of Executives*. Harvard: Harvard University Press.

Barney, J. 1991. Firm resources and sustained competitive advantage. *Journal of Management*, 17(1): 99–120.

Barney, J. B., & Hansen, M. H. 1995. Trustworthiness as a source of competitive advantage. *Strategic Management Journal*, 15(Special Issue): 175–190.

Bartlett, C. A., & Ghoshal, S. 1989. *Managing across Borders: the Transnational Solution*. Boston, MA: Harvard Business School Press.

Baskerville, R. F. 2003. Hofstede never studied culture. *Accounting, Organizations and Society*, 28: 1–14.

Baumler, J. V. 1971. Defined criteria of performance in organizational control. *Administrative Science Quarterly*: 340–350.

Bayer, L. 1996. Kulturgerechete Konzepte für das Management in Mittel- und Osteuropa. In C. Steinle (Ed.), *Management in Mittel- und Osteuropa: Konzepte, Praxis, Perspektiven*: 99–123. Frankfurt am Main: Frankfurter Allgemeine Zeitung.

Beamish, P. W., & Inkpen, A. 1998. Japanese firms and the decline of the Japanese expatriate. *Journal of World Business*, 33(1): 35–50.

Beard, V., & Al-Rai, Z. 1999. Collection and transmission of accounting information across cultural borders: The of U.S. MNEs in Jordan. *The International Journal of Accounting*, 34: 133–150.

Beatty, P. 1995. Understanding the standardized/non-standardized interviewing controversy. *Journal of Official Statistics*, 11(2): 147–160.

Becker-Ritterspach, F., Lange, K., & Lohr, K. 2002. Control mechanisms and patterns of reorganization in MNCs. In M. Geppert, D. Matten, & K. l. Williams (Eds), *Challenges for European Management in a Global Context*: 68–95. Basingstoke: Palgrave/Macmillan.

Beechler, S., & Yang, J. Z. 1994. The Transfer of Japanese-style management to American Subsidiaries: contingencies, constraints, and competencies. *Journal of International Business Studies*, 25: 467–491.

Bendak, J. 1992. *Controlling im Konzern*. München: Münchener Schriften zur angewandten Führungslehre.

Bendix, R. 1956. *Work and Authority in Industry*. Frankfurt a. M.: Europ. Verl.-Anst.

Berger, P., & Luckmann, T. 1967. *The Social Construction of Reality: A Treatise in the Sociology of Knowledge*. New York: Anchor Books.

Berland, J. 1997. Nationalism and the modernist legacy: dialogues with Innis. *Culture and Policy*, 8(3): 9–39.

Berle, A., & Means, G. 1932. *The Modern Corporation and Private Property*. New York: Macmillan.

Bernard, H. R. 2000. *Social Research Methods: Qualitative and Quantitative Approaches*. Thousand Oaks, CA: Sage.

Bewely, T. 2002. Interviews as a valid tool in economics. *Journal of Socio-Economics*, 31: 343–353.

Bhimani, A. 1999. Mapping methodological frontiers in cross-national management control research. *Accounting Organizations and Society*, 24: 413–440.

Bijlsma-Frankema, K. 2001. Faktoren des Erfolges und Misserfolges kultureller Integrationsprozesse in Mergers und Acquisitions. In G. Fink, & S. Meierewert (Eds), *Interkulturelles Management – Österreichische Perspektiven*. Wien: Springer Verlag.

Birkinshaw, J. 1997. Entrepreneurship in multinational companies: the characteristics of subsidiary initiatives. *Strategic Management Journal*, 18(3): 207–230.

Birkinshaw, J., & Morrison, A. J. 1995. Configurations of strategy and structure in subsidiaries of multinational corporations. *Journal of International Business Studies*, 26(4): 729–754.

Birnberg, J., & Snodgrass, C. 1988. Culture and control: A field study. *Accounting, Organizations and Society*: 447–464.

Birnberg, J. G., Shields, M. D., & Young, S. M. 1990. The case for multiple methods in empirical management accounting research (with an illustration from budget setting). *Journal of Management Accounting Research*, 2: 33–66.

Björkman, I., Barner-Rasmussen, W., & Li, L. 2004. Managing knowledge transfer in MNCs: the impact of headquarters control mechanisms. *Journal of International Business Studies*, 35(5): 443–456.

Black, S., Mendenhall, M., & Oddou, G. 1991. Toward a comprehensive model of international adjustment: an integration of multiple theoretical perspectives. *Academy of Management Journal*, 16(2): 291–317.

Blau, P. M. 1970. A formal theory of differentiation in organizations. *American Sociological Review*, 35: 201–218.

Blau, P. M., & Scott, W. R. 1963. *Formal Organizations*. London: Routledge and Kegan Paul.

Bleeke, J., & Ernst, D. 1993. *Collaborating to Compete: Using Strategic Alliances and Acquisitions in the Global Marketplace*. New York: Wiley.

Blumer, H. 1981. Der methodologische Standort des Symbolischen Interaktionismus. In A. B. Soziologen (Ed.), *Alltagswissen, Interaktion und gesellschaftliche Wirklichkeit*: 80–146. Opladen: Westdeutscher Verlag.

Boisot, M., & Child, J. 1999. Organizations as adaptive systems in complex environments: the case of China. *Organization Science*, 10: 237–352.

Bortz, J., & Döring, N. 2002. *Forschungsmethoden und Evaluation für Human- und Sozialwissenschaftler* (3 ed.). Berlin.

Boski, P. 2003. Polen. In A. Thomas, S. Kammhuber, & S. Schroll-Machl (Eds), *Handbuch interkulturelle Kommunikation und Kooperation Band 2 Länder, Kulturen und interkulturelle Berufstätigkeit*: 120–134. Göttingen: Vandenhoeck & Ruprecht.

Breinbauer, A., & Wakounig, M. 2003. Investieren in Osteuropa – Hintergrundwissen und Praxis Tipps für Geschäfte in den 10 EU-Beitrittsländern. Frankfurt/Wien: Carl Ueberreuter.

Brenner, B., & Reus, T. H. 2006. An Agency View on Headquarter-Subsidiary Relations of Western MNCs in Central- and Eastern Europe. Paper presented at the Annual Meeting of the Academy of International Business, Beijing.

Brislin, R. W., Cushner, K., Cherrie, C., & Yong, M. 1986. *Intercultural Interactions: A Practical Guide*. Beverly Hills, CA: Sage.

Brodbeck, F. C., Frese, M., Ackerblom, S., Audia, G., Bakacsi, G., & Bendova, H. 2000. Cultural variation of leadership prototypes across 22 European countries. *Journal of Occupational and Organizational Psychology*. 73: 1–29.

Brownell, P. 1981. Participation in budgeting, locus of control and organizational performance. *The Accounting Review*, LVI(4 October): 844–860.

Brownell, P. 1987. The use of accounting information in management control. In K. R. Ferris, & J. L. Livingstone (Eds), *Management Planning and Control: the Behavioural Foundations*: 177–196. Ohio: Century VII.

Brück, F. 1999. Österreichische, Deutsche und Schweitzer Kulturstandards. In G. Fink, & S. Meierewert (Eds), *Interkulturelles Management – Österreichische Perspektiven*: 140–155. Wien: Springer.

Brueck, F. 2002. Interkulturelles Management – Kulturvergleich Österreich, Deutschland, Schweiz, Wien: IKO-Verlag für Interkulturelle Kommunikation.

Bruns, W. J., & Waterhouse, J. H. 1975. Budgetary control and organization structure. *Journal of Accounting Research*, 5: 177–203.

Buckley, P. J., & Chapman, M. 1996. Theory and method in international business research. *International Business Review*, 5(3): 223–245.

Burns, T., & Stalker, G. M. 1961. *The Management of Innovation*. London: Tavistock Publications.

Burton, R. M., & Obel, B. 2004. Strategic Organizational Diagnosis and Design – The Dynamics of Fit (3 ed.). Boston: Kluwer.

Caligiuri, P. 2000. The big five personality characteristics as predictors of expatriate's desire to terminate the assignment and supervisor-rated performance. *Personnel Psychology*, 53: 67–86.

Calori, R., Labatkin, M., & Very, P. 1994. Control mechanisms in cross-border acquisitions: an international comparison. *Organization Studies*, 15(3): 361–379.

Capelli, P., & Sherer, P. 1991. The missing role of context in OB: the need for a meso level approach. *Research in Organizational Behavior*, 13: 55–110.

Cassell, C., & Symon, G. 1994. *Qualitative Methods in Organizational Research*. London: Sage.

Cavusgil, S. T., & Das, A. 1997. Methodological issues in empirical cross-cultural research: a survey of the management literature and a framework. *Management International Review*, 38(1): 71–96.

Chandler, A. D. 1962. Strategy and Structure: Chapters in the History of the industrial Enterprise. Cambridge, MA: MIT Press.

Chang, E., & Taylor, S. 1999. Control in Multinational Corporations (MNCs): The case of Korean manufacturing subsidiaries. *Journal of Management*, 25(4): 541–565.

Chang-Bum, C., & Beamish, P. W. 2004. Split management control and international joint venture performance. *Journal of International Business Studies*, 35: 201–215.

Chapman, C. S. 1997. Reflections on a contingent view of accounting. *Accounting, Organizations and Society*, 22(2): 189–205.

Chenhall, R. H. 1986. Authoritarianism and participative budgeting: a dyadic analysis. *The Accounting Review*, 2: 263–272.

Chenhall, R. H. 2003. Management control systems design within its organizational context: findings from contingency-based research and directions for the future. *Accounting, Organizations and Society*, 28: 127–168.

Child, J. 1972. Organization structures and strategies of control: a replication of the Aston Study. *Administrative Science Quaterly*, 17: 163–177.

Child, J. 1973. Strategies of control and organizational behavior. *Administrative Science Quarterly*, March: 1–17.

Child, J. 1984. Organization: a Guide to Problems and Practice. London: Harper and Row.

Child, J., Faulkner, D., & Pitkethly, R. 2001. *The Management of International Acquisitions*. Oxford: Oxford Univ. Press.

Child, J., & Yan, Y. 1999. Investment and control in international joint ventures: the case of China. *Journal of World Business*, 34(1): 3–15.

Child, J., & Yan, Y. 2003. Predicting performance of international joint ventures: an investigation in China. *Journal of Management Studies*, 40(2): 283–320.

Chini, T., Ambos, B., & Wehle, K. 2005. The headquarters-subsidiary trench: tracing perception gaps within the multinational Corporation. *European Management Journal*, 23(2): 134–153.

Chow, C. W., Harrison, G. L., McKinnon, J. L., & Wu, A. 1999a. Cultural influences on informal information sharing in Chinese and Anglo-American organizations: an exploratory study. *Accounting, Organizations and Society*, 24(7): 561–582.

Chow, C. W., Hwang, R. N. C., Liao, W., & Wu, A. 1998. National culture and subordinates's upward communication of private information. *The International Journal of Accounting*, 33(3): 293–311.

Chow, C. W., Kato, Y., & Merchant, K. A. 1996. The use of organizational controls and their effects on data manipulation and management myopia: a Japan vs. US comparison. *Accounting, Organizations and Society*, 21: 175–192.

Chow, C. W., Shields, M. D., & Wu, A. 1999b. The importance of national culture in the design of and preference for management controls for multinational operations. *Accounting, Organizations and Society*, 24(5–6): 441–461.

Clark, R. 1979. *The Japanese Company*. London: Yale University Press.

Coase, R. H. 1937. The nature of the firm. *Economica*, 4: 386–405.

Cohen, W. M., & Levinthal, D. A. 1990. Absorptive capacity: A new perspective on learning and innovation. *Administrative Science Quarterly*, 35: 128–152.

Collins, F., Holzmann, O., & Mendoza, R. 1997. Strategy, budgeting and crisis in Latin America. *Accounting, Organizations and Society*, 22: 669–689.

Cray, D. 1984. Control and coordination in multinational corporations. *Journal of International Business Studies*, Fall: 85–98.

Cronbach, L. 1946. Response sets and test validity. *Educational and Psychology Measurement*, 6: 475–494.

Crozier, M. 1964. *The Bureaucratic Phenomenon*. Chicago: University of Chicago Press.

Daniels, J. D., & Cannice, M. V. 2004. Interview studies in international business research. In R. Marschan-Piekkari, & C. Welch (Eds), *Handbook of qualitative*

Research Methods for International Business: 185–206. Cheltenham, UK: Edward Elgar.

Das, T. K., & Teng, B. 1998. Between trust and control: developing confidence in partner cooperation in alliances. *Academy of Management Review*, 23(3): 491–512.

Davies, H., & Ma, C. 2003. Strategic choice and the nature of the Chinese family business: an exploratory study of the Hong-Kong watch industry. *Organization Studies*, 24(9): 1405–1435.

Deci, E. D. 1980. *The Psychology of Self-Determination*. Lexington, U.S.: Lexington Books, D.C. Heath and Company.

Dedoussis, V. 1995. Simply a question of cultural barriers? The search for new perspectives in the transfer of Japanese management practices. *Journal of Management Studies*, 32(6): 731–745.

Denzin, N. K. 1989. The Research Act: A Theoretical Introduction to Sociological Methods (3 ed.). Englewood Cliffs, NJ: Prentice Hall.

Dharwadkar, R., George, G., & Brandes, P. 2000. Privatization in emerging economies: an agency perspective. *Academy of Management Review*, 25(3): 650–669.

Dickmann, M. 1999. Balancing global, parent and local influences: International human resource management of German multinational companies. University of London, London.

Dieckhaus, O.-T. 1993. Management und Controlling im Beteiligungslebenszyklus. Bergisch-Gladbach: Eul.

Dixon, N. M. 2000. Common Knowledge: How Companies Thrive by Sharing What They Know. Boston: Harvard Business School Press.

Doremus, P. N., Keller, W., Pauley, L., & Reich, S. 1998. *The Myth of the Global Corporation*. Princeton, NJ: Princeton University Press.

Doupnik, T. S., & Richter, M. 2003. Interpretation of uncertainty expressions: a cross-national study. *Accounting, Organizations and Society*, 28: 15–35.

Dowling, P. J., Welch, P. E., & Schuler, R. S. 1999. *International Human Resource Management* (3 ed.). Cincinnati, Ohio: South Western College Publishing.

Doz, Y. L., & Prahalad, C. K. 1981. Headquarters influence and strategic control in MNCs. *Sloan Management Review* (Fall) 23: 15–29.

Doz, Y. L., & Prahalad, C. K. 1986. Controlled variety: A challenge for human resource management in the MNC. *Human Resource Management*, 25 (55–71).

Doz, Y. L., & Prahalad, C. K. 1988. Patterns for strategic control with multinational corporations. *Journal of International Business studies*, Fall: 55–72.

Doz, Y. L., & Prahalad, C. K. 1991. Managing MNCs: a search for a new paradigm. *Strategic Management Journal*, 12: 145–164.

Drucker, P. 1990. *Managing the Non-Profit Organization*. London: Butterworth.

Duncan, R. B. 1972. Characteristics of organizational environments and perceived environmental uncertainty. *Administrative Science Quarterly*, 17(3): 313–327.

Durkin, T. 1997. Using computers in strategic qualitative research. In G. Miller, & R. Dingwall (Eds), *Context and Method in Qualitative Research*: 92–105. Thousand Oaks, CA: Sage.

Dyer, J. H. 1997. Effective interfirm collaboration: how firms minimize transaction costs and maximize transaction value. *Strategic Management Journal*, 18: 536–556.

Eckhardt, G. M. 2004. The Role of culture in conducting trustworthy and credible qualitative business research in China. In R. Marschan-Piekkari, & C. Welch (Eds), *Handbook of Qualitatitive Research Methods for International Business*: 402–420. Cheltenham, UK: Edward Elgar.

Eden, L., Dacin, T., & Wan, W. 2001. Standards across borders: crossborder diffusion of the arm's length standard in North America. *Accounting, Organizations and Society*, 26: 1–23.

Edstrom, A., & Galbraith, J. R. 1977. Transfer of managers as a coordinative and control strategy in multinational organizations. *Administrative Science Quarterly*, 22: 248–263.

Egelhoff, W. G. 1984. Patterns of control in U.S., U.K. and European multinational corporations. *Journal of International Business Studies*, 15(2): 73–83.

Egelhoff, W. G. 1988. Strategy and structure in multinational corporations: a revision of the Stopford and Wells model. *Strategic Management Journal*, 9(Jan/Feb): 1–14.

Eisenhardt, K. M. 1989a. Agency theory: An assessment and review. *Academy of Management Review*, 14: 57–74.

Eisenhardt, K. M. 1989b. Building theories from case study research. *Academy of Management Review*, 14: 532–550.

Erez, M., & Early, P. C. 1993. *Culture, Self-Identity, and Work*. New York: Oxford University Press.

Erramilli, K. M. 1996. Nationality and subsidiary ownership patterns in multinational corporations. *Journal of International Business Studies*, 27(2): 225–248.

Erramilli, M. K. 1991. The experience factor in the foreign market entry behavior of service firms. *Journal of International Business Studies*, 22(3): 479–502.

Erramilli, M. K., & Rao, C. P. 1993. Service firms' entry mode choice: a modified transaction cost analysis approach. *Journal of Marketing*, July: 19–38.

Esser, H. 1975. *Soziale Regelmäßigkeiten des Befragtenverhaltens*. Hain: Meisenheim an der Glan.

Esser, H. 1977. Response Set – Methodische Problematik und soziologische Interpretation. *Zeitschrift für Soziologie*, 6: 253–263.

Etzioni, A. 1961. *A Comparative Analysis of Complex Organizations*. Glencoe IL: Free Press.

Etzioni, A. 1980. Compliance structures. In A. Etzioni, & E. Lehmon (Eds), *A Sociological Reader on Complex Organizations*: 87–100. New York: Holt, Rinehardt and Winston.

Fagre, N., & Wells, L. 1982. Bargaining power of multinationals and host governments. *Journal of International Business Studies*, 13(2): 9–23.

Favere-Marchesi, M. 2001. Audit quality in ASEAN. *The International Journal of Accounting*, 36: 485–489.

Fayol, H. 1949. *General and Industrial Management*. London: Pitman, Trans. C. Scorrs.

Ferner, A. 1997. Country of origin effects and HRM in multinational companies. *Human Resource Management Journal*, 7(1): 19–37.

Ferner, A. 2000. The underpinnings of bureaucratic control systems: HRM in European multinationals. *Journal of Management Studies*, 37: 521–538.

Ferner, A., Quintanilla, J., & Varul, M. Z. 2001. Country of Origin effects, host country effects, and the management of HR in multinationals: German companies in Britain and Spain. *Journal of World Business*, 36(2): 107–127.

Ferner, A., & Varul, M. 2000. 'Vanguard' Subsidiaries and the diffusion of new practices: a case study of German multinationals. *British Journal of Industrial Relations*, 38(1): 115–140.

Filatotchev, I., Wright, M., Uhlenbruck, K., Tihanyi, L., & Hoskisson, R. E. 2003. Governance, organizational capabilities, and restructering in transition econonomies. *Journal of World Business*, 38: 331–347.

Filby, I., & Willmott, H. 1988. Ideologies and contradictions in a public relations department: the seduction and impotence of living myth. *Organisation Studies*, 9: 335–352.

Fink, G. 1971. GSSNAB SSSR, Planung und Planungsprobleme der Produktionsmittelverteilung in der UdSSR. Berlin: Duncker & Humbolt.

Fink, G. 1987. Background and Prospects on economic reforms in Eastern Europe and the USSR. In G. Fink, G. Pöll, & M. Riese (Eds), *Economic Theory, Political Power and Social Justice*: 393–405. Wien-New York: Springer.

Fink, G., Kölling, M., Meierewert, S., & Neyer, A. K. 2004a. Research on intercultural management interaction: The cultural standard method. Paper presented at the International Conference on Research Methods, Lyon, France.

Fink, G., & Lehmann, M. 2006. People's twist: performance and loyalty in former 'Socialist Economies'. In D. J. Pauleen (Ed.), *Cross Cultural Perspectives on Knowledge Management*. Portsmouth, US: Libraries Unlimited.

Fink, G., & Meierewert, S. (Eds). 2001. Interkulturelles Management – Österreichische Perspektiven. Wien: Springer.

Fink, G., & Meierewert, S. 2004b. Issues of time in international, intercultural management: East and Central Europe in the perspective of Austrian managers. *Journal for East European Management Studies*, 9(1): 61–84.

Fink, G., Holden, N., & Lehmann, M. 2007. Survival by subversion in former Socialist Economies: tacit knowledge exchange at the workplace. In K. Hutchings, & K. Mohannak (Eds), *Knowledge Management in Developing Economies: Cross-Cultural and Institutional Approach*: 35–51. Cheltenham, UK: Edward Elgar Publishing.

Fink, G., Novy, I., & Schroll-Machl, S. 2000. Tschechische, österreichische und deutsche Kulturstandards in der Wirtschaftskooperation. *Journal for Eastern European Management Studies*, 5(4): 361–376.

Firth, M. 1996. The diffusion of managerial accounting procedures in the People's Republic of China and the influence of foreign partnered joint ventures. *Accounting, Organizations and Society*, 21(7/8): 629–654.

Fisher, C. 1996. The impact of perceived environmental uncertainty and individual differences on management information requirements. *Accounting, Organizations and Society*: 361–369.

Flamholtz, E. G. 1983. Accounting, Budgeting and control systems in their organizational context: theoretical and empirical perspectives. *Accounting, Organizations and Society*: 35–55.

Flamholtz, E. G. 1996. *Effective Management Control: Theory and Practice*. MA: Kluwer Academic Publishers.

Fletcher, D. 2002. In the company of men. *Gender, Work and Organization*, 9(4): 398–419.

Flick, U. 2002a. *An Introduction to Qualitative Research* (2 ed.). London, Bonhill Street: Sage Publications Ltd.

Flick, U. 2002b. Qualitative research: state of the art. *Social Science Information*, 41(1): 5–24.

Foddy, W. 1995. Constructing Questions for Interviews and Questionnaires. Theory and Practice in Social Research. New York: Cambridge University Press.
Forsgren, M. 1990. Managing the international multi-centre firm. *European Management Journal*, 8(2 (June)): 261–267.
Freeman, J. H. 1973. Environment, technology and the administrative intensity of manufacturing organizations. *American Sociological Review*, 38: 750–763.
Froschauer, U., & Lueger, M. 1992. *Das qualitative Interview zur Analyse sozialer Systeme*. Wien: WUV-Universitätsverlag.
Fryxell, G. E., Dooley, R. S., & Vryza, M. 2003. After the ink dries: The interaction of trust and control in US-based international joint ventures. *Journal of Management Studies*, 39(6): 865–886.
Galbraith, J. R. 1973. *Designing Complex Organizations*. Reading, MA: Addison Wesley.
Galbraith, J. R. 1983. Strategy and organizational planning. *Human Resource Management*, Spring-Summer.
Galbraith, J. R. 1995. Designing Organizations – An Executive Briefing on Strategy, Structure and Processes. San Francisco: Jossey-Bass Publishers.
Galbraith, J. R., & Kazanjian, K. R. 1986. *Strategy implementation: Structure, Systems, and Process* (second ed.). St. Paul: West Publishing co.
Gamble, J. 2003. Transferring human resource practices from the United Kingdom to China: the limits and potential for convergence. *International Journal of Human Resource Management*, 14(3): 369–387.
Ganguly, A. R., & Turner, C. W. 2000. Discussion of Arnold, Bernardi, and Neidermeyer 'The association between European materiality estimates and client integrity, national culture and litigation'. *The International Journal of Accounting*, 35(1): 121–149.
Garcia-Sordo, J. B., & Wong Baren, A. 1999. National culture and preference for alternate accounting controls USA vs Mexico. *International Marketing Review*, 16(4/5): 314–325.
Garnier, G. 1982. Context and decision making autonomy in the foreign affiliates of US multinational corporations. *Academy of Management Journal*, 25: 893–908.
Gates, S. R., & Egelhoff, W. G. 1986. Centralization in parent headquarters-subsidiary relationships. *Journal of International Business Studies*, 17(2): 71–92.
Geertz, C. 1973. *The Interpretation of Cultures*. New York: Basic Books.
Geppert, M., Williams, K., & Matten, D. 2003. The Social construction of contextual rationalities in MNCs: An Anglo-German comparison of subsidiary choice. *Journal of Management Studies*, 40(3): 617–641.
Geringer, J. M., & Hebert, L. 1989. Control and performance of international joint ventures. *Journal of International Business studies*, 2nd quarter: 235–254.
Ghoshal, S., & Bartlett, C. A. 1990. The multinational corporation as an interorganizational network. *Academy of Management Review*, 15: 603–625.
Ghoshal, S., & Nohria, N. 1989. International differentiation within multinational corporations. *Strategic Management Journal*, 10(4): 323–337.
Ghoshal, S., Szulanski, H., & Korine, G. 1994. Inter-unit communication in multinational corporations. *Management Science*, 40(1): 96–110.
Ghoshal, S., & Westney, D. E. 1991. Organizing competitor analysis systems. *Strategic Management Journal*, 12: 17–32.
Gigouline, & Iouri. 2001. Ansatzpunkte zur Gestaltung des Beteiligungscontrollings westlicher Konzerne in osteuropäischen Ländern. Munic: Verlag V. Florentz GmbH.

Glaser, B. G. 2001. Doing grounded theory. *Grounded Theory Review*, 2: 1–18.
Glaser, B. G., & Strauss, A. L. 1967. Discovery of Grounded Theory: Strategies for Qualitative Research. Chicago: Aldine.
Goddard, A. 1997. Organizational culture and budget related behavior: a comparative contingency study of three local government organizations. *The International Journal of Accounting*, 32: 79–97.
Gomez-Mejia, L. R., & Palich, L. 1997. Cultural diversity and the Performance of multinational firms. *Journal of International Business Studies*, 28 (2): 309–335.
Gong, Y. 2003. Subsidiary staffing in multinational enterprises: agency, resources, and performance. *Academy of Management Journal*, 46 (6): 728–739.
Goold, M., & Campbell, A. 1987. Strategies and Styles: The Role of Centre in Diversified Corporations. Oxford: Blackwell.
Goold, M., & Quinn, J. J. 1990. The paradox of strategic controls. *Strategic Management Journal*, 11(1): 43–57.
Govindarajan, V., & Fisher, F. 1990. Strategy, Control systems and resource sharing: effects on business unit performance. *Academy of Management Journal*, 33: 259–285.
Groot, T. L. C. M., & Merchant, K. 2000. Control of international joint ventures. *Accounting, Organizations and Society*, 25: 579–607.
Guba, E. G. 1978. *Toward a Methodology of Naturalistic Inquiry in Eduacational Evaluation*. Los Angeles: Center for the Study of Evaluation, University of California.
Gudykunst, W., Hammer, M., & Wiseman, R. 1978. Dimensions of intercultural effectiveness: An exploratory study. *International Journal of Intercultural Relations*, Winter: 382–393.
Guilding, C., Lamminmaki, D., & Drury, C. 1998. Budgeting and standard costing practices in New Zealand and the United Kingdom. *The International Journal of Accounting*, 33: 569–588.
Gulati, R. 1995. Does familiarity breed trust? The implications of repeated ties for contractual choice in alliances. *Academy of Management Journal*, 38(1): 85–112.
Gupta, A. K., & Govindarajan, V. 1991. Knowledge flows and the structure of control within multinational corporations. *Academy of Management Review*, 16(4): 768–792.
Gupta, V., Hanges, P. J., & Dorfman, P. 2002. Cultural clusters: methodology and findings. *Journal of World Business*, 37(1): 11–15.
Hall, E. T. 1959. *The Silent Language*. Doubleday, New York: Anchor Press.
Hall, E. T., & Hall, M. R. 2000. Understanding Cultural Differences: Keys to Success in West Germany, France and the United States (11 ed.). Maine: Yarmouth.
Hall, F. S. 1975. Organizational goals: the status of theory and research. In J. L. Livingstone (Ed.), *Managerial Accounting: the Behavioral Foundations*: 1–32. Columbus, Ohio: Grid Publishing.
Hamilton, R. D., & Kashlak, R. J. 1999. National influences on MNC control system selection. *Management International Review*, 39(2): 167–189.
Handy, C. 1992. Balancing corporate power. A new federalism. *Harvard Business Review*, November–December: 59–72.
Harrison, G. 1992. The cross-cultural generalizability of the relation between participation, budget emphasis and job related attitudes. *Accounting, Organizations and Society*, 17: 1–15.

Harrison, G. 1993. Reliance on accounting performance measures in superior evaluation style and the influence of national culture and personality. *Accounting, Organizations and Society*, 18: 319–339.

Harrison, G., McKinnon, L., Panchapakesan, S., & Leung, M. 1994. The influence of culture on organizational design and planning and control in Australia and the United States compared with Singapore and Hong Kong. *Journal of International Financial Management and Accounting*, 5: 242–261.

Harrison, G. L., & McKinnon, J. L. 1999. Cross-cultural research in management control systems design: a review of the current state. *Accounting, Organizations and Society*, 24: 483–506.

Hartmann, F. 2000. The appropriateness of RAPM: towards the further development of theory. *Accounting, Organizations and Society*, 25(4–5): 451–482.

Harzing, A.-W. 1999. Managing the Multinationals – an International Study of Control Mechanisms. Cheltenham, UK: Edward Elgar Publishing Limited.

Harzing, A.-W. 2001a. An analysis of the functions of international transfer of managers in MNCs. *Employee Relations*, 23(3): 581–598.

Harzing, A.-W. 2002. Acquisitions versus greenfield investments: international strategy and management of entry modes. *Strategic Management Journal*, 23(March): 211–227.

Harzing, A.-W. 2003. The 'country of origin effect' in multinational corporations: sources, mechanisms and moderating conditions. *Management International Review*, 43(2): 47–66.

Harzing, A.-W. K. 2001b. Of bears, bumble-bees, and spiders: the role of expatriates in controlling foreign subsidiaries. *Journal of World Business*, 36(4): 366–379.

Harzing, A.-W. K. 2001c. Who is in charge? An empirical study of executive staffing practices in foreign subsidiaries. *Human Resource Management*, 40(2): 139–158.

Harzing, A.-W. K., & Sorge, A. 2003. The relative impact of country of origin and universal contingencies in internationalization strategies and corporate control in multinational enterprises: worldwide and European perspectives. *Organization Studies*, 24(2): 187–198.

Haspeslagh, P. C., & Jemsion, D. B. 1991. *Managing Acquisitions, Creating Value through Corporate Renewal*. New York: The Free Press.

Hedlund, G. 1981. Autonomy of subsidiaries and formalization of headquarters-subsidiary relationships in Swedish MNCs. In L. Otterbeck (Ed.), *The Management of Headquarter Subsidiary Relationships*: 25–78. New York: St. Martins Press.

Hedlund, G. 1986. The hypermodern MNE. *Human Resource Management*, 25: 9–25.

Hellmann, J. S., Jones, G., & Kaufmann, D. 2000. 'Seize the state, seize the day': State capture, corruption, and influence in transition, *Policy Research Working Paper*, Vol. 2444: The World Bank, World Bank Insitute Governance, Regulation and Finance, and European Bank of Reconstruction and Development.

Hennert, J.-F. 1991. Control in multinational firms: the role of price and hierarchy. *Management International Review*, 31(special issue): 71–96.

Hermanovicz, J. C. 2002. The great interview: 25 strategies for studying people in bed. *Qualitative Sociology*, 25(4): 479–499.

Hickson, D. J., & McMillan, C. D. 1974. The culture-free context of organizational structure: a trinational comparison. *Sociology*, 8: 59–80.

Hickson, J. D., & Pugh, S. D. 1995. Management worldwide – the impact of societal culture on organizations around the GLOBE. Harmondsworth: Penguin.

Hocking, J. B., Brown, M., & Harzing, A.-W. 2004. A knowledge transfer perspective of strategic assignment purposes and their path-dependent outcomes. *International Journal of Human Resource Management*, 15(3): 565–586.

Hoffmann, W., Niedermayr, R., & Risak, J. 1996. Führungsergänzung durch Controlling. In R. Eschenbach (Ed.), *Controlling*, Vol. 2: 3–48. Stuttgart: Schaeffer-Poeschl Verlag.

Hoffmann-Riem, C. 1980. Die Sozialforschung einer interpretativen Soziologie: Der Datengewinn. *Kölner Zeitschrift für Soziologie und Sozialpsychologie*, 32: 339–372.

Hofstede, G. 1980a. Culture's Consequences: International Differences in Work-Related Values. Beverly Hills, CA: Sage Publications.

Hofstede, G. 1980b. Motivation, leadership, and organization: Do American theories apply abroad? *Organizational Dynamics*, Summer: 42–63.

Hofstede, G. 1983. The cultural relativity of organizational practices and theories. *Journal of International Business Studies*, 14(2): 75–89.

Hofstede, G. 1993. Cultural constraints in management theories. *Academy of Management Executive*, 7(1): 81–93.

Hofstede, G. H. 1991. Cultures and Organizations: Software of the Mind. London: McGraw-Hill.

Hofstede, G. H., & Bond, M. H. 1988. The confucius connection: from cultural roots to economic growth. *Organizational Dynamics*, 16: 5–21.

Holm, U., Johanson, J., & Thilenius, P. 1995. Headquarter knowledge of subsidiary contexts in the multinational coporation. *International Studies of Management and Organization*, 25(1–2): 97–119.

Hopf, C. 1978. Die Pseudo-Exploration: Überlegungen zur Technik qualitativer Interviews in der Sozialforschung. *Zeitschrift für Soziologie*, 7: 97–115.

Horvath, P. 1986. *Controlling* (2 ed.). München: Vahlen.

Hoskisson, R. E., Eden, L., Lau, C. M., & Wright, M. 2000. Strategies in emerging economies. *Academy of Management Journal*, 43: 249–267.

House, R., Javidan, M., Hanges, P., & Dorfmann, P. 2002. Understanding cultures and implicit leadership theories across the globe. *Journal of World Business*, 37(1): 3–10.

House, R. J., Hanges, P. J., Javidan, M., Dorfmann, P. W., & Gupta, V. (Eds). 2004. *Culture, Leadership, and Organizations. The GLOBE Study of 62 Societies*. Thousand Oaks: Sage Publications.

Hunt, B. 2000. The new battleground for capitalism, *Financial Times*.

Hussein, M. E. 1996. A comparative study of cultural influences on financial reporting in the U.S. and the Netherlands. *The International Journal of Accounting*, 31: 95–120.

Inkpen, A. C., & Curral, S. C. 1997. International joint venture trust: an empirical examination. In P. W. Beamish, & J. P. Killing (Eds), *Cooperative Strategies: North American Perspectives*. San Francisco: New Lextington Press.

Inlgehart, R. 1997. Human Values and Social Change: Findings from the values survey. Brill Academic Publishers.

Jaeger, A. M. 1983. The transfer of organizational culture overseas: an approach to control in the multinational corporation. *Journal of International Business Studies*, 14(2): 91.

Jaggi, B., & Low, P. Y. 2000. Impact of culture, market forces, and legal system on financial disclosures. *The International Journal of Accounting*, 35: 495–519.

Janesick, V. J. 2000. The choreography of qualitative research design: minuets improvisations, and crystalization. In N. K. Denzin, & Y. Lincoln, S. (Eds), *Handbook of Qualitative Research*: 379–399. Thousand Oaks, CA: Sage.

Jensen, M. C., & Meckling, W. H. 1976. Theory of the firm: managerial behavior, agency costs and ownership structure. *Journal of Financial Economics*, 3(4): 305–360.

Johanson, J., & Mattsson, L. G. 1998. Internationalization in industry systems. In N. Hood, & J. E. Vahlne (Eds), *Strategies in Global Competition*, Vol. 287–314. London: Croom Helm.

Johns, G. 2001. In praise of context. *Journal of Organizational Behavior*, 22: 31–42.

Johnsen, G. 1987. *Strategic Change and the Management Process*. Oxford: Basil Blackwell.

Johnsen, G., Smith, S., & Codling, B. 2000. Microprocesses of insitutional change in the context of privatization. *Academy of Management Review*, 25: 572–580.

Johnson, R. A., & Ouchi, W. G. 1974. Made in America (under Japanese Management). *Harvard Business Review*, September–October: 61–69.

Kaplan, R. D. 1996. *The Ends of the Earth*. New York: Random House.

Kartte, W. 1994. Mein Rat an die Russen: Schmeißt alle Berater raus, *Die Welt*, 295 ed.: 7.

Keating, P. 1995. A framework for classifying and evaluating the theoretical contributions of case research in management Accounting. *Journal of Management Accounting Research*, Fall: 66–86.

Kelle, U (Ed.). 1995. *Computer-Aided Qualitative Data Analysis*. London, UK: Sage.

Kenrick, T., & Dantchik, A. 1983. Interactionism, idiographics, and the social psychological invasion of personality. *Journal of Personality*: 286–307.

Kenter, M. E. 1985. Die Steuerung ausländischer Tochtergesellschaften. Instrumente und Effizienz. Frankfurt am Main/Berlin/New York: Peter Lang.

Khandwalla, P. N. 1977. *The Design of Organizations*. Harcourt: Brace Jovanovich.

Kieser, A. 1998. *Organisationstheorien*. Stuttgart: Kohlhammer.

Kilman, R. 1985. Five steps to close a cultural gap. In K. R., M. Saxton, & R. Serpa (Eds), *Gaining Control of Corporate Culture*. San Francisco: Jossey-Bass.

Kim, B., Park, J. H., & Prescott, J. E. 2003. The global integration of business functions: a study of multinational businesses in integrated global industries. *Journal of International Business Studies*, 34: 327–344.

Kimberly, J. R. 1976. Organizational Size and the structuralist perspective: a review, critique and proposal. *Administrative Science Quarterly*, December: 571–597.

Kleps, K. 1984. Staatliche Preispolitik: Theorie und Realität in Markt- und Planwirtschaft. München.

Klitgaard, R. 1987. *Controlling Corruption*. Berkeley: University of California Press.

Kluckhohn, C. 1951. The study of culture. In L. D., & L. H.D (Eds), *The Policy of Sience*: 86–101. Stanford, CA: Standford Univ. Press.

Kluckhohn, F., & Strodtbeck, F. L. 1961. *Variations in Value Orientations*. New York: Elmsford.
Knights, D., Noble, F., Vurdubakis, T., & Hugh, W. 2001. Chasing shadows: control, virtuality and the production of trust. *Organisation Studies*, 22(2): 311–336.
Kobrin, S. 1988. Expatriate reduction and strategic control in American multinational corporations. *Human Resource Management*, 27: 63–75.
Kogut, B., & Singh, H. 1988. The effect of national culture on the choice of entry mode. *Journal of International Business Studies*, 19: 411–432.
Kölbl, C. 2001. Rekonstruktion der Forschungspraxis – eine Antwort auf die Frage, was ein Einführungstext in qualitative Methoden bringen soll. *Forum qualitative Sozialforschung (Online Journal)*, 2.
Konopaske, R., Werner, S., & Neupert, K. E. 2002. Entry mode strategy and performance: the role of FDI staffing. *Journal of Business Research*, 55: 759–770.
Kornei, J. 1992. *The Socialist System*. Princeton, NJ: Princeton University Press.
Kostova, T. 1999. Transnational transfer of strategic organizational practices: A contextual perspective. *Academy of Management Review*, 24(2): 306–324.
Kotter, J. 1982. *The General Managers*. New York: Free Press.
Kowall, S., & O'Connell, D. C. 2002. Transcribing conversations. In U. Flick, E. v. Kardoff, & I. Steinke (Eds), *Qualitative Research: A Hanbook*. London: Sage Publications.
Krippendorff, K. 1980. *Content Analysis. an Introduction to Its Methodology*. Beverly Hills: Sage Publications.
Kristensen, P. H., & Zeitlin, J. 2001. The making of a global firm: local pathways to multinational enterprise. In G. Morgan, P. H. Kristensen, & R. Whitley (Eds), *The Mulitnational Firm*. Oxford: Oxford University Press.
Kristof, A. L. 1996. Person-organization fit: an interactive review of its conceptualizations, measurement, and implications. *Personnel Psychology*, 49: 1–49.
Krotz, J. 1998. Erschließung der Märkte und Standorte in Mittel- und Osteuropa durch mittelgroße deutsche Industrieunternehmen: Rahmenbedingungen und Erfolgsfaktoren möglicher Oststrategien am Beispiel der neuen Bundesländer und Ungarn. St. Gallen.
Kuckartz, U. 1999. Computerunterstützte Analyse qualitativer Daten: Eine Einführung in Methoden und Arbeitstechniken. Opladen/Wiesbaden: Westdeutscher Verlag.
Kunda, G. 1992. *Engineering Culture*. Philadelphia: Temple University Press.
Küpper, H. U. 1987. Konzeptionen des Controllings aus betriebswirtschaftlicher Sicht. In W. Scheer (Ed), *8. Saarbrücker Arbeitstagung, Rechnungswesen und EDV*. Saarbrücken.
Kvale, S. 1996. *Interviews – an Introduction to Qualitative Research Interviewing*. Thousand Oaks, CA: Sage Publications.
Lachman, R., Nedd, A., & Hinings, B. 1994. Analyzing cross-national management and organizations: a theoretical framework. *Management Science*, January: 40–55.
Lam, A. 2003. Organizational learning in multinationals: R&D Networks of Japanese and US MNEs in the UK. *Journal of Management Studies*, 40(3): 673–703.
Lamnek, S. 1995. Qualitative Sozialforschung. Band 1: Methodologie. München.

Lane, H. W., DiStefano, J. J., & Maznevski, M. L. (Eds). 2003. *International Management Behavior. Text, Readings and Cases* (4 ed.). Oxford: Blackwell Publishing.
Langfield-Smith, K. 1997. Management control systems and strategy: a critical review. *Accounting, Organizations and Society*, 22(2): 207–232.
Lawrence, J. W., & Lorsch, P. R. 1967. *Organization and Environment*: Harvard University Press.
Lawrence, P. R. 1981. Organization and environment perspective. In A. H. Van de Ven, & W. F. Joyce (Eds), *Perspectives on Organization Design and Behavior*. Boston: Harvard Business Press.
LeCraw, D. J. 1984. Bargaining power, ownership, and profitability of subsidiaries of transnational corporations in developing countries. *Journal of International Business Studies*, 15: 27–44.
Lee, J. R., Chen, W. R., & Kao, C. 1998. Bargaining Power and the trade-off between the ownership and control in international joint ventures. *Journal of International Management*, 4: 353–385.
Levitt, T. 1983. The globalization of markets. *Harvard Business Review*, 61(3): 92–102.
Lewin, K. 1936. Some social-psychological differences between the US and Germany. *Journal of Personality*, 4(4): 265–293.
Li, J., Karakowsky, L., & Lam, K. 2002. East meets Easts and East meets West: The case of Sino-Japanese and Sino-West joint ventures in China. *Journal of Management Studies*, 39(6): 841–863.
Liessmann, K. 1990. Ziele und Strategien im Spannungsfeld der Führungsaufgaben von Konzernleitung und ergebnisorientiertem Geschäftsfeld Management. In H. Siegwart, J. I. Mahari, I. G. Caytas, & S. Sandner (Eds), *Mangement Controlling*: 105–136. Stuttgart.
Lin, K., & Chan, H. K. 2000. Auditing standards in China – a comparative analysis with relevant international standards and guidelines. *The International Journal of Accounting*, 35(4): 559–577.
Lincoln, J. R., & Kalleberg, A. 1990. *Culture, Control and Commitment*. Cambridge: Cambridge University Press.
Lipset, S. M., & Lenz, G. S. 1999. *Corruption, Culture and Markets*, George Mason University: Arlington, VA. 24–67.
Lowendahl, B. 1997. *Strategic Management of Professional Service Firms*. Copenhagen: Handelshøjskolens Forlag.
Lubatkin, M. H., Lane, P. J., Collin, S.-O., & Very, P. 2005. Origins of corporate governance in the USA, Sweden and France. *Organization Studies*, 26 (6): 867–888.
Luhmann, N. 1979. *Trust and Power*. New York: John Wiley and Sons.
Luo, Y. 2002. Building trust in cross-cultural collaborations: toward a contingency perspective. *Journal of Management*, 28(5): 669–694.
Luo, Y. 2003. Market-seeking MNEs in an emerging market: how parent-subsidiary links shape overseas success. *Journal of International Business Studies*, 34: 290–309.
Luo, Y. 2005. How does globalization affect corporate governance and accountability? A perspective from MNEs. *Journal of International Management*, 11(1): 19–41.
Lyskov-Strewe, V., & Schroll-Machl, S. 2003. Russland. In A. Thomas, S. Kammhuber, & S. Schroll-Machl (Eds), *Handbuch interkulturelle Kommunikation*

und KooperationBand 2: Länder, Kulturen und interkulturelle Berufstätigkeit: 103–119. Göttingen: Vandenhoeck & Ruprecht.

Macdonald, S., & Hellgren, B. 2004. The interview in international business research: problems we would rather not talk about. In R. Marschan-Piekkari, & C. Welch (Eds), *Handbook of Qualitative Research Methods for International Business*: 264–284. Cheltenham UK: Edward Elgar.

Macharzina, K. 1993. Unternehmensführung : das internationale Managementwissen, Konzepte, Methoden, Praxis. Wiesbaden: Gabler.

March, J. G., & Simon, H. A. 1958. *Organizations*. New York: John Wiley and Sons.

Marcus, A. 1988. Responses to externally induced innovations: their effects on organizational performance. *Strategic Management Journal*, 9: 387–402.

Marginson, P., Armstrong, P., Edwards, P., Purcell, J., & Hubbard, N. 1993. The control of industrial relations in large companies: an initial analysis of the second company level industrial relations survey, *Warwick Papers in Industrial Relations 45*. Coventry: IRRU.

Marinov, M. A., Marinova, S. T., & Morita, K. 2003. Internationalization of Japanese multinational corporations in central and eastern Europe. *Journal of East-West Business*, 9(3/4): 27–52.

Marschan-Piekkari, R., & Welch, C. 2004a. Qualitative Research methods in international business: the state of the art, *Handbook of Qualitative Research Methods for International Business*: 5–24. Cheltenham UK: Edward Elgar.

Marschan-Piekkari, R., Welch, C., Penttinnen, H., & Tahvanainen, M. 2004b. Interviewing in the multinational corporation: challenges of the organisational context. In R. Marschan-Piekkari, & C. Welch (Eds), *Handbook of Qualitative Research Methods for International Business*: 244–263. Cheltenham UK: Edward Elgar.

Martin, J., & Meyerson, D. 1988. Organizational cultures and the denial, challenging and acknowledgement of ambiguity. In L. R. Pondy, J. R. Boland, & H. Thomas (Eds), *Managing Ambiguity and Change*: 93–125. New York: Wiley.

Martinez, J., & Jarillo, J. C. 1989. The evolution of research on coordination mechanisms in multinational corporations. *Journal of International Business*, 20(3): 489–514.

Martinez, J., & Jarillo, J. C. 1991. Coordination demands of international strategies. *Journal of International Business Studies*, 22(3): 429–444.

Mayer, M. C. J., & Whittington, R. 1994. Strategy, Structure and 'systemness': national institutions and corporate change in France, Germany and the UK, 1950–1993. *Organization Studies*, 15(3): 361–380.

Mayer, R. C., Davies, J. H., & Schoorman, F. D. 1995. An integrative model of organizational trust. *Academy of Management Review*, 20: 709–734.

Mayring, P. 1999. Einführung in die qualitative Sozialforschung. Eine Anleitung zum qualitativen Denken. (4th ed.). Weinheim.

Mayring, P. 2000a. Qualitative content analysis. forum qualitative sozialforschung / forum: qualitative social research [On-line Journal] Available at: *http://qualitative-research.net/fqs/fqs-e/2–00inhalt-e.htm* date of access: 03/30/05, 1 (June)(2).

Mayring, P. 2000b. Qualitative Inhaltsanalyse: Grundlagen und Techniken (7 ed.). Weinheim.

Mayring, P. 2002a. Einführung in die Qualitative Sozialforschung – Eine Anleitung zum Qualitativen Denken (5 ed.). Weinheim und Basel: Beltz.

Mayring, P. 2002b. Qualitative content analysis. In U. Flick, E. von Kardorff, & I. Steinke (Eds), *Qualitative Research: A Handbook*. London: Sage Publications.

Mayring, P. 2003. *Qualitative Inhaltsanalyse – Grundlagen und Techniken* (8 ed.). Weinheim und Basel: Beltz.

McAllister, D. J. 1995. Affect-and cognition-based trust as foundations for interpersonal cooperation in organizations. *Academy of Mangement Journal*, 38: 24–59.

McCarthy, D. J., & Puffer, S. M. 2003. Corporate governance in Russia: a framework for analysis. *Journal of World Business*, 38(3): 397–415.

Meek, V. L. 1988. Organizational culture: origins and weaknesses. *Organization Studies*, 9: 453–474.

Meierewert, S., & Topcu, K. 1999. Ungarische Kulturstandards. In G. Fink, & S. Meierewert (Eds), *Interkulturelles Management – Österreichische Perspektiven*: 111–124. Wien: Springer.

Mendoza, R., Collins, F., & Holzmann, O. J. 1997. Central American budgeting scorecard: cross cultural insights. *Journal of international Accounting, Auditing and Taxation*, 6: 192–209.

Merchant, K., A., Chow, C., W., & Wu, A. 1995. Measurement, evaluation and reward of profit center managers: a cross-cultural field study. *Accounting, Organizations and Society*, 20(7/8): 619–638.

Merchant, K., A., Van der Stede, W. A., & Zheng, L. 2003. Disciplinary constraints on the advancement of knowledge: the case of interorganizational incentive systems. *Accounting, Organizations and Society*, 28: 251–286.

Merchant, K. A. 1981. The design of corporate budgeting system: influences on managerial behaviour and performance. *Accounting Review*, 6: 813–829.

Merchant, K. A. 1984. Influences on departmental budgeting: an empirical examination of a contingency model. *Accounting, Organizations and Society*, 9: 291–307.

Merchant, K. A. 1985. *Control in Business Organizations*. Marchfield, MA: Pitmann.

Merchant, K. A. 1996. *Modern Management Control Systems: Text and Cases*. Englewood Cliffs NJ: Prentice Hall.

Merchant, K. A., & Simons, R. 1986. Research and control in complex organizations: an overview. *Journal of Accounting Literature*, 5: 183–201.

Merten, R. K. 1995. *Soziologische Theorie und soziale Struktur*. Berlin: de Gruyter.

Meyer, J. W., & Rowan, B. 1977. Institutionalized organizations: formal structure as myth and ceremony. *American Journal of Sociology*: 340–363.

Mezias, S. J., Chen, Y. R., & Murphy, P. 1999. Toto, I don't think we are in Kansas anymore: some footnotes to cross-cultural research. *Journal of Management Inquiry*, 8(3): 323–333.

Michailova, S. 2004. Contextualising fieldwork: reflections on conducting research in eastern Europe. In R. Marschan-Piekkari, & C. Welch (Eds), *Handbook of Qualitative Research Methods for International Business*: 365–383. Cheltenham, UK: Edward Elgar.

Miles, R. W., & Snow, C. C. 1978. *Organizational Strategy, Structure and Process*. New York: McGraw Hil.

Miller, D., Droge, C., & Toulouse, J. M. 1988. Strategic Process and content as mediators between organizational context and structure. *Academy of Management Journal*: 544–569.

Mintzberg, H. 1978. Patterns in strategy formation. *Management Science*: 934–948.
Mintzberg, H. 1979. *The Structuring of Organizations*. Englewood Cliffs, NJ: Prentice Hall.
Mintzberg, H. 1983. *Power in and around Organizations*. Englewood Cliffs, NJ: Prentice Hall.
Mintzberg, H., & Quinn, J. B. 1991. *The Strategy Process – Concepts, Contexts, Cases* (2 ed.). Englewood Cliffs, NJ: Prentice Hall.
Modway, R., & Sutton, R. 1993. Organizational behavior: linking individuals and groups to organizational contexts. *Annual Review of Psychology*, 44: 195–229.
Morgan, G. 2001. The multinational firm: organizing across institutional and national divides. In G. Morgan, P. H. Kristensen, & R. Whitley (Eds), *The Multinational Firm: Organizing across Institutional and National Divides*. Oxford: Oxford University Press.
Morgan, G., & Smircich, L. 1980. The case for qualitative research. *Academy of Management Review*, 5(4): 491–500.
Morrison, T., Conaway, W. A., & Borden, G. A. 1994. *Kiss, Bow or Shake Hands*. Holbrook, MA: Adams Media Corporation.
Mueller, F. 1994. Societal effect, organizational effect, and globalization. *Organization Studies*, 15: 407–428.
Nagy, A. L., & Neal, T. L. 2001. An empirical examination of corporate myopic behavior – A comparison of Japanese and U.S. companies. *The International Journal of Accounting*, 36: 91–114.
Napier, N., & Thomas, D. C. 2004. *Managing Relationships in Transition Economies*. Westport: Praeger.
Negandhi, A. R., & Baliga, B. R. 1979. *Quest for Survival and Growth: Comparative Study of American, European and Japanese Multinationals*. New York: Praeger.
Newburry, W., & Zeira, Y. 1997. Generic differences between equity International Joint Ventures (EIJVs), International Acquisitions (IAs) and International Greenfield Investments (IGIs): implications for parent companies. *Journal of World Business*, 32(2): 87–102.
Newman, K. 2000. Organizational transformation during institutional upheaval. *Academy of Management Review*, 25(3): 602–619.
Noerreklit, H., & Schoenfeld, H.-M. 2000. Controlling multinational companies: an attempt to analyze some unresolved issues. *The International Journal of Accounting*, 35(3): 415–430.
Nohria, N., & Ghoshal, S. 1994. Differentiated fit and shared values: alternatives for managing headquarter-subsidiary relations. *Strategic Management Journal*, 15(6): 491–503.
Novy, I., & Schroll-Machl, S. 2003. Tschechien. In A. Thomas, S. Kammhuber, & S. Schroll-Machl (Eds), *Handbuch Interkulturelle Kommunikation und Kooperation Band 2: Länder, Kulturen und interkulturelle Berufstätigkeit*: 90–102. Göttingen: Vandenhoeck & Ruprecht.
O'Connor, N. G., Chow, C. W., & Wu, A. 2004. The adoption of 'Western' management accouting/controls in China's state-owned enterprises during economic transition. *Accounting, Organizations and Society*, 29: 349–375.
O'Donnel, S. 2000. Managing foreign subsidiaries: agents of headquarters, or an independent network? *Strategic Management Journal*, 21(5): 525–548.
OECD. 2005. *OECD Factbook 2005 Economic, Environmental and Social Statistics*. Paris: OECD.

Oliver, N., & Wilkinson, B. 1992. *The Japanization of British Industry – New Developments in the 1990s* (2 ed.). Oxford: Blackwell Publishing.
Omhae, K. 1990. *The Borderless World: Power and Strategy in the Interlinked Economy.* New York: Free Press.
Ondrack, D. A. 1985. International human resources management in European and North American firms. *International Studies of Management and Organization,* 9: 6–32.
Ongwuegbuzie, A. J. 2003. Effect Sizes in qualitative research: a prolegomenon. *Quality and Quantity,* 37: 393–409.
O'Reilly, C. A. I., Chatman, J., & Caldwell, D. 1991. People and organizational culture: a profile comparison approach to assessing person-organization fit. *Academy of Management Journal,* 34: 487–516.
Otley, D. 1988. The contingency theory of organizational control. In T. S., & M. Wright (Eds), *Internal Organization, Efficiency and Profit.* Oxford/New Jersey: Philip Allen.
Ouchi, W. G. 1977. The relationship between organizational structure and organizational control. *Administrative Science Quarterly,* 22(March): 95–112.
Ouchi, W. G. 1979. A conceptual framework for the design of organizational control mechanisms. *Management Science,* 25: 833–849.
Ouchi, W. G. 1980. Markets, bureaucracies, and clans. *Administrative Science Quaterly,* 25(1): 129–141.
Ouchi, W. G., & Jaeger, A. 1978. Type Z organization: stability in the midst of mobility. *Academy of Management Review,* April: 305–314.
Paik, Y., & Sohn, J. D. 2004. Expatriate managers and MNC's ability to control international subsidiaries: the case of Japanese MNCS. *Journal of World Business,* 39: 61–71.
Parker, B. 1998. *Globalization and Business Practice: Managing across Boundaries.* London: Sage.
Parkhe, A. 1993. Messy research, methodological predisposition, and theory development in international joint ventures. *Academy of Management Review,* 18: 227–268.
Parsons, T. 1951. *The Social System.* New York: Free Press.
Patton, M. Q. 1990. *Qualitative Evaluation and Research Methods* (2 ed.). Newbury Park, CA: Sage.
Patton, M. Q. 1997. *Utilization-Focused Evaluation: the New Century Text.* Thousand Oaks, CA.
Patton, M. Q. 2002. *Qualitative Research and Evaluation Methods* (3 ed.): Sage Publications.
Pauly, L. W., & Reich, S. 1997. National structures and multinational corporate behavior: enduring differences in the age of globalization. *International Organization,* 51(1): 1–30.
Pearce, J., & Branyiczki, I. 1994. Revolutionizing bureaucracies: managing change in Hungarian state-owned enterprises. *Journal of Organizational Change Management,* 6(2): 53–64.
Peemoeller, V. H., & Keller, B. 1998. Controlling / Planung. In K. Küting (Ed.), *Saarbrücker Handbuch der betriebswirtschaftlichen Beratung*: 375–428. Berlin.
Peng, M. W. 2001. How entrepreneurs create wealth in transitioning economies. *Academy of Management Executive,* 15(1): 95–108.
Peng, M. W. 2003. Institutional transitions and strategic choices. *Academy of Management Review,* 28(2): 275–296.

Peng, M. W., & Luo, Y. 2000. Managerial ties and firm performance in a transition economy: The nature of a micro-macro link. *Academy of Management Journal*, 43(3): 486–501.

Perlitz, M., Bufka, J., & Wagner, M. 1996. Erfolgsfaktoren im Management von Joint Ventures in Osteuropa. Mannheim.

Perlmutter, H. V. 1969. The tortuous Evolution of the multinational company. *Columbia Journal of World Business*(Jan/Feb): 9–18.

Perrow, C. 1970. *Organizational Analysis: a Sociological View*. California: Wadsworth Publishing Company.

Peterson, R. B. 2003. The use of expatriates and inpatriates in Central and Eastern Europe since the Wall came down. *Journal of World Business*, 38: 55–69.

Peterson, R. B., Napier, N., & Shim, W. S. 1996. Expatriate management: The different role of national multinational corporation ownership. *The International Executive*, 38(543–562).

Peterson, R. B., Napier, N., & Shim, W. S. 2000. Expatriate management: a comparison of MNCs accross four parent countries. *Thunderbird International Business Review*, 42: 145–166.

Pettigrew, A. 1985. Contextualist research: a natural way to link theory and practice. In E. E. Lawler (Ed.), *Doing Research That Is Useful for Theory and Practice*: 222–248. San Francisco, CA: Jossey-Bass.

Pettigrew, A. 1990. Longitudinal field research on change: theory and practice. *Organization Science*, 1(3): 267–292.

Pfeffer, J. 1981. *Power in Organizations*. Marshfield: Pitman.

Pfeffer, J. 1982. *Organizations and Organization Theory*. Marshfield, MA: Pitman Publishing.

Pfeffer, J., & Salancik, G. R. 1978. *The External Control of Organizations*. New York: Harper and Rowling.

Pondy, L. R. 1969. The effects of size, complexity and ownership on administrative intensity. *Administrative Science Quarterly*, 14: 47–61.

Porter, M. E. 1990. *The Competitive Advantage of Nations*. New York: Free Press.

Prahalad, C. K., & Doz, Y. L. 1981. An approach to strategic control in MNCs. *Sloan Management Review*, 22(Summer): 5–13.

Prahalad, C. K., & Doz, Y. L. 1987. *The Multinational Mission*. New York: The Free Press.

Prasad, A. 2002. The contest over meaning: hermeneutics as an interpretive methodology for understanding texts. *Organizational Research Methods*, 5(1): 12–33.

Protsenko, A., & Vinzenz, V. 1999. Direktinvestitionen und andere Kapitalströme nach Osteuropa. München.

Pucik, V., & Katz, J. H. 1986. Information, control, and human resource management in multinational firms. *Human Resource Management*, 25(Spring 1): 121–132.

Pugh, D. S., Hickson, D. J., Hinings, C. R., & Turner, C. 1969. The context of organization structures. *Administrative Science Quarterly*, 14: 91–114.

Pugh, D. S., Hickson, D. J., Hinings, C. R., & Turner, C. 1968. Dimensions of organization structure. *Administrative Science Quarterly*, 13: 65–105.

Punnet, B. J., & Shenkar, O. 1994. International management research: toward a contingency approach. *Advances in International Comparative Management*, 9: 39–55.

Puxty, A. G. 1979. Some evidence concerning cultural differentials in ownership policies of overseas subsidiaries. *Management International Review*, 19(2): 39–52.

Quinn, J. B. 1980. *Strategies for Change*. Homewood, IL: Irwin.

Ralston, D., Holt, D., Terpstra, R., & Kai-Cheng, Y. 1997. The Impact of national culture and economic ideology on managerial work values: a study of the United States, Russia, Japan and China. *Journal of International Business Studies*, 28(1): 177–207.

Rapley, T. 2004. Interviews. In C. Seale, G. Gobo, J. F. Gubrium, & D. Silverman (Eds), *Qualitative Research Practice*: 15–33. London: Sage Publications.

Reichmann, T. 1995. Controlling mit Kennnzahlen und Managementberichten: Grundlagen einer systemgestützten Controlling-Konzeption (4 ed.). München.

Reid, G. C., & Smith, J. B. 2000. The impact of contingencies on managerial accounting systems development. *Management Accounting Research*, 11: 151–158.

Richards, M. 1995. The impact of culture on the overseas operations of U.S. multinationals in the United Kingdom and Thailand. Unpublished PhD thesis, Indiana University, Bloomington, IN.

Richards, M. 2000. Control exercised by U.S. multinationals over their overseas affiliates: does location make a difference? *Journal of International Management*, 6: 105–120.

Riusala, K., & Suutari, V. 2004. International knowledge transfers through expatriates. *Thunderbird International Business Review*, 46(6): 743–770.

Robertson, M., & Swan, J. 2003. 'Control – What control' culture and ambiguity within a knowledge intensive firm. *Journal of Management Studies*, 40(4): 831–858.

Ronen, S., & Kraut, A. 1977. Similarities among countries based on employee work values and attitudes. *Columbia Journal of World Business*, 12: 89–96.

Ronen, S., & Shenkar, O. 1985. Clustering countries on attitudinal dimensions: a review and synthesis. *Academy of Management Review*. 10(3).

Rose-Ackerman, S. 1978. *Corruption: a Study in Political Economy*. New York: Academic Press.

Roth, K., & Kostova, T. 2003. Organizational coping with institutional upheaval in transition economies. *Journal of World Business*, 38(3): 314–330.

Roth, K., & O'Donnel, S. 1996. Foreign subsidiary compensation strategy: an agency theory perspective. *Academy of Management Journal*, 39: 678–703.

Roth, K., Schweiger, D. M., & Morrison, A. J. 1991. Global strategy implementation at the business unit level: operational capabilities and administrative mechanisms. *Journal of International Business Studies*, 22(3): 369–402.

Roush, C. H., & Ball, B. C. 1980. Controlling the implementation of strategy. *Managerial Planning*, 29(4): 1–12.

Rousseau, D. M., & Fried, Y. 2001. Location, location, location: contextualizing organizational research. *Journal of Organizational Behavior*, 22: 1–13.

Rousseau, D. M., Sitkin, S. B., Burt, R. S., & Camerer, C. 1998. Not so different after all : a cross-discipline view of trust. *Academy of Management Review*, 23(3): 393–421.

Rugman, A. M., & Verbeke, A. 2001. Subsidiary-specific advantages in multinational enterprises. *Strategic Management Journal*, 22: 237–250.

Salter, S. B., & Sharp, D. J. 2001. Agency effects and escalation of commitment – Do small national cultural differences matter? *The International Journal of Accounting*, 36: 33–45.

Sandholtz, W., & Gray, M. 2003. International integration and national corruption. *International Organizations*, 57: 761-800.
Sandholtz, W., & Taagepera, R. 2005. Corruption, culture, and communism. *International Review of Sociology*, 15 (March)(1): 109-131.
Sands, J. S., & Pragasam, J. 1997. The perceived importance of international accounting topics in the Asia-Pacific rim: a comparative study. *The International Journal of Accounting*, 32(2): 33-46.
Saxton, T. 1997. The effects of partner and relationship characteristics on alliance outcomes. *Academy of Management Journal*, 40: 443-461.
Scheele, B., & Groeben, N. 1988. Dialog-Konsens-Methoden zur Rekonstruktion Subjektiver Theorien. Tübingen: Francke.
Schein, E. 1992. *Organizational Culture and Leadership* (2 ed.). San-Francisco: Jossey-Bass.
Schein, E. H. 1996. Culture: the missing concept in organization studies. *Administrative Science Quarterly*, 41(2).
Schultz, J. J., & Lopez, T. J. 2001. The impact of national influence on accounting estimates: Implications for international accounting standard-setters. *The International Journal of Accounting*, 36: 271-290.
Schwab, K., & Porter, M. E. (Eds). 2004. *Global Competitiveness Report*. New York: Basingstroke.
Schwartz, H., & Davies, S. M. 1981. Matching corporate culture and business strategy. *Organizational Dynamics*, Summer: 30-48.
Schwarzburg, E. 2001. Der Einfluß der Kultur auf die Führung polnischer Tochtergesellschaften. Frankfurt am Main: Peter Lang.
Shenkar, O. 2001. Cultural distance revisited: towards a more rigorous conceptualization and measurement of cultural differences. *Journal of International Business Studies*, 32(3): 519-536.
Shetty, Y. K. 1979. Managing the multinational corporation: European and American styles. *Management International Review*, 19(3): 39-48.
Simon, H. A. 1981. *The Science of the Artificial*. Cambridge MA: MIT Press.
Simons, R. 1991. Strategic orientation and top management attention to control systems. *Strategic Management Journal*, 12: 49-62.
Simons, R. 1995. *Levers of Control: How Managers Use Innovative Control Systems to Drive Strategic Renewal*. Cambridge MA: Harvard Business School Press.
Singh, J. V. 1986. Technology, size, and organizational structure: a reexamination of the Okayama study data. *Academy of Management Journal*, 29: 800-812.
Sloan, A. 1965. *My Years with General Motors*. New York: MacFadden-Bartell.
Smith, A. 1776. *An Inquiry into the Nature and Causes of the Wealth of Nations*. London: Dent and Sons.
Snell, S. 1992. Control theory in strategic human resource management: the mediating effect of administrative information. *Academy of Management Journal*, 35(2): 292-327.
Sohn, J. H. 1994. Social knowlegde as a control system: A proposition and evidence from the Japanese FDI behavior. *Journal of International Business Studies*, 25(2): 295-324.
Sohn, J. H. D., & Paik, Y. 1996. More is better? Expatriate managers and MNC's ability to control international subsidiariesr, Working Paper.
Spitz, M. 1995. Öffnung der Märkte Osteuropas: Joint Ventures als Kooperationsform zwischen schweizerischen und ungarischen Unternehmen. Aachen.

Stede, V. d., & A., W. 2003. The effect of national culture on management control and incentive system design in mulit-business firms: evidence of intracorporate isomorphism. *European Accounting Review*, 12(2): 263–285.

Steinle, C., & Lawa, D. 1996. Internationale Unternehmensführung als interkulturelles Management. In C. Steinle, H. Bruch, & D. Lawa (Eds), *Mangement in Mittel- und Osteuropa: Konzepte, Praxis, Perspektiven*: 13–28. Frankfurt am Main.

Strauss, A., & Corbin, J. 1998. *Basics of Qualitative Research. Techniques and Procedures for Developing Grounded Theory* (2 ed.). Thousand Oaks, CA: Sage.

Symon, G., & Cassell, C. (Eds). 1998. *Qualitative Methods and Analysis in Organizational Research*. London: Sage.

Szabo, E., Brodbeck, F. C., Den Hartog, D. N., Reber, G., Weibler, J., & Wunderer, R. 2002. The Germanic Europe cluster: where employees have a voice. *Journal of World Business*, 37(1): 55–68.

Szabo, E., & Reber, G. 2001. Culture, organizational practices, and leadership in Austria. In J. J. Chhokar, F. C. Brodbeck, & R. J. House (Eds), *Cultures of the World: A GLOBE Anthology*. Thousand Oaks: Sage.

Szulanski, G. 1996. Exploring internal stickiness: impediments to the transfer of best practice within the frim. *Strategic Management Journal*, 17Winter (Special Issue): 27–43.

Takeuchi, H., & Nonaka, I. (Eds). 2004. *Hitotsubashi on Knowledge Management*. Singapore: John Wiley & Sons.

Tannenbaum, A. S. 1968. *Control in Organizations*. New York: McGraw-Hill.

Tayeb, M. H. 1994. Japanese managers and British culture: a comparative case study. *International Journal of Human Resource Management*, 5(1): 145–166.

Tayeb, M. H. 1998. Transfer of HRM practices across cultures: an American company in Scotland. *The International Journal of Human Resource Management*, 9(April): 332–258.

Taylor, F. W. 1911. *The Principles of Scientific Management*. Düsseldorf: Verlag Wirtschaft u. Finanzen.

Taylor, W. 1991. The logic of global business: an interview with ABB's Percy Barnevik. *Harvard Business Review*, March-April: 91–105.

Thomas, A. 2003. *Psychologie interkulturellen Handelns* (2 ed.). Göttingen: Hogrefe, Verl. für Psychologie.

Thompson, J. D. 1967. *Organizations in Action*. New York: McGraw-Hill.

Thushman, M. L., & Nadler, D. A. 1978. Information processing as an integrating concept in organizational design. *Academy of Management Review*, 3: 613–624.

Tomkins, C. 2001. Interdepencies, trust and information in relationships, alliances and networks. *Accounting, Organizations and Society*, 26(2): 161–176.

Tomlinson, J. 1970. *The Joint Venture Formation Process in International Business: India and Pakistan*. Cambridge MA: MIT Press.

Treismann, D. 2000. The causes of corruption: a cross-national study. *Journal of Public Economics*, 76: 399–357.

Triandis, H. C. 1983. Dimensions of cultural variations as parameters of organizational theories. *International Studies of Management and Organization*, 12(4): 139–169.

Triandis, H. C. 1995. *Individualism and Collectivism*. Boulder, CA: Westview.

Trice, H., & Beyer, J. 1984. Studying organizational cultures through rites and ceremonials. *Academy of Management Review*, 9: 653–669.

Trompenaars, F., & Hampden-Turner, C. 1997. *Riding the Waves of Culture: Understanding Cultural Diversity in Business*. London: Nicholas Brealey Publishing.

Trompenaars, F., & Hampden-Turner, C. 2000. *Riding the Waves of Culture – Understanding Diversity in Business* (2 ed.). London: Nicholas Brealey Publishing.

Tse, D., Lee, K., Vertinsky, I., & Wehrung, D. 1988. Does culture matter? a cross cultural study of executives' choice, decisiveness and risk adjustment in international marketing. *Journal of Marketing*, October: 81–95.

Tsui, J. S. L. 1996. Auditors' ethical reasoning: some audit conflict and cross cultural evidence. *The International Journal of Accounting*, 31(1): 121–133.

Tsui, J. S. L. 2001. The impact of culture on the relationship between budgetary participation (PB) management accounting systems (MAS), and managerial performance: an analysis of Chinese and Western managers. *The International Journal of Accounting*, 36: 125–146.

Turner, G. 1994. *Report*. Paper presented at the Der Osten – Aufbruch für die Wirtschaft Europas Internationales Symposium, Bildungszentrum am Müggelsee.

Uddin, S., & Hopper, T. 2001. A Bangladesh soap opera: privatisation, accounting, and regimes of control in a less developed country. *Accounting, Organizations and Society*, 26: 643–672.

Ueno, S., & Sekaran, U. 1992. The influence of culture on budget control practices in the USA and Japan: an empirical study. *Journal of International Business Studies*, 23: 659–674.

Ueno, S., & Wu, F. 1993. The comparative influence of culture on budget control practices in the United States and Japan. *International Journal of Accounting*, 28: 17–39.

Vachani, S. 1999. Global diversification's effect on multinational subsidiaries' autonomy. *International Business Review*, 8(5/6) 535–560.

Van de Ven, A. H., Delbecq, A. L., & Koenig, R. 1976. Determinants of coordination modes within organizations. *American Sociological Review*: 332–338.

Van der Stede, W. A. 2003. The effect of national culture on management control and incentive system design in multi-business firms: evidence of intracorporate isomorphism. *European Accounting Review*, 12(2): 263–285.

Van Maanen, J., & Schein, E. H. 1979. Toward a theory of organizational socialization. In B. M. Staw (Ed.), *Research in Organizational Behavior*, Vol. 1: 209–264. Greenwich CT: JAI Press.

Vance, C., M., & Paik, Y. 2005. Forms of host country national learning for enhanced MNC absorptive capacity. *Journal of Managerial Psychology*, November (Special issue on Management Knowledge Absorption and Application).

Vernon, R. 1994. Research on transnational corportations: shedding old paradigms. *Transnational Corporations*, 3(1): 137–156.

Vogel, J. 1998. Marktwertorientiertes Beteiligungscontrolling: Shareholder Value als Maß der Konzernsteuerung. Wiesbaden.

Wächter, H. 2003. The 'country of origin effect' in the cross-national management of human resources: results and case study evidence of research on American multinational companies in Germany. München: Hampp.

Wang, P., & Wee, C. H. 1999. Establishing a successful Sino-Foreign equity joint venture: the Singaporian experience. *Journal of World Business*, 34(3): 287–305.

Weber, M. 1946. *Essays in Sociology*. New York: Oxford University Press.
Weber, M. 1947. *The Theory of Social and Economic Organization*. New York: Free Press.
Weber, M. 1949. *Methodology of the Social Sciences*. Glencoe, Ill: The Free Press.
Weick, K. E. 1979. *The Social Psychology of Organizing*. New York: McGrawHill.
Weiner, N. 1954. *The Human Use of Human Beings: Cybernetics and Society*. New York: Doubleday.
Welch, C., Marschan-Piekkari, R., Penttinnen, H., & Tahvanainen, M. 2002. Corporate elites as informants in qualitative international business research. *International Business Review*, 11: 611–628.
Whitley, R. 1999. *Divergent Capitalisms. The Social Structuring and Change of Business Systems*. Oxford: Oxford University Press.
Whitley, R. 2001. How and why are international firms different? The consequences of cross-border managerial coordination for firm characteristics and behavior. In G. Morgan, P. H. Kristensen, & R. Whitley (Eds), *The Multinational Firm: Organizing Across Institutional and National Divides*. Oxford: Oxford University Press: 27–68.
Whitley, R., & Czaban, L. 1998. Ownership, control and authority in emergent capitalism: changing supervisory relations in Hungarian industry. *The International Journal of Human Resource Management*, 9(1): 99–115.
Whitley, R., & Kristensen, P. H. 1996. *The Changing European Firm*. London: Routledge.
Whitley, R., Morgan, G., Kelly, W., & Sharpe, D. 2003. The changing Japanese multinational: application, adaptation and learning in car manufacturing and financial services. *Journal of Management Studies*, 40(4): 831–859.
Wijewardena, H., & De Zoysa, A. 1999. A comparative analysis of mangement accounting practices in Australia and Japan: an empirical investigation. *The International Journal of Accounting*, 34(1): 49–70.
Williams, J. J., & Seaman, A. E. 2001. Predicting change in management control accounting systems: national culture and industry effects. *Accounting, Organizations and Society*, 26: 443–460.
Williams, M. S., & Tower, G. 1998. Differential reporting in Singapore and Australia: A small business managers' perspective. *The International Journal of Accounting*, 33: 263–268.
Williamson, O. E. 1975. *Markets and Hierarchies, Analysis and Antitrust Implications*. New York: The Free Press.
Williamson, O. E. 1981. The economics of organization: The transaction cost approach. *American Journal of Sociology*, 87: 548–577.
Willmott, H. 1993. Strength is ignorance, slavery is freedom: managing culture in modern organizations. *Journal of Management Studies*, 30(4): 515–552.
Wong, G., & Birnbaum-More, P. 1994. Culture, context and structure: a test on Hong-Kong banks. *Organization Studies*, 15(1): 99–123.
Woodward, J. 1965. *Industrial Organization: Theory and Practice*. London: Oxford University Press.
Yan, A., & Grey, B. 1994. Bargaining power, management control, and performance in United States-China joint ventures: a comparative case study. *Academy of Management Journal*, 37: 1478–1517.

Yan, A., & Yadong, L. 2001. *International Joint Ventures – Theory and Practice*. New York: Sharpe.

Yeung, R. 1995. Qualitative personal interviews in international business research: some lessons form a study of Hong Kong transnational corporations. *International Business Review*, 4(3): 313–339.

Yin, R. 1994. *Case Study Research: Design and Methods* (2 ed.). Beverly Hills CA: Sage.

Yinger, J. M. 1960. Contraculture and subculture. *American Sociological Review*, October: 625–635.

Youssef, S. M. 1975. Contextual factors influencing control strategy of multinational corporations. *Academy of Management Journal*, March: 136–145.

Zaheer, A., McEvily, B., & Perrone, V. 1998. Does trust matter? Exploring the effects of interorganizational and interpersonal trust on performance. *Organization Science*, 9: 141–159.

Zander, U., & Kogut, B. 1995. Knowledge and the speed of the transfer and imitation of organizational capabilities: an empirical test. *Organization Science*, 6: 76–92.

Index

Adler, N., 52, 100, 160, 184
age, 49
agency theory, 9
Ahrens, T., 67–8
Alvesson, M., 75, 101
Anthony, R. N., 7, 11, 15
Arrow, K., 7
Awasthi, V. N., 41, 53, 54

Bakacsi, G., 85, 86, 88–90, 175, 188, 195, 204
Baliga, B. R., 14–18, 26, 49, 64, 77
Barnard, C., 9
Barney, J., 50, 72, 210
Bartlett, C. A., 1, 16, 27, 29, 32–3, 66, 76–7, 265
Baumler, J. V., 77
Beamish, P. W., 44, 66–7, 70, 72
Beard, V., 64, 72
Beechler, S., 40, 66, 76, 81
behavior control, 16
Berger, P., 65
Berle, A., 9
Bernard, H. R., 101
Bhimani, A., 80
Birkinshaw, J., 76
Birnberg, J., 53, 106
Björkman, I., 70, 72, 75
Black, S., 104
Boisot, M., 47
Breinbauer, A., 2, 265
Brodbeck, F., 227
Brück, F., 222
Buckley, P. J., 93, 100
bureaucracy, 17, 18, 177, *see also* formal control
bureaucratic formalized control, 21
Burns, T., 28, 41, 43, 46

Caligiuri, P., 104
Calori, R., 16, 53, 55, 77
Cavusgil, S., 100

Central- and Eastern Europe, 1–3, 85–91, 115–232
political risk, 176–9
economic risk, 179–87
culture, 188–236
centralization, 24, 119, 120
Chandler, A. D., 33
Chang, E., 44, 50, 51, 66
Chenhall, R., 6, 41, 44, 46, 49, 76
Child, J., 7, 15, 18, 23–6, 34, 35, 44, 46, 47, 51–2, 66, 70
Chow, C. W., 3, 7, 41, 44, 53, 56
clan control, 17–18, *see also* control mechanisms; informal control
Coase, R. H., 8
Cohen, W. M., 184
combinations of control, 169–73
communication
  functions, 168
  headquarter, subsidiary communication, 167
communism, 91, 189
configurations of control, 172
contingency, 41–52
control by socialization and networks, 21, 23
control definitions, 7
  behavior control, 16
  combinations of control, 169–73
  extent of control, 33–8, 173
  operational control, 33–8
  strategic control, 33–8
  output control, 16
control in MNC context, 29–33
control mechanisms, 3, 5, 14–29
  centralization, 24, 119, 120
  expatriate control, 24, 119, 135–45, *see also* expatriate
  explicit control, 24, 119
  formalization, 24, 119, 129
  implicit control, 24–5, 119–20, 149
  informal communication, 24, 119, 154

303

Index

control mechanisms – *continued*
  international management training, 29, 119, 157
  intra-group networks, 24, 119, 154
  lateral relations, 24, 119, 149
  organizational culture, 29, 119, 163
  output control, 16, 24, 119, 130
  socialization, 24, 119, 149
  standardization, 24, 119, 124
content analysis, 101–7, *see also* method, qualitative content analysis
coordination, 10
corruption, 178
country of origin effect, 66–8
Cray, D., 29–30, 50
culture, 52
  cultural research on CEE, 85–91
  empirical findings on CEE culture, 188–209
  literature review on culture and control, 52–71
  moderators, 189–235

Das, T. K., 7, 23, 73, 100, 142, 155
dimensions of international control, 33–8
discussion, 240
Doz, Y. L., 1, 3, 26, 33, 34, 76, 78, 173
Drucker, P., 73

Eastern European cluster, 85–91
economic risk, 179
Edstrom, A., 23, 25, 70, 139, 155
Egelhoff, W. G., 1, 9, 29, 41, 67
Eisenhardt, K. M., 9, 71, 106
empirical research results, 115–232
environment, 42–8
Erramilli, K. M., 44, 41, 58, 67, 74
ethnocentric, 19
Etzioni, A., 12, 18
expatriate, 21, 22, 24, 27, 61, 67–72, 74, 82, 99, 107, 119, 122, 132, 134–49, 155, 156, 163–5, 171, 185, 204–5, 215–18, 226–7, 229, 240, 244–5, 247, 253, 255, 263, 269–70
expatriate control, 135–45, *see also* control mechanisms
explicit control, 120–45

Ferner, A., 8, 23, 28, 46, 47, 67, 68, 70, 71, 76, 77, 78, 106, 155
Fink, G., 87, 88, 90, 95, 96, 97, 101, 102, 105, 189, 192, 197, 199, 202, 204, 219
Flamholtz, E. G., 7, 11–14, 16, 20, 21, 27
Flick, U., 93, 95, 96
formal control, 15
formalization, 24, 119, 129, *see also* control mechanisms

Galbraith, J. R., 23, 25, 70, 139, 155
geocentric, 19
Geringer, J. M., 7, 19
Germanic cluster, 88–91
Ghoshal, S., 1, 9, 16, 27, 29, 32, 33, 76, 99, 109
Glaser, B. G., 103
GLOBE, 85–91
Govindarajan, V., 7, 17, 27
Greenfield operation, 115–18, 126, *see also* market entry
Groot, T. L., 19, 20, 22, 34, 35, 37, 51, 173
Gulati, R., 3, 7, 15, 17, 18, 70, 73, 75

Hall, E. T., 11, 104
Harrison, G., 41, 53, 59, 79
Harzing, A.-W., 8, 15, 17, 21–4, 28, 29, 33, 34, 37, 46, 47, 49, 50, 66–72, 77, 78, 94, 117, 119, 120, 124, 129, 130, 135, 137, 139, 140, 149, 155, 164, 168, 169–71, 270
headquarters, 2, 4, 5, 19, 23, 24, 29, 30, 33–9, 42, 45, 49–52, 66, 69, 71, 72, 76–8, 81–4, 88–9, 93–5, 100, 105, 108–13, 115, 119–32, 134–41, 143–75, 183–5, 188–96, 202, 205, 208–32, 234–60
Hedlund, G., 50, 77
Hofstede, G., 41, 52–4, 64–5, 79–80, 85, 88–9, 104, 239, 271–3
Holm, U., 100
Hoskisson, R., 175, 178
host-country nationals, 145–9, *see also* locals
House, R., 80, 85, 86, 88, 104, 129, 189, 195, 197, 208, 233, 247, 271–2

Index

informal communication, 24, 119, 154–7, *see also* control mechanisms
informal control, 15
institutions, 46–8
integration-responsiveness framework, 33
interdependence, 77

Jaeger, A., 14, 15, 18, 19, 26, 66, 75
Jensen, M. C., 9

Kluckhohn, C., 13, 65, 104
Kostova, T., 2, 3, 184, 193, 240, 246

Lachman, R., 79
lateral relations, 24, 119, 149–54, *see also* control mechnansims
Lawrence, J. W., 1, 15, 16, 19, 24, 25, 29, 41, 43, 45, 46, 120, 129, 239, 265
Levitt, T., 64
literature review, 39–78
locals, 145–9, *see also* host-country nationals
Lubatkin, M., 55, 85
Luo, Y., 44, 53, 70, 73, 133, 184, 197

major findings, 236–61
management control, 6, 10–14, *see also* control mechanisms
management training, 29, 119, 157–63, *see also* control mechanisms
managerial implications, 242–61
March, J. G., 25
market entry, 115–18
Marschan-Piekkari, R., 93, 98–101
Martinez, 1, 15, 16, 23, 24, 27, 29, 30, 76, 94, 120, 129, 130, 154, 155, 163
Mayring, P., 5, 93, 94, 101, 102, 103, 104, 267
Merchant, K. A., 19, 20, 22, 34, 35, 37, 51, 173
method, 92–107
  inductive categorization, 101–2
  interview bias, 97–101
  qualitative content analysis, 101–4
  reliability, 104–5

semi-structured interview, 94–7
triangulation, 100, 105, 108
validity, 105
Mintzberg, H., 14, 16–17, 26, 30, 31, 32, 46, 49, 75, 117
model, 81, 236
moderators, 69–76, 209–31
multinational corporation, 29–38

Newman, K., 2, 91, 178, 184, 193, 254, 265

operational control, 33–8
organizational culture, 29, 74, 119, 163–7
organizational design, 12–14
Otley, D., 78
Ouchi, W., 9, 14–19, 66
output control, 16, 21, 22, 24, 119, 130, *see also* control mechanisms
ownership and resource provision, 50–2

Parsons, T., 65
Patton, M. Q., 92–5, 100–4
Peng, M. W., 115, 175, 190, 197
personal centralized control, 21, 22
personality traits, 75
Peterson, R. B., 51, 66, 70, 72, 160
Pfeffer, J., 16, 40, 41, 43, 77, 78, 163
planning, 11, 130–2
political risk, 176
polycentric, 19
power, 76, 78
Prahalad, C. K., 1, 3, 26, 33, 34, 76, 78, 173
Pugh, D. S., 1, 15, 40–3, 49, 85, 120, 265

qualitative content analysis, 101–7, *see also* content analysis; method

regiocentric, 19
reliability, 104–5
research question, 1–3
research results, 115–232, *see also* empirical research results
Richards, M., 45, 47, 67, 70, 96
Ronen, S., 85

Roth, K., 2, 9, 31, 65, 71, 88, 91, 193, 265
Rousseau, D. M., 101

sample, 108–14
Schein, E., 23, 65, 75
Shenkar, O., 65, 85, 100
Simon, H. A., 25, 31, 35
Singh, J. V., 43, 66
Snell, S., 17
Sohn, J., 27, 66, 70, 72, 143
standardization, 24, 119, 124, *see also* control mechanisms
strategic choice, 29, 115
strategic control, 33–8
strategy, 30–5
Strauss, A., 103, 104
summary, 262–70
Szulanski, G., 99, 246

Thushman, M. L., 184
transaction cost theory, 8–9

Triandis, H. C., 79, 239
triangulation, 100, 105, 108
Trompenaars, F., 65, 85, 86, 197, 202, 225, 233, 271, 273, 275
trust, 72
Tsui, J. S., 7, 61, 64

Ueno, S., 53, 61–4, 44, 47, 50–2, 78
uncertainty, 46

validity, 105

Weber, M., 15, 17, 40, 42, 43, 65
Williamson, O., 8, 9
Wong, G., 40, 44, 49, 50, 53, 59, 63, 64

Yan, A., 6, 29

Zaheer, A., 72, 142, 210
Zander, U., 246